ON THE MARCH

LABOUR REBELLIONS IN THE BRITISH CARIBBEAN, 1934-39

'It is now possible to ask what has emerged from these years of working class upheaval, with their tale of strike and riot, death and victimisation. Two things: the rise of trade unions, and the entry of the working classes into West Indian politics... The Labour Movement is on the march.'

(W. Arthur Lewis, Labour in the West Indies, 1939).

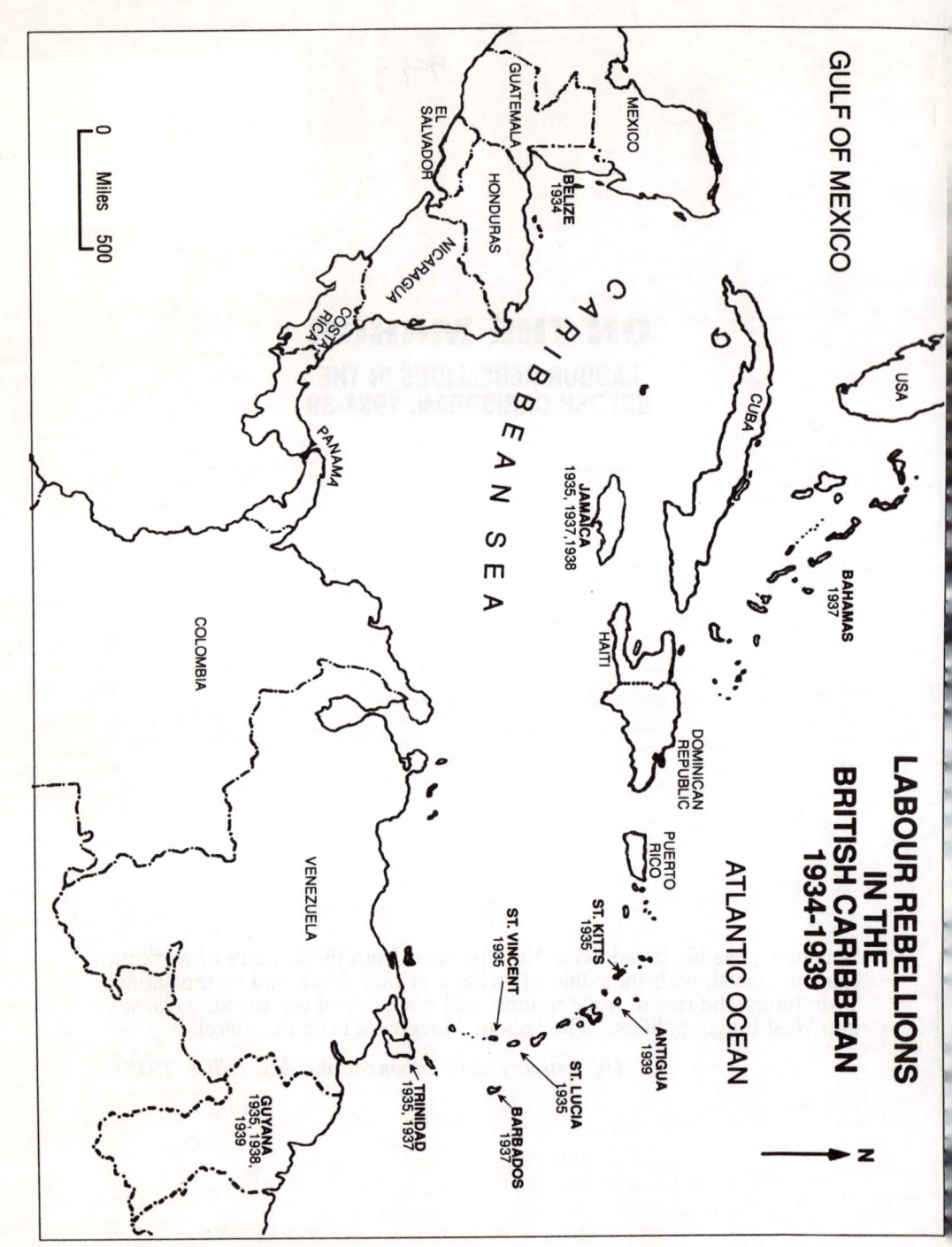

LABOUR REBELLIONS
IN THE
BRITISH CARIBBEAN
1934-1939

GULF OF MEXICO

ATLANTIC OCEAN

CARIBBEAN SEA

USA

MEXICO

BELIZE
1934

GUATEMALA

EL SALVADOR

HONDURAS

NICARAGUA

COSTA RICA

PANAMA

COLOMBIA

VENEZUELA

CUBA

HAITI

DOMINICAN REPUBLIC

BAHAMAS
1937

JAMAICA
1935, 1937, 1938

PUERTO RICO

ST. KITTS
1935

ST. VINCENT
1935

ANTIGUA
1939

ST. LUCIA
1935

BARBADOS
1937

TRINIDAD
1935, 1937

GUYANA
1935, 1938, 1939

N

0 Miles 500

ON THE MARCH

LABOUR REBELLIONS IN THE BRITISH CARIBBEAN, 1934-39

O. Nigel Bolland

IAN RANDLE PUBLISHERS
KINGSTON

JAMES CURREY PUBLISHERS
LONDON

First published 1995 by

Ian Randle Publishers Limited
206 Old Hope Road, Kingston 6, Jamaica
ISBN 976-8100-52-4
and
James Currey Publishers
54b Thornhill Square, London
ISBN 0-85255-730-2

Catalogue records for this book are available from the National Library of Jamaica and the British Library.

Book and cover design by Michael Gordon
Manufactured in the Jamaica by Stephensons Litho Press

CONTENTS

ACKNOWLEDGEMENTS

I should like to thank many scholars who have given comments and encouragement during thecourse of this project, including David Abdulah, Fitzroy Baptiste, Hilary Beckles, BridgetBrereton, Roy Bryce-Laporte, Mary Butler, Ashton Chase, Colin Clarke, Donna Coombs-Montrose, Edward Cox, Michaeline Crichlow, Peter Fraser, Richard Hart, Alistair Hennesey,Paget Henry, Gad Heuman, Barry Higman, Percy Hintzen, Howard Johnson, Roberta Kilkenny,Linden Lewis, Richard Lobdell, Jay Mandle, Woodville Marshall, Luis Martinez-Fernandez,Teresita Martinez-Vergne, Roderick McDonald, Sidney Mintz, Robert Morris, Ivar Oxaal, KenPost, Kenneth Ramchand, Rhoda Reddock, Glenn Richards, Gail Saunders, Gabby Scott, Verene Shepherd, Assad Shoman, Arnold Sio, Mary Turner, and Swithin Wilmot. Richard Hart deserves my special thanks for contributing the Introduction of this book.

I am grateful to the staff of the following archives and libraries, who provided a professional and friendly service: the Barbados Department of Archives, the Barbados Workers' Union, the National Archives of Belize, the Colgate University libraries, the Institute of Commonwealth Studies of the University of London, the Oilfield Workers' Trade Union, San Fernando, and the University of the West Indies libraries.

I wish to thank Macmillan Publishers for permission to use material from my article, The Labour Movement and the Genesis of Modern Politics in Belize, in Labour in the Caribbean, edited by Malcolm Cross and Gad Heuman (1988).

For their financial assistance, I thank the National Endowment of the Humanities, for providing funds to visit some of these libraries and for a generous fellowship in 1994, and the Colgate University Research Council.

I owe a special debt of thanks to my colleagues and my family, and especially to my wife, Ellen Bolland, for their sustained support.

INTRODUCTION

Although, as the title states, this is primarily a study of the labour rebellions of the 1930s in the anglolphone Caribbean area, it contains a first chapter on two preceding waves of trans–regional labour unrest which provides useful background information. These earlier waves occurred c. 1895–1910 and 1917–1925. The term 'Caribbean' is used elastically to include not only the Antilles and mainland territories washed by the Caribbean Sea but also British Guiana (now Guyana) lying just outside the Caribbean perimeter and the Bahamas Islands to the north of Cuba and Hispaniola.

The events of the 1930s, including those in British Honduras (now Belize) and the Bahamas, areas ignored by most authors when discussing labour unrest in the region, are reported in some detail. That this wave of labour rebellions commenced not in St Kitts, as is often supposed, but in British Honduras in 1934 has now been firmly established by the author. At the same time he mentions demonstrations and strikes in Trinidad and British Guiana in 1934 and 1935 and strikes in Jamaica in 1935 which could be regarded as part of the beginnings of, or as early warnings of, the 1930s labour rebellions.

The labour rebellions of the 1930s occurred in almost every colony of the anglophone Caribbean area. This regional character was also a feature of the two earlier manifestations of labour unrest. The trans-regional flow of these waves of working-class upheaval requires an explanation, especially in view of the fact that at the time trans-regional contacts were very limited. Before the 1940s there was little contact, and none at the working-class level, between the eastern Caribbean islands and British Guiana on the one hand and Jamaica and British Honduras on the other. Indeed the only contacts that existed were those between Indian cricketers. Nor had the earlier contacts which had existed between British Honduras and Jamaica continued into the twentieth century.

How can the fact that these waves of labour unrest and rebellion flowed right across the region be explained? It is to the author's credit that he has, where others have failed or made no attempt to, offered a satisfactory explanation of the regional nature of the labour unrest and rebellions.

The contributory factors of low levels of wages, oppressive working conditions, which existed for a long time and were in themselves inadequate to explain why social explosions should have occurred at roughly the same time in colonies separated by thousands of miles of the Caribbean Sea. There must have been other factors responsible for the regional nature of the outbreaks that occurred.

One such factor was the repercussions of the world economic depression which occurred in the wake of the 1929 financial crisis in the USA. This adversely affected world trade and had serious effects in the import-export monoculture economies of the Caribbean colonies. Another common factor was the repatriation of labourers who had gone to work in the Latin American countries and the closure of the possibility of future employment there. A third factor was the increase in internal migration from rural to urban areas, resulting in greater population concentrations and increased unemployment.

There were also common social factors. These included the increasing racial self-respect of the black masses, to which the educational and agitational activities of Marcus Garvey and the Universal Negro Improvement Association had contributed, and the growth in class solidarity resulting from the advocacy of trade unionism and the spread, however limited, of Marxist ideas. These in turn increased resentment at the disparity between the standards of living of the upper and upper-middle classes on the one hand and that of the manual workers and peasants on the other, a disparity which had both class and racial aspects.

Then there were factors resulting from the more widespread dissemination of information, particularly audio and visual information through greater access to radio broadcasts and news reels at the cinemas, which, in situations of widespread illiteracy, provided an important supplement to the newspapers. The increase in access to external news facilitated the growth of tremendous resentment over the Italian invasion of Ethiopia, which was seen in terms of a black-white conflict. Also of some agitational significance (though the author does not mention this) was the impact of reports, which had begun to filter through in the early 1930s, that the workers had taken power and property from the capitalists in a country called Russia.

A factor present in the period following the first World War, which was perhaps of diminished significance by the 1930s, had been the return of soldiers who had been recruited for service abroad. Many of these ex-servicemen, who had had romantic illusions of their importance to the glorious British Empire, had returned to their respective homelands disillusioned and embittered by discriminatory treatment they had received overseas and neglect on their return by their respective governments.

These then are the common factors explaining a regional phenomenon. What they do not explain is why similar social upheavals did not occur in the island of Grenada and Dominica, two apparent exceptions to the general pattern. A labour rebellion did occur in Grenada, but not until 1950–51, a decade after the rebellions of the 1930s had subsided. Can these exceptions be explained by a higher than average peasant component in the populations of these two colonies? Is the greater politicisation of Grenada under the popular leadership of T. Albert Marryshow and the workers' resultant belief that problems could be solved by means of political representations rather than strikes a possible additional explanation?

Richard Hart

PART ONE

The Regional Character and Historical Roots of the Labour Rebellions

Introduction

A series of strikes, riots, and other labour disturbances swept through the British Caribbean in the 1930s, beginning in Belize (British Honduras), Trinidad, and Guyana (British Guiana) in 1934, and culminating in Jamaica in 1938, and Antigua and Guyana in 1939. During these years there were disturbances also in St Kitts, St Vincent, St Lucia, Barbados, and the Bahamas. As W. Arthur Lewis noted in 1939, it was not until then that there was 'anything that could be called a movement' among the working people of the British West Indies.[1] There had been many ostensibly similar events prior to the period 1934–39, disturbances which began in the late nineteenth century and contributed to the development of a greater consciousness of class and race among the working people of the British colonies in the Caribbean. However, these earlier disturbances, while they did produce some labour organisations, did not give rise to a lasting labour movement, as such. The British Guiana Labour Union was the only important organisation of manual workers in existence in the British Caribbean in the early 1930s, but by the end of the 1930s there were trade unions throughout these British colonies. This rise of organised labour became the basis for subsequent political developments in the 1940s and 1950s. It is these consequences that give the labour rebellions of the 1930s their importance and distinctive socio-historical meaning.

This book, which is the first study to describe and analyse these labour rebellions regionally and comparatively, aims to contribute to our understanding of the historical sociology of the Caribbean and specifically to the emergence of the labour movements and nationalist movements in the 1930s and 1940s. This book is part of a larger study that will trace the social origins of authoritarianism and democracy in the British Caribbean, with a particular focus on the two decades from 1934 to 1954. The purpose of this larger study is to trace the sources, evolution, and problems of key aspects of the political culture of the region, particularly as they have become institutionalised in trade unions and political parties during the process of decolonisation.

The history and culture of Caribbean societies, as is well known, have been shaped by centuries of colonialism and slavery. It is a history of systems of extreme domination that resulted in a rigid social hierarchy and pervasive authoritarianism. Throughout the British Caribbean colonies the slaves, who constituted the majority of the population, were exploited and oppressed by a small and mostly white minority. Even after slavery was finally abolished in 1838, labour relations were generally characterised by domination and subordination, not least in those colonies where large numbers of indentured workers took the place of many former slaves on the plantations. Violence, aggression and authoritarianism have pervaded these colonial societies in innumerable ways, but especially in connection with the coercion and exploitation of labour. 'The labour relationship is so central' in the political culture of these societies 'that it is inevitably bound up with processes of historical change'.[2]

For a century after emancipation 'the economic foundations of slavery, especially in the general picture of land ownership, had remained basically untouched'.[3] There were countless protests and acts of resistance against the injustices and abuse that prevailed in the colonies after 1838, and particularly after the first great depression hit the sugar industry in the 1880s, but these protests were largely ineffective so long as they failed to develop into a more coherent, sustained and powerful movement. Within a few years in the 1930s, the working people in all these colonies, with or without middle-class allies, challenged these systems of domination. Old traditions of resistance to slavery and the experience gained in labour struggles from the 1880s to the 1920s provided a basis for new tactics and the emergence of a new political culture. More democratic procedures and institutions emerged to organise and channel this labour movement into trade unions and political parties. What began as a labour movement thus developed into a widespread human rights movement in which people struggled for participation in their societies as citizens, and then for decolonisation and independence. Several of the early leaders of this movement, such as Grantley Adams of Barbados, Vere Bird of Antigua and Alexander Bustamante and Norman Manley of Jamaica, who were all active by 1939, subsequently became the beneficiaries of political reforms in the 1940s.

There are several studies of the labour rebellions and the growth of trade unions and political parties in individual colonies. Some of these are outstanding, both in the thoroughness of their research and the insights of their analyses. However, the narrowly national focus of such studies, which reflects the collapse of the Federation of the West Indies in 1962 and the subsequent independence of most of the former colonies as individual units, tends to obscure the regional character of the early labour movement. Indeed, the aspiration to a regional federation was initially rooted in the labour movement itself and connections existed between several of the labour rebellions in the 1930s and, subsequently, between the labour organisations in these colonies. Most notably, the Caribbean Labour Congress emerged from meetings held in Guyana in 1926, under the auspices of the British Guiana Labour Union and in 1938, when the British Guiana and West Indies Labour Congress was attended by delegates from Barbados, Suriname and Trinidad, as well as Guyana.

The labour movement in the British Caribbean was profoundly affected by common economic factors as changes in metropolitan capital penetrated these dependent colonial economies. British policies, such as the system of sugar preferences, affected the colonies throughout the region and specific firms had branches in more than one colony. Tate & Lyle, the giant British sugar company, for example, acquired major plantations in Jamaica and Trinidad in the 1930s. The modernising orientation of this firm, along with the impact of oil companies and the United Fruit Company in Trinidad and Jamaica, respectively, shaped the labour process in new ways. In particular, the economic and social pressures engendered by the second great depression after 1929 had common explosive consequences throughout the region, as sugar prices collapsed, unemployment and poverty increased and emigrants returned home from overseas. To a large extent the labour rebellions were in response to the economic distress of these depression years.

There were other regional connections. Some labour leaders and activists were involved in more than one colony. For example, Clement Payne, who was the major figure in the Barbados labour rebellion in 1937, was active also in Trinidad in the National Unemployment Movement, the Negro Welfare Cultural and Social Association and subsequently was a founder and leader of the Federated Workers' Trade Union in Trinidad. A large number of the labour activists were people who had worked as migrants in other countries and colonies and several leaders were immigrants. For example, Elma François and Uriah Butler in Trinidad were from St Vincent and Grenada, respectively, and A.A. Thorne, leader of the British Guiana Workers' League, was from Barbados. Many working people in the Caribbean, then as now, were pan-Africanist in orientation and knew about and responded to events in the region as well as further afield. The influences of Marcus Garvey's movement and of the Italian invasion of Ethiopia in 1935 were seen throughout the region in the developing racial and anti–colonial consciousness. At the other end of the spectrum, some colonial officials were transferred from one Caribbean colony to another, most notably Sir Edward Denham who was governor of British Guiana before his last post as governor of Jamaica from 1934 to 1938. The experiences and responses of these officials to the labour rebellions were not confined to single colonies. The Colonial Office increasingly treated the Caribbean colonies as a region in terms of developing responses and policies to economic, political and social problems, not least with the appointment of the Royal Commission, known as the Moyne Commission, which travelled there in 1938 and 1939. Sir Walter Citrine, secretary of the British Trades Union Congress and a prominent member of this commission, was one of several British trade unionists and Labour MP's who sought to influence the development of trade unions in the British Caribbean by sending information, giving advice and offering scholarships to selected people.

The historical roots of this regional labour movement of the 1930s lay in the nineteenth century, particularly in the working people's resistant responses to the impact of the first great depression in the 1880s and 1890s.[4]

Notes

1. W.M. Macmillan, *Warning from the West Indies* (London, 1936), does not mention Belize.
2. D.A.G. Waddell, *British Honduras: A Historical and Contemporary Survey* (London, 1961); Narda Dobson, *A History of Belize* (London, 1973).
3. C.H. Grant, *The Making of Modern Belize: Politics, Society and British Colonialism in Central America* (Cambridge, 1976), pp.61, 67; Peter D. Ashdown, "Antonio Soberanis and the Disturbances in Belize 1934-1937", *Caribbean Quarterly* 24:1/2 (1978), pp.61-74.
4. Bolland 1986a: 33, 105-06; 1988a: 258-84; 1991.
5. Major G. St J. Orde Browne, *Labour Conditions in the British West Indies* (London, 1939); *West India Royal Commission Report* (London, 1945).

Chapter ONE

CLASS STRUGGLE, CLASS FORMATION AND EARLY LABOUR ORGANISATIONS

A rise in class consciousness, appearing in conjunction with increasing racial consciousness, was manifest in parts of the British Caribbean from the late nineteenth century. Some forms of class struggle, including strikes and collective verbal protests, had occurred since emancipation and even before,[1] but the first major wave of working-class activity was between the late 1890s and the beginning of the First World War.[2] Several labour protests and strikes, together with the emergence of the early unions and other working-class organisations, accelerated proletarianisation at the same time that middle classes were developing in these colonies.

Though there were generally racial and ethnic as well as educational and occupational divisions within the middle strata, these people shared the goal of a secure income and material standard of living that would support their claims for a 'respectable' status in a system of prestige that was still largely dictated by the 'mother country'. Even members of the intelligentsia who sought more rights and privileges for themselves generally did so in terms of the values of a civilisation that was defined by the British. A diffuse group of occupations including some wealthy peasants and farmers, professionals such as teachers, civil servants, clergymen, lawyers, doctors and nurses, as well as some merchants and the upper echelons of artisans and some members of the police and armed forces, lay between the European-dominated elite and the mostly black masses. Though members of this middle stratum made some fine distinctions between each other in terms of education, colour and consumption patterns, their shared goal of 'respectability' distinguished them, in their own minds at least, from the poorer peasants and workers who they believed were less 'civilised'.

The chief problems for this emerging middle class were the threat that the depression of the late nineteenth century posed to their material circumstances and the fact that, however educated and culturally assimilated they became, they were still subject to racial discrimination from those who were whiter than themselves.[3] Anxiety and resentment about these issues fed their growing class and race consciousness and their incipient sense of nationalism. The first labour organisations of workers and the growing propensity of poor people to demonstrate and even to strike, while more respectable people only petitioned to maintain or extend their social and political privileges, augmented the feeling in this middle stratum that they constituted a distinct class. Class, after all, is a social relationship, so the evolution of the class consciousness of this middle strata and of the working people were connected to each other, as well as to the persistence of the white and increasingly absentee or expatriate colonial elite.

The depression and the reorganisation of the sugar industry in the late nineteenth century increased unemployment, lowered wages and heightened suffering throughout the British Caribbean. Angry protests broke out in many colonies in the 1890s and the first years of the twentieth century. While each disturbance responded to local problems, their increasing frequency shows that they were caused by 'overarching issues of economic inequality buttressed by colonial control'.[4] At least 16 serious disturbances occurred between 1884 and 1905, most of them in Jamaica (1884, 1894, 1895, 1901 and 1902) and Guyana (1889, 1896, 1903, 1905). Others occurred in St Vincent (1891), Dominica (1893, 1898), Belize (1894), St Kitts-Nevis (1896), Montserrat (1898) and Trinidad (1903). Further disturbances occurred in 1908 in St Lucia and in 1912 in Kingston, Jamaica.

For most black Jamaicans, who were extremely poor, 'the struggle was not against racism defined as such but against class oppression, heavy taxation and injustice'.[5] Strikes on estates in St Thomas, Portland, St Elizabeth, St James and Hanover in 1867, 1868 and 1878 were directed against low wages, or the planters' irregularity or failure to pay wages due. In February 1884 sugar workers and stevedores sought higher wages in St Ann and, during this bad year in the sugar industry, several strikes broke out. The inspector of police reported that an agent recruiting labourers for work in Panama had agitated people by promising them higher wages. Workers crowded into the town of St Ann's Bay, some of them waiting to embark to Colon and others planning their struggle for better wages at home. Planters and their managers conceded increased wages in order to end the strikes and slow the loss of labour to Panama. In September 1884 some recently imported Chinese workers rioted at the Gray's Town Estate in St Mary, resulting in one being killed and five wounded.[6] These events show the complexity of the relationship between labour supply and wages, immigration and emigration and the crisis in the sugar industry. The planters responded to the fall in sugar prices, from 25s. 6d. per hundredweight in 1873 to 19s. in 1883 and 13s. 3d. in 1884, by lowering wages and importing indentured labourers, while the Jamaican workers sought higher wages, if not at home then abroad.

Trade unions were illegal and the colonial administration saw labour conflict as a matter for the police. The colonial state strengthened its police forces in order to coerce workers and suppress disorders. Riots at Cumberland Penn in 1894, provoked by the attempt of the police to arrest a poor young man for gambling illegally at the races, convinced the governor that the constabulary would not have been able to contain a more serious disturbance. Playing on the elite's fears of a race war, he sought to strengthen the police by importing white sergeants and sergeant-majors from the Royal Irish Constabulary. Conflicts between soldiers of the West India Regiment and members of the Jamaica

Constabulary, which was created after the Morant Bay rebellion of 1865, sometimes resulted in riots. On 8 June 1894, for example, soldiers, joined by women and men of the town, attacked two police stations and roughed up the police at Fletcher's Land and Sutton Street. A similar pitched battle occurred in 1900 and in 1901 police intervened in riots in Portland and St Mary, which were sparked by disputes over the sale of bananas and wage rates, respectively.[7] Coercion was a standard mode of social control, as it was in the period of slavery, because any protest or demonstration by the working people of Jamaica was defined by the authorities as a riot.

Jamaican workers, however, developed strike action 'as a legitimate method of protest against conditions'[8] and they were even supported by some middle-class Jamaicans. Dr Robert Love, the editor of the *Jamaica Advocate*, described the strike by wharf workers in Kingston in May 1895 as a 'new chapter' in Jamaica's social history. For four days some 800–1,000 dock workers 'continued to maintain, with more or less obstinacy, their hostile attitude.... Strikes are in reality the mode of warfare adopted by the labourers against the capitalist. It is the former's method of bringing the latter to terms'.[9] The dock workers sought wages of 5–6s. per day. When employers sought to break the strike by employing sailors at 6s. per day, the sailors would not cooperate, 'partly as a gesture of solidarity, but mainly out of fear of reprisals from angry workers'.[10] Love encouraged workers to form associations all over the island, to 'organise themselves everywhere into Labour Clubs, or Labour Unions (or whatever else they may choose to call it)',[11] in order to make their collective voice heard in the Legislative Council, where they were unrepresented. Despite the growing class conflict and class consciousness, however, this did not happen until the 1930s.

Other sources of class conflict in Jamaica were over land and taxes. In 1901 and 1902 several attempts were made by poor people to seize land from large landowners. In 1901 in St Mary, a major banana-producing parish, small settlers tried to possess land owned by the Hon. Dr John Pringle. The police report stated this was one of several attempts, 'The persons so acting in all cases try to put forward some bogus title, and incite the more ignorant portion of the peasantry by telling them that the lands in St Mary were belonging to the black people'.[12] Additional taxes were imposed on land in 1901 and by 1902 taxation was a burning issue. Many poor taxpayers in Montego Bay were taken 'before the resident magistrate for the non-payment of taxes, and given the alternative of either paying their obligations in full within a certain period or going to prison'.[13] As these people borrowed money from friends and relations to avoid going to prison, there was widespread indignation and anger in the area.

Montego Bay was a rapidly growing town, whose population increased from 4,803 people in 1891 to 6,616 in 1911, but unemployment was a major problem because of the depression in the sugar industry. On 5 April 1902, a market day when the town's population was swollen with people from its environs, a constable tried to arrest a drunken sailor. People disliked this policeman in particular and a crowd of about 2,000 gathered around the court house. They pelted the building with stones and other missiles, breaking the windows and then attacked the policeman's home. The sailor whose arrest had sparked the protest was released, but people continued to attack the police in the town after dark. The police had to retreat and released others they had arrested. Special constables were sworn in and 60 armed men and other police officers arrived the next day to reinforce the local police. Rioting was renewed the next night, the police barracks was attacked and police were forced to seek shelter in houses. An inspector then ordered the crowd to be attacked with fixed bayonets and bullets. After two and a half hours of skirmishing, one man, who was not a rioter, had been shot dead and another died subsequently of his wounds, before the people dispersed. Some of the fighting was at close quarters, one person was wounded by a bayonet and one of the injured police was knocked senseless by a bottle. HMS *Tribune* came from Port Royal and its 300 sailors increased the security forces to 750 armed men, who effectively crushed the protest.[14]

The *Jamaica Advocate* of 12 April 1902[15] blamed the Montego Bay disturbances on the 'chronic irritation and discontent which have for some time existed among the poorer classes as the consequence of the grinding, crushing, weight of the taxes which they are unable to pay, and of the prosecutions which have been recently instituted against them for not being able to pay'. The harsh efforts of the police and magistrates to enforce this oppressive taxation made them prime targets of the protest. If 'the police were simply the uniformed symbol of a system of justice which was unduly oppressive on the poor',[16] they were also the front line of the system. Like at Morant Bay in 1865, the police barracks and court house, which were not merely the symbols but the actual vehicles of domination, were attacked. The white officers and colonial officials, no doubt haunted by the example of Morant Bay, were anxious about the loyalties of their black constables. One of the inspectors who helped suppress the Morant Bay disturbances, obsessed with fears about a race war, was reassured that his men were willing to 'use their weapons against their kith and kin. I am proud to have had the honour of thus "blooding" the Jamaica Constabulary, especially in such trying circumstances....They proved their loyalty to the hilt on the night of 6 April, 1902; and they have done so repeatedly since then'.[17] The use of black police by the colonial state to repress poor black people divided the majority racial group, but also showed how the force of the law was used to maintain class dominance in the colony. Such prominent events as the Montego Bay disturbances of 1902, therefore, may have strengthened the emerging sense of class consciousness at the expense of racial solidarity, though it was clear that race remained a central component in the maintenance of this extremely unjust society.

In St Vincent, Dominica, Belize, St Kitts and Trinidad, also, the disturbances in this period concerned wages, prices, taxes and frustration with the local colonial authorities. In St Vincent 'a frightening show of force by rural estate workers, an incipient capacity by these workers to organize', and a near-riot in Kingstown in November 1891 that was provoked by an impending poll tax, led to considerable violence and the landing of marines who were summoned from Trinidad.[18] In Dominica, where a substantial peasantry developed after 1838, access to land and taxation were key issues. The governor sought to extend taxes throughout the colony in 1886 and set a land tax which led to a confrontation with the authorities in 1893. Pierre Collard, who lived in La Plaine, in a very poor region of Dominica from which the peasants took arrowroot and farine to sell to the merchants in Roseau, could not pay his taxes. His house lot was ordered to be sold, but when the bailiff and police inspector arrived to take possession an angry crowd forced them to flee. The governor arrived with additional police and 25 armed soldiers, and when Collard refused to vacate his property he ordered him to be ejected. The police and soldiers were stoned by the villagers. They opened fire, killing four men and wounding two others.[19] The crowd dispersed because as unarmed peasants they lacked the means to resist the armed force of the state successfully.

In Belize, the small elite that controlled the land, commerce and administration of the colony was divided between expatriates and an emerging creole elite, some of whom were the descendants of the old settler families. Some of the local elite pressed for constitutional change, including a return to the elective principle, but they succeeded only in obtaining a majority of unofficial members, all nominated by the governor, on the Legislative Council in 1892. The governor appointed some creole members to the council but whites remained the majority. Two years later, the linking of the colony's currency to the gold standard effectively devalued it. This increased the price of imported goods, on which people were highly dependent, and hence reduced their real income. Mercantile clerks in Belize Town received salary raises of about 25 percent, but government workers and forest workers did not. A strike by government workers was unsuccessful. A group of workers petitioned Governor Moloney, saying,

> That there has been a great fall for sometime past in the price paid for labour in this Colony....Your petitioners are the real inhabitants of this Colony, the men by the sweat of whose brow in the forests, all its prosperity has been achieved. Yet they are without a voice in the Legislative Council of this Colony, without anyone to protect their interests while both Councils are filled with merchants and other employers of labourers.[20]

The merchants denounced the petitioners as 'loafers' and called their leader, John Alexander Tom, a 'public house politician', while the governor advised the workers to wait for a revival of trade to restore their wages to their pre-1894 levels. Some would not wait. Frustrated by the responses to their peaceful petition and angered by the attitude of the merchants who continued to profit while they were forced into increasing poverty, about 100 forest workers attacked the chief stores in Belize Town on 11 December 1894. Some stores were looted. After the governor called in an armed detachment from HMS *Partridge* and the workers were offered a 50 per cent wage increase, the disorders quickly subsided.[21] This episode, though sparked by a currency issue, was really about wages and prices. It showed that the working people were developing a sense of themselves as a distinct class, whose particular interests were unrepresented in the Legislative Council, and that when their petition was rudely dismissed they could react more aggressively to obtain results.

In St Kitts and Nevis in the 1890s, working people were said to be starving and forced to resort to begging for food. Wages were severely depressed, the rate for cutting cane having been reduced from 8d. per ton to 7d. in 1895 and then to 6d. in 1896, and emigration did not sufficiently relieve the persistent distress. Demands for higher wages erupted into disorders during the sugar crop in 1896.[22] Unrest broke out on 28 January at the adjoining estates of Ponds and Needsmust, east of Basseterre, when canefields were set alight and onlookers impeded attempts to extinguish them. These estates were owned by Joaquin Farara, a Portuguese planter who was widely disliked for having reduced wages below the prevailing rate. When the harvest was due to begin on 10 February, the factory workers at Needsmust refused to work until their original wages were restored. They were joined in their strike by the fieldworkers and by the workers at Ponds estate and they mounted pickets. Farara was forced to concede wage increases and news of the concessions stimulated similar action on other estates. Over 400 acres of cane had been burned by 17 February. When the manager of Walter R. Boon's estate at Stone Fort tried to put out a fire on 16 February he was stoned by onlookers. He fired his revolver at the crowd, wounding two women, and required police protection.

Bands of strikers and demonstrators patrolled the roads, accompanied by the sounds of fifes, drums and conchshells, and armed with sticks. Three weeks of this rural unrest climaxed on 17 February when waterfront workers in Basseterre went on strike. A warship, HMS *Cordelia*, had anchored in the harbour that morning, but the demonstrators were not intimidated. A large crowd of strikers, joined by unemployed men and women and workers from the estates, took over the streets of the town for the day, armed with sticks and machetes, and playing fifes, drums and conchshells. The police inspector felt he could not challenge them because he would incite further disorder and risk defeat. In Old Road village, police who tried to arrest a worker who was accused of breaking an overseer's arm were overpowered by the villagers and forced to retreat to their barracks. Other unrest, involving stone-throwing, was reported from Challengers Village and from the north-eastern districts.

At the administrator's urgent request, 60 armed marines were landed from the warship to assist the police, but when he drove into town at 7.30 pm his carriage was stoned and bottles smashed on it by an angry crowd. Several properties belonging to the 'better classes' were attacked, including stores owned by Farara, and street lights were smashed, so another 26 marines were landed. When the marines charged the crowd with their bayonets fixed they were met with a barrage of stones and bottles, and when the fire brigade tried to put out fires their hoses were cut. An eye-witness reported that the struggle was so fierce that a 'whole body of rioters charged the marines and there was a hand to hand fight for a minute or two'. After the marines fired two volleys the people dispersed, but then they formed smaller groups and continued to throw stones and bottles from behind house fences. Some marines were said to have fired with revolvers. The unrest did not subside until after 3 am on 18 February, by which time two young men had been shot dead and several other people had received gun shot wounds. Many marines were struck by missiles and two were badly injured. Some 11 stores, most of them owned by Portuguese, were burned during the night.

Even when Basseterre had been quieted, labour protests continued in the countryside, with large crowds of estate workers and villagers patrolling the roads, shouting in chorus, 'Higher wages! Higher wages!' and entering estates in an attempt to enforce a general strike. Parties of marines were dispatched to restore order in the countryside where estate managers and Portuguese shopkeepers felt vulnerable. At a meeting of planters and merchants on 18 February, a resolution was passed calling for the retention of a warship and the establishment of a 'permanent protective force'. Meanwhile, 43 special constables and 83 rural constables were sworn in, most of them store owners or estate managers, and 216 people were arrested. A British warship remained in harbour while the cases were being tried. Several of the 99 people who were convicted received harsh sentences of as long as seven years in prison with hard labour. A detachment of marines was sent to Nevis in response to rumours of similar protests there.[23] The ruling elite and the colonial administration responded to the working people's strike as if this was primarily a civil disorder, and thereby provoked what they were ostensibly trying to prevent. Not everyone was intimidated, however, as reports of lawlessness and disorder, including further outbreaks of canefires, persisted throughout the year. In St Kitts-Nevis, as elsewhere, the severe depression in the sugar trade had provoked labour protests and resulted in violence and death, without resulting in any long-term gains by the working people.

Some of the largest and most persistent disturbances occurred in Guyana between 1889 and 1905. The expansion of plantation production and the massive import of indentured workers after emancipation resulted in persistent poverty and widespread hardship among the majority of people in Guyana. The social structure, in which the working people were divided between peasants and rural and urban wage earners, and those who were both 'peasant' and 'proletarian',[24] as well as by race and ethnicity, made the process of class formation very complex. Nevertheless, as Walter Rodney and others have shown in detail, the Guyanese working class began to constitute itself through its own activities immediately after the period of slavery: 'it was through political struggle that the working people (and the middle class) clarified their identity and tested their relationship with other classes and strata'.[25] While members of the middle strata periodically sought an alliance with working people in the late nineteenth century to support such goals as constitutional reform, the interests of the working class were distinct and frequently diverged from those of the middle classes. This can be seen in the protests and disturbances that culminated in the 'Ruimveldt Riots' of 1905.

Disturbances and strikes occurred in nineteenth-century Guyana among the largely Indian indentured immigrants as well as the ex-slaves, though the former could not legally cease work. Immigrant discontent rose in the 1860s and at least seven large-scale strikes and demonstrations broke out on the estates between August 1869, when immigrants rioted at Plantation Leonora, and January 1870. Even when not on strike, 'immigrants massed in delegations of one hundred or more became a common sight in Georgetown',[26] and strikes on five plantations in November 1870 were suppressed by armed police. In 1872 and 1873 there were other waves of strikes at several estates. In September 1872 five Indian workers were shot dead by the police at Plantation Devonshire Castle, and in just six weeks in July and August 1873 there were at least 14 strikes, some of which involved assaults on overseers and managers, arson in the canefields and open rioting.[27]

With this recent history and experience of labour disturbances, it is not surprising that labour relations in Guyana were tense and strikes frequent during the sugar depression in the late nineteenth century. A hundred strikes on sugar estates were recorded between 1886 and 1889, 49 between 1895 and 1897, and another 60 between 1899 and 1903.[28] Every stoppage or demonstration by indentured workers was regarded by their employers and the state as a 'riot' and 'as such was usually brought to an abrupt end through the use of armed police'.[29] The police had been armed and reinforced after the disturbances at Leonora in 1869, and in 1881 the force was reorganised along military lines. The presence of this paramilitary force and its proven readiness to fire on crowds may have deterred some workers, but it is evident that many remained highly active and militant throughout this period despite these threats.

African Guyanese, also, were active in the late nineteenth and early twentieth centuries. In March 1889 they became angry when a Portuguese merchant brutally beat a black boy in a dispute over a pennyworth of bread in the Stabroek market. 'Over the preceding months, Creoles had taken note of the tendency to treat very lightly the taking of a black man's life.'[30] Their frustration with racial discrimination in the judicial system, which favoured whites at their expense, erupted in an attack on Portuguese shops and other properties in Georgetown, resulting in considerable damage. This event, which was spontaneous and unorganised, 'was analogous to the enraged attacks by sugar workers on overseers and drivers on the estates.'[31] Demonstrations, which were sometimes violent, were one of the few resources of poor African and Indian Guyanese who could find no justice in the courts and had no representation in the government. Moreover, 'given the heavy-handed, authoritarian responses of those in power',[32] strikers and demonstrators who may have started their protests peacefully were often incited to fight back in self-defence. The pattern became a vicious circle, as the police saw any protest as a 'riot' that must be suppressed with armed force, and demonstrators became violent when they anticipated that the police would open fire.

The dialectic between the authoritarian colonial system and workers' resistance is clearly demonstrated in the events that took place at Plantation Non Pareil on the east coast of Demerara in October 1896. Indentured immigrants' wages had been lowered beyond the statutory rate, yet the workers were willing to negotiate with the plantation manager and with immigration officials. They would tolerate lower wages if they received cheap rations and access to provision grounds in compensation. The manager, however, asked for five of the workers who had been identified as promoting grievance claims to be transferred, a standard practice for people who had been defined as 'troublemakers', in order 'to avoid breaches of the peace'.[33] Four of them were arrested on 13 October when they were returning from participating in a deputation to the Immigration Office. The chief spokesman of the Non Pareil workers was Gooljar, an Indian who had arrived in Guyana in 1871, served his indenture, sold clothing and worked in the police force, returned to Calcutta in 1890, and then reindentured and returned to Guyana in 1894 .[34] The planters and colonial officials anticipated that such an experienced man would give them trouble. Workers who were defined as 'rioters' were dealt with peremptorily, though the colonial administration made a pretence of following legal formalities. The governor claimed to have issued instructions that arrests should be made only with proper warrants issued by a stipendiary magistrate and in the normal course of the law, that immigrants who came to state their grievances before the officials in town should not be interfered with, and that armed force was not to be used for the removal of any immigrant. Captain de Rinzy, who was in charge of the armed police party, broke all these instructions. When fellow estate workers tried to stop the arrest of the men, the police opened fire without even the formality of reading the Riot Act. Two workers died on the spot. Three others died later of the injuries they received, one of them a well-known militant named Jungali, and 59 others were wounded. De Rinzy, as Rodney stated, 'was acting within the planter milieu and according to certain accepted norms',[35] though the governor tried to disassociate himself. De Rinzy, who became notorious as a trigger-happy officer, had obtained a warrant from a local justice of the peace, who was a planter, and he was later vindicated for ordering his men to fire on the grounds of self-defence before a riotous mob.

Perhaps each act of violent repression intimidated some workers for a while, but the tradition of resistance persisted despite these murderous reprisals. Violent clashes became inevitable, whether or not they were preceded by legal formalities. In another case, in 1903, police violence was followed by legal formalities that clarified the nature of class legislation and power in this brutal colonial society. A gang of indentured workers at Plantation Friends in Berbice, which had been working on the rows for the replanting of cane tops, struck work on 6 May 1903 and marched to New Amsterdam to seek justice at the magistrate's court. They had been earning $1 per opening and asked for $1.44. Management had offered them $1.20 and then refused the compromise of $1.28, which the workers were willing to accept. Some workers were then charged with threatening the manager, on the word of a driver, and were arrested. The Riot Act was read outside the court and six workers were promptly shot dead and seven seriously wounded. Four leaders were subsequently convicted of threatening the overseer and sentenced to 6–12 months' imprisonment each. One of the workers' leaders in this dispute was a veteran indentured woman, Salamea, who was said to 'urge the coolies who had assembled to fight'.[36] In this case, again, 'indentured resistance was met with preemptive force by the state apparatus acting on behalf of the plantation capitalists'.[37] While police violence and prison sentences were intended to intimidate the workers, each such incident must have increased class consciousness and hardened class lines as it contributed to the history and tradition of militant resistance to oppression.

The widespread strikes and disturbances in Guyana in 1905 were the most serious in the British Caribbean in the period before the First World War.[38] The central issue of the 1905 labour disturbances was the persistent low rate of wages, which resulted in depressed living standards for the working people. Two decades of depression resulted in endemic low wages, high unemployment and poverty on the sugar estates, in the villages and in Georgetown. Social and environmental factors, including poor and overcrowded housing, swampy conditions and lack of sanitation, resulted in high mortality rates, especially among infants, in Georgetown and the countryside. Families were crowded into single rooms, roofs leaked, cesspits overflowed and yards flooded. The infant mortality rate was over 200 per 1,000 live births, so mothers had a one in five chance of losing a new baby before it was a year old.[39] A mortality commission held public hearings in Georgetown in November 1905 and this publicised the problems of which many people were all too well aware from their personal experience. The commissioners stated what was obvious:

> We are of the opinion that the excessive mortality in the colony occurs chiefly among the poorer classes of the community...and the high rate among the poorer classes is in part due to the absence of adequate measures of sanitation; overcrowding in rooms, in ranges of tenement rooms and in tenement houses .... It is also due to poverty.[40]

While the sugar industry was beginning to emerge from its slump in the two years before the 1905 disturbances, wages were generally the same as they had been for 30 years, the cost of living was higher and work more scarce. Rent for the inadequate tenement rooms could consume at least a quarter of the $3 or $4 a labourer might earn in a week, and one of the chief problems was that many workers were casually employed and might get only one or two days of work per week. Changes in the organisation of labour and technological innovations were making labour more productive and restoring the employers' profits, but many workers suffered *de facto* wage reductions and intensified exploitation. On the docks, for example, stevedores were loading ships with sugar in one and a half to two days in 1905 that they had previously loaded in four or five days. They got the same rate of pay, yet less work was available. Large numbers of unemployed workers gathered around the Georgetown docks hoping for some work, even if only for a day or two in the week, and this enabled employers to keep wages down. The stevedores felt that the shipping companies owed them back pay because they had been so underpaid for years.

It was on the Georgetown wharves, among stevedores who were poor and resentful, and who were in touch through sailors with the outside world, that the disturbances in 1905 began. There had been strikes among them in 1890, a year after the great London dock strike, and in 1905 they were the centre of militancy in Guyana. The stevedores had several complaints about their wages: first, that they had been too low for far too long; second, that they should be paid at a higher rate than the prevailing *pro rata* of 6 cents per hour for part of a day when work ran out; and third, that adults were often classed as 'boys' and paid at a rate of 48 cents per day rather than the general rate of 64 cents for casual labourers. When the New Colonial Company offered a special rate of 16 cents per hour to complete the loading of a steamer, other workers went on strike on 28 November to back their demands that wages be raised to that level. The next day, the number of strikers increased and about 300 of them marched under a banner, saying '16 cents an hour or no work'. Some strikers intimidated workers on the wharves who had not joined them and others met in groups of 50 or 60 in parts of the business district.

Meanwhile, porters at Plantation Ruimveldt, the nearest estate just south of Georgetown, went on strike at midday. There was clearly contact between strikers in Georgetown and workers on several sugar estates on the East and West Banks of the Demerara and up the river, and strikes started among porters, sugar boilers, stokers and other workers near the sugar factories as well as some Creole cane cutters. These estate workers often were friends, relatives, or former neighbours of some of the urban workers, many of whom had only recently moved to town in search of work. Though these occupations and places of residence are distinguishable, the mobility that was provoked by the depression emphasised the fluid nature of a casual workforce, and this fluidity encouraged the working people to make links and develop a broader class consciousness.

On 30 November large numbers of people demonstrated in the streets of Georgetown. Many of the strikers were joined by domestic workers and unemployed people. Some workers, like those in the Railway Goods Wharf, were intimidated, but there was little violence and no arson. By the evening the bakers had joined the strike because of a wage dispute and they marched down Carmichael Street. Around 6 pm the Riot Act was read at four points in the town and the crowds dispersed into smaller groups and outlying areas. The colonial state was over reacting, as if this was already a general labour rebellion, whereas it was still only a series of quite spontaneous and unorganised strikes and demonstrations, chiefly in Georgetown. As strikes spread in the next few days, however, there seems to have been some communication and perhaps even coordination among groups of workers.

At about 5 am on 1 December work ceased at the Ruimveldt Plantation factory. The manager rejected the strikers' wage demands and sent for the police, alleging that the workers were rioting. By 7.55 am the police and a detachment of artillery were in position by the Ruimveldt bridge. The Riot Act was read and the police opened fire, seriously wounding four workers, including a militant known as Long Walk and a porter named Haynes, both of them factory workers who were in the forefront of the demonstration. Police deliberately singled out those whom they considered ringleaders as targets. De Rinzy, who had been promoted to major since he fired on Indian workers at Non Pareil in 1896, ordered his men to shoot Robert Chapman, another leader. When one policeman missed, another was ordered to shoot him and Chapman died of his wounds.

News of the shooting and the sight of the wounded being brought to hospital inflamed people in Georgetown and, despite the reading of the Riot Act, thousands of people converged on the public buildings, seeking the inspector-general of police. Stones were thrown at magistrates, three of whom were injured, and some white people were beaten. Other people were shot by the police, who regained control of the western part of the town. People continued to resist by throwing stones and other missiles, and the police fired back. By the end of the day, which was dubbed 'Black Friday', seven or eight people had been killed and 30 wounded, 17 of them seriously.

On 2 December the strikers and demonstrators were more cautious and moved in smaller groups. Women, in particular, engaged in stone throwing and a band attacked the police station in Hadfield Street at midday, scattering the meal that was being brought to the men besieged inside. Several women were arrested and the demonstrators split into smaller groups of four or five persons, thereby making the task of the police to control them harder. While Georgetown became quieter, however, the sugar estates of the East Bank,

Demerara, became more affected. At Houston, adjacent to Ruimveldt, the deputy manager was stoned, and at Plantation Diamond, further up the river, factory porters demanded an increase in wages from 36 cents per day to 48 cents per day, and sugar curers asked for 56 cents instead of the current rate of 40 cents per day. A force of 27 police and special constables was sent to Plantation Diamond to quell these demands.

On 3 December, a Sunday, while most workers were at rest, the tram conductors struck for more pay. Conductors received 5 or 6 cents an hour, depending on whether they had been employed for less or more than one year. By 5 December Georgetown was quieter but the wharves were still practically at a standstill. On 6 December, however, most of the strikes were over and the governor said that Georgetown was back to normal. Some sugar factory workers were still on strike in West Bank estates and workers at Peter's Hall on the East Bank struck for higher wages. On the West Bank, Phillip Washington of Toevlugt became a recognised strike leader. He mobilised in Bagotstown and brought out the workers at Plantations Nismes, Schoonord and Wales. Workers at Plantation Versailles were also involved and some managers were now prepared to negotiate. On 12 December about 225 workers employed at an American-owned quartz mine in the Purumi River district went on strike, demanding $1.50 per day for men working underground, instead of their current wages of between 64 cents and $1.20. By that time, however, the colonial state, strengthened by almost 600 men from HMS *Diamond* and HMS *Sappho*, had reacted with such repression that the labour disturbances subsided. So-called ringleaders were arrested and others were intimidated. Another problem was the strikers' 'sheer want, since the workers had no means of surviving without employment',[41] and they lacked organisation and strike relief funds.

The colonial state's coercive apparatus was effectively brought to bear on the working people of Guyana in 1905. Without plans, organisation, or support systems, this spontaneous workers' rebellion quickly ebbed. 'At best, ad hoc committees of workers sought audience with employers and with the colonial authorities. Alternatively, middle-class spokesmen presented themselves as negotiators'.[42] The state's forces, acting on behalf of the employers to intimidate strikers, killed several people and jailed others, while reinforcing the authoritarian response to the workers' reasonable demands for wage increases, demands that were interpreted as criminal acts. As Rodney states, 'There was certainly no plan to stage a violent rebellion. The corollary to this was that state agencies were largely responsible for forcing the wage protests in the direction of mass violence'.[43] This pattern was repeated all too frequently in later years. Hardliners among the employers, who were unwilling to negotiate with their workers, were effectively supported by the state, while managers who were willing to compromise were undermined by the general show of force. Governor Hodgson, accompanied by troops from the naval ships, visited several West Bank plantations and forced the managers to renege on new wage rates they had promised their workers, on the grounds that such concessions would encourage further wage demands. 'The governor told them plainly that they should follow his advice or he would withdraw the armed forces from their estates and leave them to the mercy of the "rioters"'.[44]

The colonial government did not try anyone by a jury because it was convinced that no jury would convict. Instead, using the Summary Convictions Ordinance of 1893, which was effective as soon as Georgetown was 'proclaimed' on 30 November, dozens of people were charged with 'disorderly conduct', possession of 'dangerous weapons', 'throwing stones', and 'assaulting police'. Many people were fined and imprisoned; some men were flogged and women had their heads shaved as additional punishments. These archaic and brutal penalties were possible under an amendment to the Summary Criminal Offences Ordinance in 1904, which had been passed with the intention of dealing with street people who were known as 'centipedes'. In this way, the working people who struggled for better wages were defined and treated as common criminals and social refuse by the authoritarian colonial state. The agents of the state, meanwhile, were not punished for their excesses. Patrick Dargan, a lawyer whose newspaper, the *Creole*, criticised the colonial administration for its handling of the disturbances, brought charges against Inspector-General Lushington and Major de Rinzy, alleging that they were criminally liable for the deaths of people at the hands of the police. These cases were dismissed.

The colonial administration could not be too complacent about these events, however, as there was evidence of quite widespread disaffection among the middle classes. A military tribunal dealt with some of the many militiamen who deserted or failed to answer the call to arms. Several were sentenced to imprisonment but were released after one month, and other pending cases, including one against Sergeant William Dathorne, a schoolteacher who had urged his fellow militiamen not to turn out, were dismissed. Over 100 men of this middle-class militia had failed to answer the call, and these defections suggest that many middle-class Guyanese sympathised with the strikers and could no longer be counted on as subalterns by the colonial authorities. Some middle-class people showed that they could be active as allies in the workers' cause. Some educated people were alienated from the colonial regime because they were excluded from participation in the political process and discriminated against within the colonial establishment. A.A. Thorne, an educator from Barbados who became one of Guyana's trade union leaders in the 1930s, publicised the workers' grievances, but he was careful to disassociate himself from the 'centipedes' who were alleged to have committed the violence. Thorne and some other members of the People's Association, which had been formed in 1903, including Patrick Dargan and Dr J.M. Rohlehr, won the respect and support of many working people. However, the People's Association, which had unsuccessfully called for the formation of a trade union, failed to organise the workers.

The actual leaders of this labour rebellion were themselves workers, who seem to have emerged at the local level in the course of the disturbances, and 'did not reappear subsequently as national trade unionists'.[45] Phillip Washington, Long Walk and Robert Chapman have already been mentioned. Another local leader was George Henry or George Beckles, a cane cutter who led his mates out of the fields when he heard the factory workers had struck. Police stopped them and told them to give up their cutlasses. This they did, until the police tried to gather them up, when they objected. There was a scuffle and Henry, who had previously been identified as a ringleader, was arrested. He was subsequently sentenced to six months in prison with a flogging. Women, too, were active. Of the 105 people convicted in the magistrates' courts as a consequence of these disturbances, 41 were women, many of whom were probably domestic workers, washerwomen, street vendors and seamstresses in Georgetown. Though there were fewer Afro-Guyanese women working on the sugar estates, one of them, Dorothy Rice, was part of a workers' delegation from Ruimveldt. She explained that, though she worked cutting cane up to 7 pm each day and to midday on Saturdays, and had two daughters assist her with fetching the canes, she earned no more than 6 or 7s. per week.[46] These workers were evidently militant and courageous, but without organisation they could not win in a struggle that was not only against their employers but also the power of the colonial state.

One major problem that the workers faced in Guyana in 1905 was the racial split in their ranks. Though they succeeded to some extent in bringing together urban and rural workers, employed and unemployed, women and men, and they obtained some sympathetic support from members of the middle classes, the 1905 disturbances seem to have been limited to Guyanese workers of African descent. The workers who went on strike in the sugar estates were factory workers and cane cutters who, according to the prevailing ethnic segmentation of the labour force, were largely Africans. Though management at Plantation Versailles promised wage increases to Indian as well as African workers, 'Indians were absent from the demonstrations'.[47] Some employers tried the old tactic of making Indians fill the places of Africans who were on strike, thereby fostering tensions between them. At Ruimveldt striking Africans kept Indians away from the job site, but no major conflict was provoked between them.

It was clearly official policy, as well as the employers' goal, to confine the disturbances to the African Guyanese and to 'prevent the spread of strike action and combination across racial lines',[48] and in this they were largely successful. However, the need for a massive show of force, including two imperial warships, and the defection of so many members of the militia and middle classes in this critical time, indicate that, though the working class was not united, the colonial state was not entirely secure. The response of the state was to increase and reorganise its local armed forces, the chief function of which was to suppress the expression of discontent by working people. In place of the unreliable militia, a mounted police branch, comprising initially 40 mounted policemen, was created for riot control and the government tried to start 'a volunteer force from among locally resident whites and senior employees of the large merchant firms'.[49] The resort to such means of force, however, was tantamount to an admission of failure by the colonial regime to establish its authority as legitimate. Moreover, the class and racial basis of this force was quite transparent to all concerned, which further undermined the regime's legitimacy in the minds of the majority.

Although the Guyanese labour rebellion of 1905 was not successful, it should not be seen as a complete failure. The divisions among the working people of Guyana, and particularly the great racial split which coincided with the division of labour, could not be easily overcome, so the rebellion never came close to becoming a general strike or uprising so long as the Indians did not participate.

However, in the context of 1905, and viewed in comparison with other parts of the British Caribbean at the time, it contributed to the development of an especially militant class consciousness and the early formation of organised working-class institutions in Guyana.

The grievances of men and women from the sugar estates and Georgetown were articulated and fought for in 1905 and, though their leaders were victimised, the experience surely provided a basis for future action for many people. In 1906 the governor was still concerned that so many people in Georgetown showed disrespect to him, the representative of the king and the empire. Groups of people openly discussed the court cases of the militia and of Lushington and de Rinzy. In this way, what had started as a specifically labour issue concerning wages was becoming a more generally political affair. Then in September 1906 there was another strike among Georgetown's stevedores. Because the grievances that had caused the disturbances of 1905 remained unresolved, they continued to ferment.

Dock workers at Bookers Brothers McConnell and Company and at Sandbach Parker and Company went on strike at 1 pm on 25 September 1906. This time it seemed that 'a secret underground movement was being built up'[50] as the workers acted without warning, but also in a controlled way, without violence. This was a quiet, determined and organised strike, timed to coincide with the arrival of several ships in the port. On the second day the strike spread but, with mounted police patrolling the streets, there was no public disturbance. Some workers at Plantation Providence stopped work and came to Georgetown to make a complaint, but this was only a temporary stoppage and no other sugar workers joined them. The employers on the docks used strike-breakers and after three days the strike collapsed. Many strikers who returned to work were 'told with frigid politeness that their services were not required'.[51] During the strike a 22-year old dock worker named Hubert Nathaniel Critchlow was charged with assault on 27 September. The magistrate dismissed the case and 'Critchlow left the Court a hero'.[52] Critchlow was born in Georgetown on 18 December 1884, the son of a dock worker who had immigrated from Barbados. He had left primary school at the age of 14, but he became the greatest of the early leaders of organised labour in the British Caribbean.

There were several other strikes in Guyana in the following years, but it was during the First World War, when shortages provoked more demonstrations and disturbances, that Critchlow became more prominent. In 1916 he led a demonstration and delegation to the governor, Sir Wilfred Collet. As a result the dock workers gained a 10 per cent increase in wages and a reduction of their working day from ten and a half to nine and a half hours. Critchlow continued to agitate for reduced working hours, seeking an eight hour day. A strike in 1917 obtained a nine hour day, with a lunch break and rest period, and overtime pay for work after 5 pm and on Sundays and holidays. Many other strikes followed, at sawmills, on the railway, in the ice, match and soda factories, and among sea defence and road workers. These early efforts at collective bargaining led others, including post office workers, to petition for higher wages. Later, Critchlow negotiated a further wage increase with the chamber of commerce, but he lost his job in 1918 and was unable to find other work at the wharves as a result of being victimised by the chamber of commerce.

Critchlow was the recognised leader of Guyanese workers at this time. He led a massive demonstration in 1918, held talks with Governor Collet and on 11 January 1919 announced the formation of the British Guiana Labour Union (BGLU). Critchlow was the union's secretary, treasurer and organiser. By the end of the year the BGLU had about 7,000 members, including porters and labourers, tradesmen, sea defence and road workers, railway employees, factory workers, government employees, sugar estate workers and interior workers such as balata bleeders and miners, as well as dock workers, with branches in villages on the East and West Demerara Coasts, on the Essequibo Coast and in Berbice.[53] Critchlow's BGLU hosted the first regional labour conference in 1926 and was still active in the 1930s and 1940s. There are thus clear and direct connections between the waterfront strikes in Georgetown in 1905 and 1906 and the emergence of the first major trade union and the regional labour movement in the British Caribbean. The labour rebellion of 1905, far from being a failure, therefore, played an important part in the formation of a working class in Guyana and of organised labour in the Caribbean.

During this early phase of working-class activity, several small unions of skilled artisans were formed in Jamaica. Among them was the Carpenters, Bricklayers and Painters Union, organised in 1898, which became known as the Artisans Union, officers of which helped form the Tailors and Shoemakers' Union in 1901. Short-lived unions of printers, in which Marcus Garvey was involved, and of cigar makers were formed in 1907. A carpenter, W.G. Hinchcliffe, started the Jamaica Trades and Labour Union in 1907, but two years later it ceased to function because its most 'zealous' members had emigrated to Haiti and Central America. None of these early Jamaican unions survived into the second decade of the century. [54]

One of the earliest and longest lasting organisations of working people in the British Caribbean was the Trinidad Workingmen's Association (TWA), formed in 1897. Its core consisted of skilled workers, like the early Jamaican unions, but the TWA also sought to include unskilled workers employed on the railway and waterfront, and to engage in reformist politics as well as trade union activities. Its first president, Walter Mills, was a druggist. He opposed Indian immigration but advocated free grants of five acres of land to labourers from Barbados, Tobago and Grenada. 'Labour by compulsion', he told the Royal Commission in 1897, 'can be nothing else but a state of half-slavery'. [55]

The TWA was quite inactive until 1906, when Alfred Richards, an Afro-Chinese pharmacist, became president. The other members of the 1906 executive committee were a tailor, a mason, a carpenter, a planter and a commission agent. The chief activities of this largely petty bourgeois and skilled artisan group were in political reform rather than trade union affairs. The TWA worked in close association with the Ratepayers' Association and sought affiliation with the British Labour Party in 1906. It remained an urban-based organisation and its failure to recruit Indians was 'a major shortcoming, reflecting prejudice or neglect, or both'.[56] Attempts were made in 1910 to form the Trinidad Bakers' Association and the Progressive Crafts Union of artisans, but both soon disappeared. Despite these efforts, by the First World War there was 'no combination of workers or body genuinely concerned with building a close-knit rank-and-file workers' organisation in Trinidad'.[57] In 1914 there was a split in the TWA when one faction, led by J. Sidney de Bourg, tried to end Richards' leadership, and by 1916 there were two 'branches' of the TWA, neither of which 'could honestly claim to represent any important section of the people'. [58]

The first wave of working-class unrest in the British Caribbean which had begun in the depression years of the nineteenth century had ebbed away by about 1907 and little was left to show for it by the time the war began. The most militant activity was in Guyana, but the most serious attempts at organisation before the war were in Jamaica and Trinidad. Though there were many self-help organisations, such as friendly societies and fraternal lodges, there were no trade unions in the smaller colonies. In some respects, the friendly societies served as 'proto-unions', providing some security in the form of sick and death benefits, and opportunities for working people to develop organisational skills and a sense of self-reliance. In some cases the friendly societies handled considerable sums of money, including contributions from overseas, like 'Panama money'.

More labour agitation occurred during the war. In addition to the working-class demonstrations and strikes in Guyana in 1916 and 1917, there were disturbances and strikes in Trinidad, St Lucia, St Kitts, and Antigua in 1917 and 1918, but the war-time atmosphere and official restrictions were not conducive to organised labour or radical ideas, and political mobilisation did not progress until after the war had ended. The chief cause of discontent was 'the rapid increase in the prices of imported items of popular consumption during the course of the war, against a background of little or no increase in the level of wages'.[59] According to Peter Fraser, the price of flour, salted fish, salted beef and cotton manufactures rose in Guyana from a base of 100 in 1914 to 227, 228, 229 and 400, respectively, in 1918, while imports of flour, salted beef and cotton manufactures fell over this period to about two-thirds of the 1914 level and of salted fish by over 39 per cent. The governor of Guyana wrote to the Colonial Office on 31 January 1917, 'In view of the undoubted increase of prices due to the war, I fear the labour unrest in the Colony cannot yet be regarded as at an end'. [60]

This situation, which was common more or less throughout the British Caribbean during the war, caused considerable hardship and increasing discontent. In St Lucia, there were several strikes both in the rural areas and in Castries in 1917. Stevedores obtained average wage increases of 25 per cent and the coal carriers 15 per cent. In St Kitts-Nevis workers tried to form a trade union in 1917. A small shopkeeper, J.A. Nathan, who had experienced trade unionism when he lived in the United States, was one of the organisers of the St Kitts-Nevis Universal Benevolent Association, registered under the Friendly Societies Act, and J. Matthew Sebastian, its president, began a labour-oriented newspaper, *The Union Messenger*, in 1921. Unions were illegal, however, and when some St Kitts workers went on strike in 1918 they were arrested and imprisoned for breach of contract, which was still a criminal offence. There was also a strike in Antigua in March 1918, provoked by an attempt to reduce the wages of cane cutters. Canefields were burned and some planters were attacked. When protests spread to the town of St John, the police fired into a crowd, killing two people. An administrator alleged that one man, Arlington Newton, was behind the efforts to form a trade union in St Kitts in 1917 and the strike in Antigua in 1918.[61] This may have been true, or it may reflect the administrator's paranoia about labour agitators.

In Trinidad war-time restrictions checked the workers' protests, but in March 1917 workers in the oil and asphalt industries were involved in serious disturbances. Despite the fact that they were better paid than most labourers, they suffered as the others did from rising prices. Workers at the Point Fortin oilfields and the Asphalt Company refinery at Brighton went on strike between 19 and 26 March. Armed police went to other oilfields at Tabaguite and Fyzabad and the management dismissed and evicted some strikers at Fyzabad. George Richardson, the strikers' leader, rejected the oilfield company's effort to get them to resume work at the current rate of pay, but the strikers were at a great disadvantage because they had no strike funds or union organisation and they lived on company property. The leaders were ejected from the area and 50 soldiers were drafted to replace the strikers. In five days the Point Fortin strike collapsed. At Brighton, where the asphalt workers went on strike on 21 March, buildings and refined asphalt were destroyed by fire, but most of the 540 strikers returned to work by the sixth day. Three strikers and several other people, including a Seventh Day Adventist preacher who allegedly urged the men to strike, were arrested, and some received prison sentences. The strikes had failed.[62]

The TWA, meanwhile, was still divided into two factions. On the one hand, Alfred Richards tried to keep the TWA as a strictly political organisation involved chiefly in municipal politics, while, on the other hand, the rebel branch, whose leaders included David Headley, James Braithwaite, William Howard Bishop, and J. Sidney de Bourg, behaved more as if it were a trade union. Several of these leaders were immigrants and hence vulnerable to threats of deportation. De Bourg, for example, who was from Grenada, and had been active in radical Trinidad politics since the 1880s, was deported in 1920. Braithwaite, a Barbadian dock worker, who became secretary of the TWA in 1918, and Bishop, a Guyanese journalist and teacher, were also vulnerable. These rebel leaders took over the TWA in 1918.

Though it was neither large nor well organised, the TWA 'became the main agency through which worker grievances were articulated, and it taught Trinidadians the methods of collective political and industrial action'.[63] In the first months of 1919 there were strikes by dockers, railwaymen, city council employees and workers at the Electric and Telephone companies, and the TWA leaders played an active role in the agitation for higher wages. When asphalt workers at La Brea asked TWA leaders to negotiate for them, the team achieved a 33 per cent wage increase, a reduction of working hours by one hour, and an increase in overtime rates of 150 per cent. This victory was important because it 'boosted TWA's status among workers, leading to an increase in its membership, and the establishment of two branches at La Brea and San Fernando'.[64] Though trade unions remained illegal, organised labour in Trinidad was clearly progressing by 1919.

In Jamaica workers at the Kingston Ice Factory went on strike in 1917 and several were imprisoned.[65] Cigar makers, led by J. A. Bain-Alves, who had been a member of their short-lived union in 1908, went on strike and formed a new union. In 1918 Bain-Alves organised unions among dock workers and tram workers in Kingston, and A.J. McGlashan organised waiters. In the same year several strikes erupted in Kingston, among employees of the fire brigade in April, and then among the longshoremen and coal heavers on the wharves and the sanitation workers. A strike among sugar workers at Amity Hall plantation at Vere in Clarendon, resulted in violent police action: three workers were shot and killed and a dozen wounded in 1918.[66] Other strikes occurred at estates in Golden Grove in St Thomas and Annotto Bay in St Mary, but no attempt was made to organise agricultural workers at this time. In 1919 W.G. Hinchcliffe, a carpenter who had been secretary of the early Artisans' Union, was again trying to organise workers in the building trades. Workers employed on the railway went on strike and in 1919 formed a 'union under cover' called the Workingmen's Co-operative Association in 1919.[67]

Bain-Alves, the founder and president of the Longshoremen's Union, with the help of Alfred Mends, who had been vice-president and secretary of the Artisans' Union in 1908, formed the Jamaican Federation of Labour (JFL), a group of embryonic unions under his presidency.[68] The JFL petitioned Governor Sir Leslie Probyn to give legal and official recognition to trade unions. As a result, the Trade Union Law, introduced into the Legislative Council in March 1919, became law on 25 October 1919. This law conferred legal status on registered trade unions and protected them from prosecution for conspiracy or unlawful combinations, but it did not confer immunity for unions and workers from liability for tort or breach of contract, nor did it legalise peaceful picketing.[69] Prior to this legislation trade unions were illegal throughout the British Caribbean. Similar legislation was passed in Guyana in June 1921, but not in Trinidad and other parts of the British Caribbean until the 1930s and 1940s.

The strikes and organisation of workers in Jamaica in 1917 and 1918 provided the necessary pressure that resulted in the significant, though still limited, legalisation of trade unions in 1919. They also show that there was important continuity, albeit interrupted, between the first, second and third waves of labour unrest in Jamaica, between the 1880s and 1908, 1917 and 1919, and the 1930s. Some people, including Bain-Alves, Mends, Hinchcliffe, McGlashan[70] and Garvey, were active as organisers in more than one of these periods, and some of them in all three.

Notes

1. Turner 1988.
2. Hart 1988: 43-50.
3. Bryan 1991: 226.

4. Richardson 1992a: 179.
5. Bryan 1991: 266.
6. *Ibid.*, 266-67, 276.
7. *Ibid.*, 270-71.
8. *Ibid.*, 268.
9. 'Wharf Labourers' Strike in Kingston', *Jamaica Advocate*, 1 June 1895, quoted in Bryan 1991: 268.
10. Bryan 1991: 269.
11. 'Wharf Labourers' Strike', *op.cit.*, quoted in Bryan 1991: 269.
12. Quoted in Bryan 1991: 271.
13. *Ibid.*, 271.
14. *Ibid.*, 272-74.
15. Quoted in Bryan 1991: 275.
16. *Ibid.*
17. Thomas 1927: 122, quoted in Bryan 1991: 276.
18. Richardson 1992b: 182.
19. Baker 1994: 121-22.
20. Cited by Ashdown 1979.
21. *Ibid.*, 79-86.
22. This account is largely based on Richards 1993.
23. Richardson 1983: 106.
24. Frucht 1967; Rodney 1981: 218.
25. Rodney 1981: 220.
26. Adamson 1972: 130.
27. Moore 1987: 173.
28. Adamson 1972: 155.
29. *Ibid.*, 154.
30. Rodney 1981: 163.
31. *Ibid.*, 164.
32. *Ibid.*, 158.
33. Gov. Hemming to Joseph Chamberlain, 4 March 1897, Colonial Office records, hereafter CO, CO 111/493.
34. Adamson 1972: 156.
35. Rodney 1981: 159.
36. *Ibid.*, 157.
37. *Ibid.*, 159.
38. This account is based largely on Chase n.d.: 20-27 and Rodney 1981: 190-216.
39. Infant mortality rates fell to about 190 per 1,000 live births between 1911 and 1920, and then declined steadily to about 175 per 1,000 in 1921-25, to 146 per 1,000 in 1931-35, to 110 per 1,000 in 1941-45, and 64 per 1,000 in 1956-60 (Mandle 1973: 88).
40. MCC Special Session, 1906, 'Report on General Mortality and Infant Mortality', quoted in Rodney 1981: 195.
41. Rodney 1981: 194.
42. *Ibid.*, 198-99.
43. *Ibid.*, 199.
44. *Ibid.*, 200.
45. *Ibid.*, 208.
46. *Ibid.*, 207.
47. *Ibid.*, 212.

48. *Ibid.*, 213.

49. *Ibid.*, 215.

50. Chase n.d.: 36.

51. *Ibid.*, 37.

52. *Ibid.* It has also been said that Critchlow was arrested for disorderly behaviour and assault, and later released, during the 1905 disturbances (Harry 1977: 14).

53. Chase n.d.: 50.

54. Hart 1988: 43-44.

55. Quoted in Ramdin 1982: 43.

56. *Ibid.*, 46.

57. *Ibid.*, 49.

58. *Ibid.*, 48.

59. Hart 1988: 50.

60. Cited in Fraser 1981.

61. *Ibid.*, 6.

62. Ramdin 1982: 49-51.

63. Brereton 1981: 160.

64. *Ibid.*, 161.

65. Hart 1988: 52.

66. Eaton 1975: 20.

67. Hart 1988: 52.

68. *Ibid.*; Post 1978: 212.

69. Eaton 1975: 20; Hart 1988: 74.

70. A.J. McGlashan, a seaman who organised waiters in 1918, was a champion of Jamaican seamen in the mid-1930s, and a member of the committee of a labour union created by the Permanent Jamaica Development Convention in June 1935 (Post 1978: 241).

Chapter TWO

Demobilised soldiers from the British West Indies Regiment

A new factor after the First World War, which was manifested in several parts of the British Caribbean, was the role of demobilised soldiers returning home from service with the British West Indies Regiment (BWIR). Bitterly disillusioned with the racial discrimination they had encountered during their war-time service for the 'mother country', and coming home to face unemployment and poverty, these men 'swelled the ranks of the discontented'[1] and as ex-soldiers they were not easily intimidated by the standard show of force. Strong racial feelings, in addition to the concern about worsening economic conditions, were responsible for popular unrest in several British Caribbean colonies in 1919.

Thousands of West Indians volunteered for service in the First World War and most of them, 397 officers and 15,204 other ranks, served in the BWIR, which was created in 1915. The largest contingent by far, consisting of 303 officers and 9,977 other ranks, came from Jamaica. Another 40 officers and 1,438 other ranks came from Trinidad and Tobago, and 20 officers and 811 other ranks from Barbados. Even the small colonies contributed men, with 441 men from the Bahamas, 533 from Belize, 445 from Grenada, 700 from Guyana, 229 from the Leeward Islands, 359 from St Lucia, and 305 from St Vincent. By 1917, Belize had sent 12.8 men per 1,000 of its population, well above the regional average of 4.9 per 1,000, so recruiting was suspended in that colony in order not to further affect the local labour supply.[2] Of the total of 15,601 men, 1,256 were killed or died of wounds or sickness, and 697 were wounded.[3]

Two battalions of the BWIR were involved in fighting in Palestine and Jordan against the Turkish army, but the War Office was determined that black colonial troops would not fight against Europeans. Consequently, most of the BWIR functioned as labour battalions, employed in handling ammunition and digging cable trenches and gun emplacements in France, often under heavy shell fire, and working on the quays in Taranto, in southern Italy. Many West Indian soldiers served garrison duties in Egypt, and small parties were sent to East Africa and Mesopotamia, also in non-combatant roles. The racist policy of using West Indian soldiers primarily as labour battalions was compounded by the policy that the officers of these black troops must be white.[4] Further, towards the end of the war, when British soldiers received pay increases of 50 per cent, the War Office ruled that West Indians were not eligible because they were 'natives'.[5]

The pattern of discrimination continued after hostilities ceased, when the battalions of the BWIR from France and Egypt joined those already in Taranto. There the West Indians were not treated like British troops, but were 'humiliated and badly treated', some of them having to wash dirty linen and clean latrines for other troops, as if they were labour battalions.[6] On 6 December 1918, members of the 9th Battalion of the BWIR attacked their officers, and 180 sergeants petitioned the secretary of state for the colonies, protesting against the discrimination they suffered. After several days of 'insubordination', during which the men refused to work, the 9th Battalion was disbanded and a machine-gun unit of the Worcestershire Regiment was sent to Taranto.[7] There were several other incidents of 'insubordination', as some West Indians refused to carry out the duties they were assigned, and on 17 December some 50 or 60 sergeants of the BWIR secretly formed the Caribbean League at Cimino camp. At several meetings through into early January 1919, they discussed their grievances, including the replacement of black by white non-commissioned officers. They demanded that 'the black man should have freedom to govern himself' and declared that they were prepared to use force to that end, and to strike for higher wages after demobilisation. The Caribbean League was betrayed to the officers and disbanded.[8] Some soldiers were convicted of mutiny and received sentences of 3 or 5 years in prison. One was sentenced to 20 years in prison and another was executed by firing squad.[9] The decision was made to disarm the West Indian soldiers and to repatriate them as soon as possible.[10]

The Colonial Office was concerned that these men would promote disorder when repatriated and warned the West Indian governors of such a danger. In February 1919 the Colonial Office secured the pay increases previously denied to the BWIR, and applied them retroactively in order to allay their resentment, but also asked the Admiralty to make a warship available near Jamaica at the time of demobilisation. In March there was discussion about issuing machine-guns to West Indian police forces, provided they were supervised by white officers, to meet any disorders that might arise on the return of men from the BWIR. C.L. Joseph states that: 'The disturbances expected in the early post-war period did not materialize, despite the fact that many ex-soldiers experienced difficulty in obtaining their pay and pensions'.[11] In fact, however, there were some serious disturbances, in which demobilised soldiers of the BWIR played a major role, in Belize in July 1919 and in Trinidad in November and December 1919. These disturbances, in turn, contributed to the development of racial and class consciousness and incipient nationalism in those colonies in the interwar period.[12]

The situation in Belize, where 339 demobilised soldiers from the BWIR returned on 8 July 1919, had been growing increasingly tense with racial feeling. The tensions of race and class that had erupted in 1894 continued to cause disturbance. During the administration of Governor Sir Wilfred Collett, between 1913 and 1918, there were several racial incidents, including the exclusion of H.H. Vernon, a prominent middle-class Creole, from the governor's reception prior to the departure of the first Belizean volunteers to the BWIR in 1915. When the public buildings in Belize Town caught fire in August 1918, the colonial officials felt that the creole public was indifferent.[13] Copies of Garvey's paper, the *Negro World,* had been entering Belize in large numbers since 1918, and in January 1919 Acting-Governor Walter proscribed its circulation. This ban, which was ineffective as copies continued to be smuggled in, 'created much local resentment'.[14] A deputation, led by a black radical, Herbert Hill Cain, demanded a revocation of the ban as the paper was allowed to circulate elsewhere in the West Indies.[15] Walter's dismissal of the deputation and maintenance of the ban was subsequently held to be one of the grievances that provoked the disturbances in July.[16] Cain published a newspaper, the *Belize Independent,* that emphasised black achievements and included a column called 'The Garvey Eye', written by L.D. Kemp. Samuel Haynes, who had been a corporal in the BWIR, wrote to the *Belize Independent* in 1919, complaining of their treatment by British soldiers in Egypt in 1916. Arriving hungry and tired, the Belizean soldiers were singing 'Rule Britannia' when British soldiers demanded, 'Who gave you niggers authority to sing that? Clear out of this building, only British troops admitted here'.[17]

The demobilised soldiers were reviewed and addressed by the new governor, Sir Eyre Hutson, and given a meal and $10 to keep them going, but some resented their exclusion from a social event at the golf club. On the night of 22 July, resentment erupted in violence when ex-soldiers, led by Sergeant Hubert Vernon, raged through the town smashing windows in the principal stores and assaulting some officials and employers. Joined by other working people of the town, a crowd of perhaps 3,000 people rioted through the night. The government remained helpless to stop them because it could not trust the local police and only some members of the volunteer Territorial Force responded to the authorities. Then some of the former soldiers, led by Samuel Haynes, helped to stop the looting and violence. Order was restored by the next morning, and the arrival of HMS *Constance* on 24 July brought the disturbances to an end. Haynes, as secretary of the British Honduras Contingent Committee, subsequently sought the release of several soldiers who had been imprisoned but, as an associate of Cain, he was seen by the governor as 'a troublesome agitator'.[18]

The chief consequence of these disturbances was the heightening of racial and anticolonial feeling in general, and of support for Garvey's philosophy in particular. In April 1920 a group of Belizean Creoles created a local branch of the UNIA. Haynes was the general secretary, and he subsequently became one of the principal leaders of the UNIA.[19] Others involved in the UNIA were Cain and Kemp of the *Belize Independent,* and Calvert Staine, who later became a city councillor and a nominated member of the Legislative Council from 1942 to 1947. This local UNIA branch received a visit from Garvey himself in 1921, when he held several public meetings, exhorting his supporters to purchase shares in the Black Star Line. Though Garvey's visit encouraged interest in the UNIA, when Samuel Haynes left with him for the United States the Belize branch lost its most able member. A successful branch of the Black Cross Nurses was created in Belize by Vivian Seay in 1920,[20] but a split developed in the UNIA local in 1927 between L.D. Kemp, the executive secretary, and Benjamin Pitts, the president.

When Garvey again visited Belize, in 1929, his organisation was in decline internationally as well as locally. Nevertheless, his ideas influenced racial consciousness in Belize and several Garveyites, including Cain, Kemp and Staine, continued to be politically active, while some of the leaders of the labour movement that began in 1934 were also followers of Garvey. In fact, the development of racial and class consciousness was so closely interrelated in the interwar years in Belize that it is somewhat artificial to try to distinguish between them. The emergence of racial and class consciousness, together, was a resistant response to the prevailing colonial political economy and began to shape a new anti–colonial and nationalist ideology in Belize.

There were demonstrations also in Jamaica in July and August 1919. F.E.M. Hercules, a Trinidadian resident in London, who was the secretary of the Society of Peoples of African Origin, arrived in Jamaica in June and addressed several public meetings, advising workers to press for a minimum wage law. During his visit, railway workers went on strike for a higher wage, white sailors were attacked, and there were demonstrations in Kingston.

In Trinidad, as in Belize, the return of soldiers from the BWIR played a major part in the development of racial feeling and of serious unrest in 1919 and 1920. In July 1919, there was already evidence of anti-white feeling when British sailors were attacked in the streets of Port-of-Spain. The local press, particularly the *Argos*, reported racial incidents in Britain, including the anti-black riots in Cardiff and Liverpool in which hundreds of black people were attacked and a Trinidadian sailor who had served in the navy during the war, Charles Wotten, was murdered.[21] Hercules, who was well-known for his defence of blacks in Britain, visited Trinidad in September 1919, where he 'contributed to the development of black nationalism'.[22] While unrest escalated, the governor refused to allow Hercules to return to Trinidad at the end of the year.

The *Argos* and the *Negro World* promoted race-conscious views in Trinidad and many sailors brought in Garveyite and socialist ideas. Members of the white community urged the colonial secretary to suppress the *Argos*, arm the white people, and station British troops in the colony because of what they saw as the hostility of the black population. Returned soldiers who found it hard to obtain jobs and were annoyed at the delays in settling their claims for pay, allowances and pensions, formed the Returned Soldiers and Sailors Council, and contributed 'to the already deteriorating and explosive situation'.[23]

The dock workers of Port-of-Spain, supported by the TWA, took the initiative in November 1919 and started what was to become virtually a general strike. The dock workers in Trinidad, as elsewhere, were a radical element in the emerging working class. They were concentrated on the waterfront and were in regular contact with international news and ideas, including radical ideas about trade unionism, socialism and Garveyism, disseminated through the sailors who brought in literature and engaged them in discussions. Many of the dock workers, like James Braithwaite of the TWA, were immigrants from other colonies who brought with them broader experience and a wider perspective on local issues. They suffered in their work from irregular employment and great insecurity, as well as suffering from low wages and high inflation like other workers. In 1919 they demanded a wage increase, overtime pay, and an eight hour day, and were probably encouraged in this by the efforts of Critchlow and his BGLU in Guyana. The TWA, whose president and secretary were stevedores, sought to negotiate on the dock workers' behalf, but the shipping agents refused, saying this was 'a piece of impudence on the part of those who had no authority from the men to make such representations'.[24] On 15 November the dock workers went on strike. It was

> a well-planned strike, with a high level of collective organization and action among the workers on the waterfront. Scab labour was used to keep the docks functioning, and on 1 December dockers attacked warehouses, ran the scabs off the waterfront, and marched through the city forcing businesses to close. City council employees and coal carriers joined the strike. [25]

The employers' attempt to use strike-breakers from rural Trinidad and Venezuela and to fire strikers backfired. Instead of intimidating the workers, it angered them and made them more determined, thus escalating the confrontation.

The strikers achieved extensive public support. Even the governor acknowledged that workers had been hit hard by uncontrolled inflation and price-gouging:

> the scandalous prices charged by the dry goods merchants have added to the difficulties of the poorer classes in maintaining themselves. As an illustration of the profits they are making, I may mention that one John Smith, owner of a business called Bonanza, who was supposed to be on the brink of bankruptcy when the war broke out in 1914, died six months ago leaving £250,000.[26]

On 1 December, thousands of supporters joined the strikers in a march through Port of Spain that brought the city to a standstill. While the police, Volunteers and Mounted Infantry were mobilised and a warship and white troops were requested, Dr Stephen Laurence, a popular coloured member of the Executive Council, urged Governor Chancellor to compromise.

The TWA provided a structure within which the strikers and protesters could operate, encouraged collective action and became an agency through which grievances were articulated. A conciliation board was created, consisting of two shipping company representatives, two TWA leaders representing the strikers and two government appointees. The evident strength of the strike and support for the TWA had forced the employers and government to accept the TWA as the collective bargaining agency, effectively a union, of the workers. After a single meeting of the board, on 3 December, the shipping companies granted a 25 per cent wage increase to the waterfront workers.[27] This victory encouraged other workers to strike throughout Trinidad and Tobago. HMS *Calcutta* was sent to Tobago where estate workers struck and marched through Scarborough. The Riot Act was read and the police fired, killing one striker, Nathaniel Williams, and wounding seven others. Order was restored only after the marines landed. In Port of Spain, city council employees struck for higher wages and chose the TWA to represent them. Meanwhile, Indian estate workers went on strike at Montserrat, Couva, Cunupia, Esperanza, Sangre Grande, D'Abadie and Chaguanas. In a strike at Woodford Lodge an Indian worker was killed by a white plantation official.[28] Workers took to the streets in San Fernando, and at Central Oilfields in southern Trinidad fitters and labourers went on strike, demanding a 25 per cent wage increase. On 5 January oil workers on strike at Point Fortin returned to work only after the secretary of the TWA persuaded them to do so, but two weeks later the Asphalt Company workers at La Brea struck.

The governor and the chamber of commerce felt that black police and militia were unreliable in the circumstances as they could not be counted on to protect strike-breakers or to suppress riots. A white volunteer force of businessmen and their friends, called the Colonial Vigilantes, was formed and 350 soldiers of the Royal Sussex Regiment were despatched from Britain to ensure the maintenance of law and order in the colony. It became increasingly apparent that this was class law and a racist order as the colonial government, feeling more secure with these white reinforcements, cracked down on the strikers and their leaders.

In the period of repression that followed the strikes and demonstrations of late 1919 and early 1920, 99 people were arrested and 82 of them were subsequently convicted and fined or imprisoned, among them the secretary and assistant secretary of the TWA, James Braithwaite and James Phillips. Four leading members of the TWA who were not natives of Trinidad were deported for committing seditious activities: Brutus Ironman (Guyana), Bruce McConney (Barbados), J. Sidney de Bourg (Grenada) and E. Sellier Salmon (Jamaica). The colonial government as yet saw 'little difference between industrial agitation and sedition'.[29] The *Trinidad Guardian* of 21 and 28 March 1920 published alarmist reports, lacking any factual foundation, that there was a conspiracy to massacre whites, overthrow the government and establish a black republic.

In this atmosphere, the colonial government passed the Seditious Publications Ordinance in April 1920, banning the *Negro World*, *The Monitor*, *The Crusader* and *The Recorder*. One Colonial Office adviser saw this as an attack on 'fundamental liberties' but it received approval anyway.[30] The Strikes and Lockout Ordinance, passed in January 1920, prohibited strikes by workers and provided for compulsory arbitration in wage disputes. The head of the West India Department in the Colonial Office opposed this repressive legislation, on the grounds that something should be done to improve the economic situation and thereby reduce people's 'legitimate grievances'. He concluded,

> while the cost of living is more than doubled, wages have increased in general decidedly less than one half. The existing standard of living for the labourers is much below the standard prevailing in Cuba and San Domingo. No doubt racial feeling has played a considerable part in the troubles.... But experience in St Kitts, Sir Frederick Maxwell's report from British Honduras and the Admiral's telegram...just received from Trinidad all go to show that the predominant cause was economic. The labourer is badly paid and short of clothes and cash, and he sees the planters, with sugar trebled in price, making more money than they know how to spend. Evidently this position tends to exaggeration of the racial factor in the business.[31]

He followed these comments a year later with a more specific criticism of the steamship agents, who

> in spite of the great increase in the cost of living...asked for trouble by leaving the stevedores on pre-war wages, and even this they aggravated by refusing to receive the men's representatives when the strike broke out, and by importing Venezuelans and other foreigners in order to crush it. The result has been to provoke disorder, to stir up racial feeling and to inflict upon the whole colony the expense of maintaining white troops for a long period... I cannot suppose that mob rule would have gone to such lengths if it had not been for the existence of genuine and serious grievances.[32]

While it is true that there were serious economic grievances that needed to be addressed, the 'racial factor' should not be underestimated. Racial feelings were stirred up by the way the business community responded to the strikes in Trinidad and Tobago, but these feelings were already present and had a long history. Moreover, while racial feelings were heightened before these strikes by the return of angry soldiers of the BWIR, by the circulation of the *Negro World* and similar literature and by the agitation of men like Hercules, they were endemic in the colonial situation itself. Economic and labour grievances overlapped with issues of racial oppression in colonial societies. When these issues fused in people's consciousnesses their political demands became more radical and anticolonial, as in the period immediately after the First World War.

Notes

1. Hart 1988: 50.
2. Joseph 1971: 110–11.
3. *Ibid.*, 124.
4. *Ibid.*, 103.
5. Elkins 1970: 100.
6. Joseph 1971: 119.
7. Elkins 1970: 101.
8. Joseph 1971: 120.
9. Elkins 1970: 102.
10. Joseph 1971: 118.
11. *Ibid.*, 121.
12. Elkins 1970: 103.
13. Ashdown 1981: 44.

14. *Ibid.*, 45.

15. Later, the *Negro World* was banned in 1919 and 1920 in Guyana, St Vincent and Trinidad, but after 1920 "the British rulers in the Caribbean generally did not consider the *Negro World* to be a serious threat to the colonial system" (Elkins 1971: 346).

16. "Report of the Commission appointed by the Governor to enquire into the origin of the riot in the Town of Belize which began on the night of 22nd July 1919", 10 Oct. 1919, CO 123/296.

17. Quoted in Foster 1987: 57.

18. Quoted in Ashdown 1981: 47.

19. He wrote the words of "Land of the Gods", which has become Belize's national anthem.

20. Herrmann 1985: 39-46.

21. Brereton 1981: 161.

22. *Ibid.*

23. Basdeo 1983: 15.

24. Quoted in Hart 1988: 53.

25. Brereton 1981: 162.

26. Gov. Sir John Robert Chancellor to Grindle, 20 Dec. 1919, CO 295/523. "John Smith" and "Bonanza" were presumably pseudonyms.

27. Chancellor to Milner, 7 Dec. 1919, CO 295/523.

28. Chancellor to Milner, 27 Jan. 1920, CO 295/526.

29. Basdeo 1983: 29.

30. *Ibid.*, 29.

31. Minute by C.R. Darnley, 13 Dec. 1919, CO 318/352.

32. Minute by Darnley, 23 Dec. 1920, CO 295/530.

Chapter THREE

Labour organisations in the 1920s

There is no doubt that race and class consciousness were increasing in many parts of the British Caribbean in the years immediately after the First World War, as a result of great economic hardship and the influence of Garveyism and the returning soldiers from the BWIR. What was lacking in most colonies was an organised structure that could effectively channel this consciousness into social action. However, paradoxically, two of the colonies with the most racially divided working class, namely Guyana and Trinidad, were in 1919 and 1920 the most advanced in terms of organised labour. The BGLU was the only union created at this time in the British Caribbean that continued to function in the 1930s and 1940s, while the TWA pioneered the way for future political and labour organisations in Trinidad and Tobago. Together, these early labour organisations began to conceive and coordinate a regional labour movement in 1926, when the first British Guiana and West Indies Labour Conference was held in Georgetown. Yet both the BGLU and the TWA suffered from the fact that their members and support were drawn largely from the African segments of their respective societies and that they neglected to organise the Indians.

Despite the repression in 1920, the TWA emerged with greater prestige and membership. By early 1920 the TWA had about 6,000 members and by 1921 it was 'the sole representative organization of the Trinidad workers, recognized as such by the British Government and, reluctantly, by the local officials'.[1] However, just at this time the TWA became less of a trade union and more of a reformist political party. This change was reflected and reinforced by a change in the organisation's leadership. Howard Bishop, the new secretary, began to publish a paper, the *Labour Leader*, in 1922 and to forge an alliance with middle-class liberals. The key figure became Captain Arthur Cipriani, a hero of the BWIR soldiers, who had defended them against racism, joined the TWA in 1919 and was elected its president in 1923. The shift from black working-class leaders like Headley and Braithwaite to this white middle-class officer influenced the organisational transformation of the TWA, but it was also affected by the fact that in Trinidad, unlike Jamaica and Guyana, trade unions remained illegal in the 1920s. 'Cipriani's bias was towards reformist politics rather than working class struggles... [As the TWA's president] he discouraged the trade union side of its activities and concentrated its attention on the achievement of political reforms'.[2]

Cipriani had great faith in the British Labour Party and believed that constitutional reforms would enable the people of Trinidad and Tobago to achieve improvements. Of course, this may be seen as merely self-serving, at least in part, because Cipriani based his own political career on reformist politics. He entered the Legislative Council in 1925 when the TWA won three of the five elected seats under the new constitution. While the TWA expanded and consolidated as an organisation in the 1920s, with at least 13 branches outside Port-of-Spain, 'the trade union activities declined under Cipriani's leadership'.[3] Even after legislation legalised trade unions in Trinidad and Tobago in 1934, Cipriani would not allow the TWA to register as a trade union, but instead changed its name to the Trinidad Labour Party (TLP). This 'merely confirmed a change of function that had long since been achieved in practice'.[4] The constitutional reform of 1925 had thus opened the way for middle-class political activity and confirmed the transformation of the TWA, while leaving the majority of working people unenfranchised and without an organisation that was really their own. This pattern occurred in similar fashion in other parts of the British Caribbean in subsequent decades.

Barbados in the 1920s lacked an organisation or pressure group as significant as the TWA or BGLU, but similar social and political forces were at work. A Barbados Labour Union was formed in 1919, and a branch of Garvey's UNIA in 1920. The two major figures involved in the 1920s were Clennell W. Wickham and Dr Charles Duncan O'Neale. Wickham's experience in the services in the First World War contributed to his anticolonial consciousness, just as it did for others. He became the editor of the *Barbados Herald*, a weekly newspaper started in 1919 by Clemment Innis. Wickham 'developed a socialist agenda for action, and came close to being the country's first Marxist theoretician and activist'.[5] It was O'Neale, however, who launched the Democratic League (BDL), Barbados' first political party, in October 1924. Though O'Neale and other League leaders emphasised the moderate and Christian character of their goals, they were branded 'racists' and 'bolsheviks' by their conservative opponents.[6] In December 1924, C.A. (Chrissie) Brathwaite won a seat in the Assembly in a by-election for the League, and several others were won in the next decade.

O'Neale also started the Barbados Workingmen's Association (BWA), modelled on the TWA and acting as the 'industrial and business arm' of the League, in 1926. Working closely with the UNIA, led by John Beckles, the BWA spawned two working-class organisations, the Barbados Workers' Union Cooperative Company and the Workingmen's Loan and Friendly Investment Society. Trade unions were still illegal in Barbados, but during a dock workers' strike in April 1927 the BWA and O'Neale supported the strikers. Others, including a young lawyer named Grantley Adams, attacked O'Neale and other League leaders for supporting the strike. Representing a Bridgetown merchant, Adams won a libel suit in 1930 against Wickham for his editorials in the *Herald*. The judgment ruined Wickham financially and was 'a major blow for the Democratic League and the workers' movement'.[7] The BWA, which was created at a time when trade unionism was in decline elsewhere in the region, 'did not succeed in mobilising the workers for sustained trade union activity'.[8] Adams, who was elected to the House in 1934, took up some liberal causes, but the reformist efforts of the League were frustrated in the Assembly and the

Legislative Council remained dominated by the island's conservative merchant-planter elite. The BDL and its associated organisations did not survive after O'Neale's death in 1936, though friendly societies, lodges and UNIA branches maintained some political activity at the local level.[9]

In Guyana, Critchlow's BGLU, which was formed in 1919, became the first legally recognised trade union in the British colonies. However, the union barely survived a crisis in the early 1920s. A group of middle-class people tried to take over the union in 1920 and in the struggle for leadership the workers' confidence and membership declined. In an economic crisis in 1921 the labour force was reduced by about 40 per cent and wages reduced by about 20 per cent. The BGLU, too weak to resist, gave in without a strike. The Trades Union Ordinance was enacted in June 1921 and the BGLU was formally registered on 21 July 1922. By March 1923 the union had lost its headquarters because it was unable to make the mortgage payments, and it had only 205 members. By 1924, membership had recovered to 1,129, though only 418 of these were financial. The BGLU was open to all workers but its strongest support was on the docks, where the workers were the most militant.[10]

On 31 March 1924 the stevedores demanded an increase from $1.60 to $2.00 per day, truckers from 84 cents to $1.20, and packers from $1.12 to $1.44. The BGLU also demanded double time for night work, Saturday afternoons, holidays and for work done between 4 pm and 6 pm. Another problem was the shortage of work, since most people got only one and a half days work per week on the waterfront, and the price of food had again been raised. The union called out the workers and, though the law still did not permit picketing, organised a picket line to help dissuade strike-breakers and to keep the strikers orderly. On the second day of the strike, 1 April, there was a huge demonstration of support in Georgetown, joined by several hundred sugar workers, and the saw mill, tram cars and sewage works were closed down. When they heard that strike-breakers were unloading a Canadian vessel, the crowd rushed to the wharf and drove them off. Other demonstrators closed the electric power company, the sewerage works and the railway, stopped the barges of the Demerara Bauxite Company, and middle-class homes were 'invaded' and servants told to quit work. Carpenters left their jobs and water supplies were interrupted. Governor Sir Graeme Thomson, facing widespread unrest, issued a Proclamation that invoked the provisions of the Summary Convictions Offences Ordinance of 1898, called out the Active and Reserve Military Forces, and banned all open-air meetings and demonstrations, though there was little evidence of any violence. A conspicuous show of military strength and the arrest of many men and women was intended to intimidate the demonstrators, and Critchlow was pressured to urge the strikers to return to work before any wage increases had been conceded. Placing their trust in Critchlow, they resumed work and calm returned to Georgetown, but on 4 April the shipping agents and employers rejected the workers' demands. Critchlow appealed to the governor for arbitration, but this, too, was promptly rejected.[11]

Meanwhile, sugar workers went on strike on 2 April at Plantations Houston, Farm and Providence on the East Bank of the Demerara. Creole and Indian workers marched to Diamond Estate and stopped the factory and field workers. A procession of Indian and Creole men, women and children, met by armed soldiers and police with machine-guns, chanted, 'We ain't want to see soldier with gun and revolver, we want see money'.[12] On the next day, when about 4,000 people from several estates on the East Bank headed to Georgetown, where the dock workers were still on strike and the Proclamation was in effect, their way was barred at Ruimveldt. The Riot Act was read, the crowd tried to push through the guard, and the police charged them. The crowd then stoned the police, slightly injuring one of them, and the police fired. Within a few minutes 12 people were killed and many injured, 15 of them seriously. Some Barbadian workers from Diamond, members of the BGLU, were reported to be 'ringleaders' of the crowd at Ruimveldt. Once again, 'the state machinery was firm and merciless in dealing with the workers',[13] and by the next day the East Bank was quiet. Work resumed, without any workers in the city or on the estates having made any immediate gains. The failure of the BGLU in 1924 'led to a slowing down in the recovery of the union',[14] as feelings of frustration and powerlessness rose. Nevertheless, the BGLU survived and it was the only union in Guyana in the 1920s. In fact, it was the only 'functioning trade union of manual workers' in the British Caribbean at the time the great depression hit the region.[15]

Critchlow was a regionalist and internationalist. In 1925 he attended the British Commonwealth Labour Conference in London and was inspired to organise the first regional conference in the British Caribbean. From 12 to 14 January 1926, the BGLU hosted the first British Guiana and West Indies Labour Conference in Georgetown. Critchlow was joined by Cipriani and Bishop from Trinidad's TWA and two representatives from Surinam, W.J. Lesperan and W.H. Bastick. The participation of F.O. Roberts MP, representing the British Labour Party and International Trades Union Congress, initiated a long-term relationship between the British labour movement and West Indian trade unions. Roberts' reports to the British Labour Party and TUC were 'a glaring indictment of labour conditions' in the British Caribbean, including workers' wages and welfare, and the lack of labour legislation and of protection for working women and children.[16] A.K. Amin and W.D. Dinally represented the BG East Indian Association, and a message was received from the Indian Congress urging Guyanese Indians to 'organise in alliance with workers of other nationalities to build up a Socialist State'.[17]

On Critchlow's initiative, the conference approved a resolution to form a labour federation to be called the Guianese and West Indian Federation of Trades Unions and Labour Parties, and a committee was formed to draw up a constitution and rules. They passed many other resolutions, specific to both labour and political reform issues.[18] Critchlow represented the BGLU at another Commonwealth Conference in London in 1930 and at an international trade union conference in Germany in 1931, and visited the Soviet Union in 1932. On his return to Guyana, the papers branded him a Communist and the governor referred to him as a 'Bolshie agitator'.[19] The regional Labour Federation remained an embryonic aspiration until 1938, when a similar conference was held in Trinidad. When it eventually gave rise to the Caribbean Labour Congress (CLC) in 1945, Critchlow was elected the 1st vice president. In this way, this pioneering labour organiser linked the militant strikes in Guyana at the turn of the century to the emergence of this regional Caribbean labour organisation.

Notes

1. Brereton 1981: 164.
2. Hart 1988: 57.
3. *Ibid.*
4. *Ibid.*
5. Beckles 1990: 156.
6. *Ibid.*, 157.
7. *Ibid.*, 159.
8. Hart 1988: 58.
9. Beckles 1990: 161.
10. Chase n.d.: 56, 62-63, 69.
11. *Ibid.*, 66-70.
12. *Ibid.*, 71.
13. *Ibid.*, 72.
14. Hart 1988: 59.
15. *Ibid.*, 61.
16. Basdeo 1983: 6.
17. Chase n.d.: 73.
18. *Report of the First British Guiana and West Indies Labour Conference* (Georgetown, BGLU, 1926).
19. Gov. Denham to Sir Cosmo Parkinson, 25 Sept. 1933, CO 111/712/15140.

Conclusion

The period 1880 - 1930 was not a dead time for labour history in the British Caribbean. On the contrary, it was a period marked by great, if erratic, activity on the part of working people. It was during this half century that developing class and race consciousness prepared the way for the formation of an active working class with its own labour organisations. However, as we have seen, the process was very uneven in different colonies, and there were many setbacks and tragic events, many frustrations and casualties. Though the aspiration for trade unions and political parties representing labour was emerging throughout the Caribbean — and was even expressed in 1926 as an aspiration for a regional labour federation and some form of self-government — the only two organisations with any real staying power, the TWA and the BGLU, were less effective in the late 1920s than they had been in the early 1920s.

The experience gained in the half century from the 1880s through the 1920s however, proved to be important when economic distress and social disruption devastated the entire region in the 1930s and ushered in the third and greatest wave of working-class activity. The modern trade unions , political parties and the CLC, that were created during and soon after the wave of labour rebellions between 1934 and 1939, grew out of these efforts and organisations that had preceded them.

PART TWO

Labour Rebellions in the British Caribbean, 1934-39

Introduction

That the late 1930s constitute a kind of watershed in the modern history of the British Caribbean is not in dispute. However, my claim that this period began in Belize, Trinidad and Guyana in 1934 is not so widely accepted. The assertion that these upheavals began in St Kitts early in 1935, which was first made apparently in W.M. Macmillan's *Warning from the West Indies* in 1936[1] and repeated in Lewis's booklet for the Fabian Society in 1939, continues to be made. Meanwhile, some scholarly studies of Belize either omit any mention of the 1930s events[2] or fail to link them to the later labour and nationalist movements.[3] However, the labour movement that began in Belize in 1934 is crucial in the political history of that country, as well as being one of the earliest manifestations of the labour rebellions that swept through the British Caribbean.[4] Moreover, it is clear that the unrest that began in Trinidad and Guyana in 1934 and 1935 was linked to subsequent developments in those colonies.

My case for considering Belize to be one of the first of the West Indian labour rebellions is based on two points. First, Belize, though often viewed apart from the 'sugar colonies', should be considered as part of the British Caribbean with which it shares several socio–historical, cultural, economic and even political links. Certainly, during the 1930s and 1940s, Britain considered its Central American colony as part of the West Indian region. Belize was included in Orde Browne's official *Report of Labour Conditions in the West Indies* and in the *West India Royal Commission Report* chaired by Lord Moyne.[5] Belize was also included within the West Indies by the Colonial Development and Welfare Organisation after 1940 and in the discussions concerning the formation of the West Indies Federation. Moreover, in the 1940s there were links between Belizean labour organisations and those in the other British colonies, including participation in the regional Caribbean Labour Congress from 1947. Second, in Belize, as elsewhere in the British Caribbean, there were direct links, in terms of personnel and organisation, between the labour disturbances of the 1930s and the subsequent development of trade unions and political parties that formed the basis of the decolonisation movement. The Belizean developments of the 1930s and 1940s were not only a similar socio–historical phenomenon to those occurring elsewhere but were also a part of the regional labour movement that grew from those more discrete riots, strikes and disturbances that had preceded them.

So, while the strikes and demonstrations in Trinidad and Guyana in 1934 and 1935 will be described in connection with their later rebellions, this study begins with an account of Belize, to be followed by St Kitts, St Vincent, St Lucia, Trinidad, Barbados, the Bahamas, Jamaica, Antigua and Guyana.

Notes

1. Macmillan 1936 does not mention Belize
2. Waddell 1961, Dobson 1973
3. Grant 1976, Ashdown 1978
4. Bolland 1986a: 33, 105 06; 1988a; 1993.
5. Orde Browne 1939, West Indian Royal Commission Report 1945.

Chapter FOUR

Belize

The early labour rebellion in Belize had three phases. The first, between February and October 1934, constituted the rise of the movement, and the second, from November 1934 to 1936, witnessed its decline. In the third phase, between 1938 and 1939, there was a revival of activity, in which the basis for the formation of the first trade union and the emergence of anticolonial and nationalist sentiments in the 1940s and 1950s was established.

The great depression and a devastating hurricane that destroyed Belize Town on 10 September 1931,[1] shattered the already fragile colonial economy and further aggravated the chronically poor living conditions of the majority of people. The economy of Belize had been based on the export of forest products since its colonisation in the seventeenth and eighteenth centuries.[2] First logwood and then mahogany predominated, and as they declined the export of chicle propped up a flagging economy after the 1880s. The timber trade revived briefly in the 1920s when tractors, bulldozers and mechanical saws were introduced, but the mechanisation of felling and hauling stripped forest resources and required less labour. Forest products accounted for over 80 per cent of exports by value and the 'forestocracy', led by the Belize Estate and Produce Company, which owned over 1 million acres, suppressed agriculture and dominated the colony.

In 1931 most woodcutters and chicle gatherers were out of work and exports were half what they had been in 1930. The hurricane, which killed more than 1,000 of the 16,000 inhabitants and destroyed at least three-quarters of the housing in Belize Town, came on top of the economic disaster caused by the great depression. As the economy continued to decline after the hurricane, living conditions worsened and people became increasingly desperate. By 1932 the volume of exports was less than half of those in 1931, and the *Colonial Report* stated that, 'mahogany cutting was entirely stopped' and there was 'no market for the Colony's staple products, mahogany and chicle, and unemployment was more severe than in 1931'.[3] After the hurricane the government opened soup kitchens and established a temporary camp and opened public buildings to shelter the homeless, but many people had to make their own shelters from the wreckage, pathetic shacks that they called 'dog-sit-downs'. Labour conditions and living standards in the 1930s were similar to what they had been in the nineteenth century. Yet such conditions in themselves could lead to despair rather than social action, so what accounts for the politicisation of the people of Belize in the 1930s?

Many people in the 1930s remembered the two previous popular protests in Belize Town, in 1894 and 1919, when the colonial system of government had been openly criticised. Judging by the nature of the protests and demands in the 1930s, the people seemed to hold the colonial administration increasingly responsible for their situation. Resentment against the administration's apparent callousness in delaying and imposing conditions over the Hurricane Loan increased when relief measures for the hungry and homeless proved woefully inadequate and insulting. The measures taken to quell the protests and restore order, which were initially quite successful, included relief work. While, on the one hand, this increased people's dependency and hence the government's ability to control them, on the other hand the working people's demands escalated beyond the ability or willingness of the government to meet them. The resulting resentment smouldered throughout the 1930s and 1940s, providing the basis of the first protests, petitions and organisations, and eventually exploded when the governor used his reserve powers to impose devaluation in 1949.[4]

In the early 1930s there was little agitation in Belize. The branch of Garvey's UNIA that had been formed in 1920 was not very active, though Garveyites still ran the newspaper, *The Belize Independent*, owned by Herbert Hill Cain. The related organisation of the Black Cross Nurses (BCN) was engaged in community health and welfare activities and their leader, Vivian Seay, as a member of the Belize Town Board in 1933, tried to establish a Women's Employment Bureau. However, the social welfare approach of the BCN was soon eclipsed by a new radical critique and more militant politics, initiated by the unemployed workers. When a group calling itself the 'Unemployed Brigade' marched through Belize Town on 14 February 1934 it started a broad movement that had a lasting effect on Belizean politics.

Still in the depths of the depression, and two and a half years after the hurricane had destroyed the town, unemployment and poverty remained widespread and housing was deplorable. Though the people were desperate, this demonstration was orderly. The superintendent of police, who was present, reported:

> Leaders were appointed and a march round the town arranged. After the march the leaders met the Governor by appointment. The leaders were men of the artisan and labouring classes.... The deputation represented to the Governor that their families were starving because the men could not get work.[5]

In answer to their appeal, Governor Kittermaster promised immediate outdoor relief for the hungry, told the unemployed to register at the Belize Town Board offices, and said that the Hurricane Loan Board would not foreclose on debtors. The police superintendent reported that the deputation 'was not too pleased with the result of the interview' as they wanted a cash dole of $1 a day. Moreover, the artisans were discontented with the unskilled nature of the relief work offered. A daily ration of 1lb of cooked rice and 3oz of local sugar, issued at the prison gate, was started on 21 February when 85 persons took the supplies. Within a week nearly 300 persons had accepted the rations but the number declined to 35 as a result of complaints that the food was not cooked properly, and on 10 March it was discontinued. At this time people were allowed to break rocks in the Public Works Department yard for 5 - 10 cents each day, or 20 cents for married people, to 'keep them from starving'. These inadequate measures, redolent of the nineteenth century, provoked further bad feeling. Even the usually pro-government *Clarion* called the proffered relief 'degrading and humiliating'.

The inadequacy of the governor's response can be gauged by the fact that 1,100 men and 300 women registered as unemployed as soon as the list was opened and this was recognised by the governor to be a 'large proportion' in a town of 16,000 people.[6] 'By this time', according to the police superintendent, 'the masses of the unemployed had become restless', though the Government was not doing all it should for them, and 'commenced to be dissatisfied with their leaders. The leaders were not extreme enough for them and violence began to be talked about'.[7] A new leader emerged at a meeting held in front of the court house, in an open square called the 'Battlefield', on 16 March 1934.

Antonio Soberanis Gomez, a barber by trade, denounced the Unemployed Brigade's leaders and took over the movement. Soberanis' father, Canuto Soberanis, had come to Belize from Yucatan in 1894 and lived in San Antonio, Orange Walk, and his mother, Dominga Gomez, was born in Corozal, northern Belize. Antonio, the eldest of seven children, was born on 17 January 1897. He attended Roman Catholic primary school in Belize Town until 1912, was a member of the Volunteers Guard in the First World War and served on the Cayo expedition in 1914. He had travelled in all the Central American countries and the USA.[8] Soberanis, who died in 1975, has only recently been identified as a patriot and unofficial national hero.[9]

Soberanis held frequent meetings in the Battlefield, two or three times a week, when 600 - 800 people attended. He was joined by a group of self-styled 'colleagues' who constituted the co-leaders: Benjamin Reneau, John Lahoodie, James Barnett, Chano Lovell, James Middleton, Fred Allen and Alfred Hall.[10] The meetings in the Battlefield began at 8 pm and sometimes lasted until 1 am. According to the police superintendent, 'the more violent the language used from the rostrum the more the crowd enjoyed it. Soberanis was called the Moses of British Honduras who had been sent by God to lead the people to better things'. He noted that at least half of his followers were women and 'they were always more truculent than the men'.[11]

Though the governor first thought of him as a man of no importance, the organisation that Soberanis created and led, called the Labourers and Unemployed Association (LUA), soon became a significant political force in Belize and was the prototype of future trade unions and political parties. It was reported that he 'always said that he was forming a labour Union',[12] though unions could not be legally registered at that time. His association, though not quite a union, was nevertheless far more political than the numerous friendly societies that existed to provide mutual aid and support for their members. The LUA organised food and medical care from time to time but its chief orientation from its inception was political in so far as it used such techniques as petitions, demonstrations, pickets, strikes and boycotts to pressure the employers, merchants and colonial officials into making concessions in favour of working people. Soberanis's attacks on the governor and various colonial officials, which were said 'to please the people immensely',[13] increasingly became an attack on the colonial government itself.

In April 1934 Soberanis was convicted of making a threatening remark about the police superintendent and was cautioned. Undeterred by the police, who were present at all the meetings, he organised a petition signed by several hundred people, demanding that the government find work for the unemployed at a minimum wage of $1.50 per day. He led a procession of about 500 people around the town and the crowd waited outside the court house while their leader presented the petition to the governor. The language of the petition gives some idea of the tone as well as the content of Soberanis's demands. He called for 'British Honduras for British Honduraneans.... We are a new People...we are only asking for our rights. Justice to all men... British Honduras has been sleeping for over a century, not dead only sleeping.... Today British Honduras is walking around.'[14] While the specific demands were for relief work and a minimum wage, they were couched in broad moral and political terms that began to develop a new nationalistic and democratic political culture hitherto unknown in Belize.

Kittermaster replied that wages were governed by the world market price. A minimum wage of $1.50 a day, he said, would force enterprises to close for lack of profit, so 'It is better to get work steadily at 50 or 75 cents a day all the year'. This was an astonishingly provocative recommendation since hundreds of Belizeans could obtain no work at all and most labourers had never had contracts that lasted all year. The governor said he could do no more about the unemployed: 'It is only by asking for charity from England that there will be enough money this year to pay for services such as schools and hospitals. England herself has 4,000,000 unemployed and yet she is generously helping us here in our difficulties'.[15]

Soberanis rejected Kittermaster's argument and pointed out that many colonial officials drew large salaries while 50 cents per day is considered 'sufficient for the poor man and his family'. He also rejected the notion of English charity: 'What we are receiving from England is only what belongs to us.... We will not throw up the sponge, but continue to agitate for our rights'.[16] At his next public meeting, when describing his interview to the crowd, Soberanis referred to the governor as a damn fool. At about this time he produced a flag in green and red, the colours of Garvey's movement, and said that 'he had no King, and no Queen, nor no Prince, but only his green and red flag, for which he was prepared to die'.[17] Soberanis and the LUA continued to agitate and developed new and successful tactics in the next few months.

In July Benjamin Reneau was prosecuted for resisting arrest and was fined $25. The police superintendent reported that 'Soberanis and his colleagues considered they were their own law', and they publicly criticised the district commissioner, Denbigh Phillips, who had fined Reneau.[18] Meanwhile, Kittermaster obtained only $2,000 to provide relief work building the Northern

Highway. Eighteen men were sent up every week on a rotation basis, each being given ten days' work; for each eight-hour day they received 60 cents, mostly in the form of credit for provisions at local stores. About 1,500 men were registered for work, so this was a hopelessly inadequate response.

On 1 August 1934 a march was held to celebrate the centenary of emancipation. Led by the UNIA and the BCN, the marchers were joined by friendly societies and a 'Workers' Union', which was probably the LUA.[19] It was reported later in August that: 'unemployment will get worse shortly. The Belize Estate and Produce Company are practically closing down'. The Chairman of the Belize Town Board observed that there was 'considerable want and even distress', especially hungry children, among the unemployed.[20] Soberanis and the LUA responded to their urgent need by pressuring local merchants and tradesmen to donate to the poor. When some merchants refused (among the largest were Harley, Brodie and Melhado), the LUA organised a boycott. People bearing placards saying 'Don't buy from this store' paraded around the stores but were careful not to loiter or break the law in any way. According to the police superintendent, 'it was very evident that Soberanis was receiving legal advice as to how far he could go in various matters'.[21] A 'boycott procession', in which 50 banners were paraded around the town, showed who had and who had not contributed to the poor fund. During the celebrations on 10 September, commemorating the Battle of St George's Caye in 1798, the town was full of unemployed people and their families. Soberanis, on a horse, led a march of about 3,000 people, with many LUA members dressed in red and green, that culminated in a huge picnic for the poor. Even his opponents acknowledged that: 'This procession and feed added greatly to the prestige of Soberanis and he was referred to as a "Moses" more than ever'.[22]

Encouraged by his success and widespread support, Soberanis broadened his attack and became increasingly militant. He demanded that Denbigh Phillips, a notoriously severe magistrate, should be removed from the bench, and that C.S. Brown, the manager of the Belize Estate and Produce Company and a member of the Legislative Council, should not be allowed to live in Government House. The acting governor refused to comply with these demands. Soberanis frequently held meetings in Stann Creek (now Dangriga), which was then the second largest town with a population of about 3,000, chiefly Garifuna. On 27 September he organised a strike there among the stevedores who loaded grapefruit and achieved another encouraging victory when their pay was raised from 8 cents to 25 cents per hour.

Returning to Belize Town on 29 September, he was reported to have threatened to drag Phillips off his bench and to organise a strike at the Belize Estate and Produce Company sawmill.[23] The police arrived at the sawmill at 6.15 am on 1 October, before Soberanis and 200 of his followers, so the mill started as usual at 7 am. When all seemed quiet the police dispersed, but by 8.45 some 500 people 'armed with sticks' succeeded in closing the mill. When the police returned, the crowd split and went to different parts of the town. One group broke down the gates of the Public Works Department and told the director he should pay his labourers more; another group closed the office of Mr Esquivel, a coconut exporter; another stopped the dredger working at Fort George; and another closed Harley's lumber yard. According to the police superintendent, 'it was not a case of workmen striking for more pay but a case of unemployed men forcing employed men to strike for more pay'.[24]

By 10.40 am about 300 men and women, armed with sticks, went to the Belize Town Board. When Superintendent Matthews tried to arrest a man for threatening the deputy chairman of the board, a struggle ensued. Eight men and one woman were arrested and, when the crowd increased to about 1,500, the police, in two ranks, pushed it back down Queen Street. Several constables were assaulted, shots were heard and one of the crowd, Absolom Pollard, was wounded.[25] At 10.50, when the situation threatened to get out of control, the acting governor ordered the police to halt and return to their station while he talked to six of the crowd's leaders. It is not clear who these leaders were, or if, indeed, there were any at this point. None of the LUA leaders were named, nor were any of them among those arrested during the riot. At noon, Soberanis arrived at the police station, enquired who had been arrested, told the crowd to behave, and went away. At 2 pm he returned in a 'very truculent' mood and demanded bail for all those arrested. At 5 pm he bailed out 16 of the 17 persons who had been jailed, but he was promptly arrested himself and charged with threatening Phillips on 29 September. As news of this spread, the crowd increased to about 2,000. Several efforts to release Soberanis on bail were refused, and he remained in custody. One Christopher Velasquez brought two large snakes and told them to 'go and get Tony', but the police beat them off. Heavy rain dispersed the crowd, a planned meeting at the Battlefield was abandoned, and the night passed peacefully.

The next day, in a court 'guarded by every available man', Soberanis was charged and refused bail.[26] About 500 people abused the magistrates and 1,000 gathered in the market square. Some, it was said, 'were inclined to be disorderly', and 'it was the women who were the most virulent', but no one was armed.[27] At 8.00 am on 3 October, about 150 men who were assigned jobs refused to work for 60 cents a day and, demanding $1, they dispersed. On the following day a 'large gang of men' failed to stop others from working for 60 cents a day. The crisis was over and the British cruiser that the acting governor had inquired about was not needed. The sawmill remained closed until 18 October and the people obtained a promise of $3,000 for immediate outdoor relief. Meanwhile, 26 of the 32 persons who had been prosecuted for participating in the riot were convicted, receiving sentences of between three days and one year of hard labour. The jurors having failed to agree, Soberanis was released on bail on 6 November and his freedom was celebrated by a big rally at Liberty Hall. In January 1935 Soberanis was acquitted of the charge of threatening Phillips, who, it transpired, had threatened to horsewhip him. Soberanis continued to lead the LUA, but the movement was weakened by a split that had occurred while he was in jail. From the time that Lahoodie and Reneau formed the British Honduras Unemployed Association (BHUA), which was more like a friendly society than a union, the movement declined.

Shortly after the peak of the disturbances in October 1934, a new governor, Alan Burns, arrived. He viewed Soberanis as a professional agitator who should be locked up, and refused Soberanis's request to meet to discuss the franchise. Nevertheless, Burns was shocked by the people's condition and he made an effort during his six years in Belize to bring relief. In March 1935 the senior medical officer reported that the people, especially the children, were dangerously undernourished and hence susceptible to disease. Burns commented that the unemployment situation was still acute, that those who were employed were receiving lower wages, and that when their contracts ended in June these wages would not tide them over the season. He considered that 'the situation is most serious and that it will shortly become desperate.... The people have behaved, in the circumstances, with admirable restraint, but their temper is rising and matters must come to a head within a few months unless something is done'.[28] Soberanis continued to hold mass meetings and his speeches became increasingly 'offensive and inflammatory',[29] so Burns prepared legislation to facilitate control, namely a law to prohibit processions without police permission, one to give the governor emergency powers to maintain order, and a seditious conspiracy bill so that 'Soberanis could be successfully prosecuted for sedition'.[30]

In May 1935 Soberanis helped organise a strike among railway workers in Stann Creek, whose wage of 65 cents per day was below the rate for government workers elsewhere, which ranged between 75 cents and $1. Soberanis had made several visits to the Stann Creek and Toledo Districts in southern Belize, 'holding meetings and preaching discontent'.[31] On 20 May, following a meeting in Stann Creek Town, a crowd of about 300 unemployed men and women stopped the railway workers at Havana Bridge and told them to strike for $1 per day. The workers went home and made no attempt to go to work the next morning. That afternoon four railway employees who tried to pass the bridge were beaten by pickets and the police could not make arrests because of 'the very threatening attitude' of a crowd of about 400 people. Later, the crowd dispersed peacefully and the district commissioner spoke to two local leaders, Abraham Dolmo and Zacharias Flores, since Soberanis had already left by boat. That night, police reinforcements arrived from Belize Town 'to crush the disorders without bloodshed'. One woman and five men were convicted of impeding passage and disorderly conduct and were fined. None of the strikers was re-employed and those workers who were hired received the usual 65 cents per day. The police force had crushed the strike effort and Burns felt that 'in consequence Soberanis has suffered in repute as a leader'.[32] Burns claimed that Soberanis's support and influence in general was waning as a result of the colonial development grants that employed people in road work and thus changed people's attitude to the government, but he still kept the police 'constantly on the alert in case of a possible sudden outbreak'.[33] By July, Soberanis himself acknowledged that the LUA was declining. He blamed Lahoodie and Reneau for splitting the organisation, and suggested 'that they must have been paid to do so'.[34]

When Burns refused to allow Soberanis or any member of the LUA to Government House on the anniversary of emancipation or on the anniversary of the Battle of St George's Caye, Soberanis responded in a rather quieter manner than usual. The LUA, he stated, was 'organised to agitate for a living wage and justice for the workers of British Honduras. The average personel [sic] of the General Membership earns between 1/50 to 1/200 part of Your Excellency's salary. We of the L. & U.A. do not believe God intended this to be so'. He insisted that they had the right to try to better their situation. He pointed out that, by organising a band of 22 nurses, they helped and cheered up the workers and unemployed and that the LUA's community work had benefited hundreds of people.[35]

Shortly after the seditious conspiracy ordinance was passed on 24 October 1935, Soberanis was charged for using 'abusive and seditious language' at a public meeting in Corozal, though this meeting was held on 1 October, the first anniversary of the riot, before the bill was passed.[36] Burns was determined to put Soberanis behind bars, and to do so without provoking further disturbances. He instructed E.A. Grant, the magistrate of Orange Walk, to try Soberanis at Corozal because the Corozal magistrate was 'suffering from cold feet'. He added: 'One of my reasons for sending Grant to try 'Tony' was that he was a black man. I did not want the trial to be a black v. white affair'.[37] He wanted Soberanis 'put away for a good long sentence'.

The trial was, as anticipated, a tense affair. People in Corozal and nearby Maya villages contributed over $200 to Soberanis's assistance and, because of 'a state of civil commotion which threatens the public safety', meetings were prohibited in the district. Soberanis was fined $85 (or four and a half months' hard labour), plus $30 costs, for using insulting words about various people. In January 1936 Soberanis was acquitted by the Supreme Court on the charge of attempting to 'bring His Majesty into hatred, ridicule or contempt', but the Corozal conviction, along with the prior split in his organisation, the muzzling effects of the new laws, the governor's efforts to expand relief work,[38] and a temporary improvement in the economy in 1936, combined to spell the decline of his influence and the LUA. While the LUA continued to hold meetings and processions in 1936, much of Soberanis's efforts consisted of attacking Lahoodie's BHUA.

The LUA disappeared, but Soberanis did not, and when another slump occurred in the economy in 1938 and 1939 he and several associates continued to agitate and organise until they had created a trade union. At a Battlefield meeting attended by about 500 people on 20 June 1938, Soberanis, along with James Barnett alias Bangula (who had helped in the Stann Creek strike in 1935), John Neal and Thomas Sabal, a Garifuna from Stann Creek, complained about wages and rations and demanded that Governor Burns must go. Neal said that in Jamaica Alexander Bustamante had demanded that Governor Denham must go 'and Denham go flying and Bustamante got what he wanted'. This refers to the fact that Bustamante started a 'Denham must go' campaign in 1937, and the governor's death after an abdominal operation during the labour rebellion was widely seen as a fulfilment of the labour leader's charge.[39] Soberanis addressed the crowd as 'Citizens of B.H. Comrades'. Speaking in Spanish and English, he said he had collected $40 from people in Stann Creek to register a union,'we want a union and we must get it', but when he asked for donations people began to leave. He chastised them and said they needed more loyalty, like the Jamaicans who had demanded Bustamante's release, if they were to get what they wanted.[40] As the Jamaican labour rebellion had begun scarcely a month earlier, and Bustamante was released from jail on 30 May and Denham died on 2 June, Neal's and Soberanis's comments on this occasion show that they knew what was happening in labour movements in some other parts of the Caribbean.

Later that year, Burns reported that unemployment was much worse and that he needed to provide work for more men so as to prevent disorder. On 19 November, over 600 men gathered to apply for work at the Public Works Department where only 200 could be hired. One man was arrested for assaulting the clerk, but danger of serious trouble was 'averted by a promise to the men that more would be taken on in a few days'.[41] Burns organised a series of roadworks, reclamation and drainage projects, as relief schemes for the unemployed. Under the *quicena* system, gangs of labourers were hired for two-week periods so that, by rotation, all the unemployed were given a chance of intermittent work. At one time there were about 600 men so employed, but Burns, concerned that about 1,000 fewer men would be hired in the mahogany industry in 1939, proposed opening a quarry at Gracy Rock to provide work for 300 men and stone for the Belize-Cayo road. The development of better communications in Belize through road construction was clearly of secondary importance to Burns, whose primary concern was to avoid trouble in the streets. 'This year there appears to be very little money and crowds of unemployed men are in the streets. The local agitators have not missed the opportunity to stir up trouble'.[42] While the governor's strategy seems to have been largely successful, as further widespread disorders were avoided, it was not because Soberanis and his colleagues had retired. On the contrary, their continued agitation was clearly a factor in pushing Burns and the Colonial Office to expand the relief schemes.

The economy deteriorated further in 1939 and Burns had to lay off half of the men working on the Northern Highway, leaving 847 men in Belize Town seeking work.[43] In March, a telegram was sent from a public meeting to the secretary of state for the Colonies:

> Suffering and uneasiness acute Belize. Due to unemployment. Developing into dangerous situation. Cannot continue without disastrous results. Government approached and admits situation grave but unable to help. Wholesale laying off by Government on public works not understood by the masses. Population pray for immediate intervention.[44]

Burns attempted to belittle this by saying that the chairman of the meeting, L.D. Kemp, was 'trying to make capital out of the situation'.[45] Kemp, an associate of Soberanis and cousin of Lahoodie, was a journalist who, under the *nom de plume* of 'Prince Dee', had for years attacked the colonial administration and supported Soberanis in his column, called 'The Garvey Eye', in the *Belize Independent*. Kemp continued to be politically active and influential in the 1940s.

Soon after this meeting a crowd became disorderly when only 75 men were engaged for road work out of 591 applicants and was ejected from the Public Works Department by the police.[46] Burns' letter to the secretary of state in April makes it clear that he viewed relief work as a way to avert further disturbances, but that the rate of wages paid for such work could itself become a cause of unrest:

> the steps taken with your approval to relieve unemployment have averted what might have been serious disturbances, and have had an immediate effect on

the people...I considered it possible that the Belize labourers might refuse to work for 50 cents a day, and that rioting might result if Government should insist on paying no higher wage for relief work.... Your decision that the normal rate of wages should be paid for relief work relieves me of any anxiety regarding possible disturbances.[47]

The number of unemployed men registered in Belize Town alone rose from 1,200 in April to 1,953 in August.[48] Once again, public anxiety and the prospect of unrest were relieved by announcements of continuing relief work, though everyone knew this was only a palliative in a sick economy. It was in this context that early in 1939 Soberanis and R.T. Meighan, a former member of the Belize Town Board, founded the British Honduras Workers and Tradesmen Union (BHWTU), the first organisation to be called a union in Belize, though it could not then be legally registered as such. So, some five years after the labour movement had started in Belize, it began to become institutionalised.

Throughout these years the increasing involvement of the colonial administration in relief work, made necessary by the deterioration of the economy and widespread hardship, had resulted in popular attention becoming focused on its responsibilities and shortcomings. Soberanis and his colleagues succeeded in channelling this attention into a labour movement and the first stirring of Belizean nationalism. Soberanis linked the pressing concerns of his followers, which were chiefly with wages, prices, employment, food, health and housing, to an attack on the colonial administration and the merchant elite, whom he characterised as incompetent and overpaid, ruthless and callous in their relations with workers and the poor and as the cause of much of the poverty and injustice experienced by most Belizeans. Soberanis, who organised the working people who were unrepresented in the Legislative Council, developed a variety of techniques to help the voiceless be heard, namely petitions, processions, boycotts, strikes and mass meetings, as well as mutual aid efforts. Though the core of these activities was in Belize Town, where a third of the colony's population was concentrated, Soberanis was active in the districts from north to south, among the Maya Indians around Corozal and the Garifuna in Stann Creek.

Never having been allowed to represent itself, the working class of Belize was used to looking to members of the elite to represent it. The 1936 constitution, which readmitted the electoral principle for the first time since 1871, though with high property and income qualifications and reserve powers for the governor, encouraged this, with the result that much of the political activity of the working people and the LUA in 1936 was focused on supporting the 'people's men' in the elections. Endorsed by the LUA and a middle-class Citizens' Political Party, these men became the chief 'parliamentary opposition' after 1936. With support from working people, who had neither votes nor candidates of their own, some of these early nationalists, like Arthur Balderamos, a black lawyer, Robert S. Turton, a chicle millionaire, and L.P. Ayuso, a local businessman, developed a 'Natives First' orientation because they resented the control of land, commerce and government by a coterie of expatriates. As working-class agitation continued, all six seats on the Belize Town Board, which was elected with a broader franchise, went to middle-class

Creoles who appeared sympathetic to labour in 1939. It was Soberanis who, in 1934, had initiated this growing working-class consciousness and proto-national movement, in which labour issues and interests were in the forefront of a critique of colonial government, thereby presaging the labour and national movements developing elsewhere in the British Caribbean.

Notes

1. Bolland 1993.
2. Bolland 1973, 1977.
3. Colonial Report for 1932, No.1 1647 (London, 1933), pp.12, 31.
4. It is to this explosion that the beginning of modern politics is generally attributed (see Waddell 1961: 109). However, as I have shown, the 'birth of the nationalist movement' cannot be understood without consideration of the long period of gestation on which it depended.
5. P.E. Matthews report to the Governor, 27 Nov. 1934, CO 123/346/35524.
6. Gov. Sir Harold Kittermaster to Secretary of State (SS), 7 March 1934, CO 123/346/35524.
7. Matthews report, *op. cit.*
8. See the autobiographical letter, A. Soberanis to Vernon Leslie, 10 July 1973, Belize Archives, hereafter BA, BA, SP 27; also "Oral History: The L. and U.A.", *National Studies*, 2:3 (1974), 3-10.
9. A government-sponsored school textbook lists him as a 'Belizean hero'; see *A History of Belize: Nation in the Making* (Belize City, 1983), p.53.
10. Matthews report, *op. cit.*
11. *Ibid.*
12. *Ibid.*
13. *Ibid.*
14. "Memorial in regard to conditions in the Colony", Soberanis to Kittermaster, 17 May 1934, BA, MP 700-34.
15. Kittermaster to Soberanis, 18 May 1934, BA, MP 700-34.
16. Soberanis to Kittermaster, 21 May 1934, BA, MP 700-34.
17. Matthews report, *op. cit.*
18. Matthews report, *op. cit.*
19. *Belize Independent*, 1 Aug. 1934.
20. See reports enclosed in Acting-Gov. Hunter to SS, 14 Aug.1934, CO 123/346/35524.
21. Matthews report, *op. cit.*
22. *Ibid.*
23. *Ibid.*
24. *Ibid.*
25. He recovered from the wound and it was never discovered who shot him. The police contended that it was a member of the crowd but it was widely believed that Corporal Building was responsible.
26. Matthews report, *op. cit.*

27. *Ibid.*

28. Gov. A.C. Burns to SS , 31 March 1935, CO 123/352/66554.

29. Burns to SS, 26 July 1935, CO 123/353/66571.

30. Att. Gen. S.A. McKinistry to Burns, 22 July 1935, CO 123/353/66571.

31. Superintendent Matthews report, 12 June 1935, included in Burns to SS, 13 June 1935, CO 123/253/66568.

32. Burns to SS, 13 June 1935, CO 123/253/66568.

33. Burns to SS, 23 May 1935, CO 123/353/66571.

34. See Serg. A.B. Clarke's report, 20 July 1935, CO 123/353/66571.

35. Soberanis to Burns, 23 Sept. 1935, CO 123/353/66571.

36. Burns to SS, 30 Oct. 1935, CO 123/353/66571.

37. Burns to Beckett, 15 Nov. 1935, CO 123/354/66648. A Colonial Office official approved of Burns's action: 'The Governor took the right line in putting Mr. Grant on to try Tony, so as to avoid any suspicion of colour clash,' Rootham's minute, 13 Dec. 1935, CO 123/354/66648.

38. The amount spent on outdoor relief, distributed largely in Belize Town, had increased rapidly from $2,600 in 1931 to about $10,000 in 1935 and 1936; see Cheverton and Smart 1937: 47.

39. Eaton 1975: 223.

40. Corporal Cornelius A. Building to Supt. of Police, 21 June 1938, CO 123/367/66648.

41. Burns to SS, 22 Nov. 1938, CO 123/366/66553.

42. *Ibid.*

43. Burns to SS, 5 Jan. 1939, CO 123/366/66553.

44. Enclosed in Burns to SS, 13 March 1939, CO 123/373/66553.

45. *Ibid.*

46. Burns to SS, 24 March 1939, CO 123/373/66553.

47. Burns to SS, 3 April 1939, CO 123/373/66553. The same issue arose in Jamaica at this time; see below.

48. Acting-Gov. Johnston to SS, Aug. 1939, CO 123/373/66553.

Chapter FIVE

St Kitts

The labour rebellion that exploded in St Kitts in January 1935 had been preceded by some efforts to raise the consciousness of the working class. As the law did not permit the formation of trade unions as such, the first popular organisation was the St Kitts-Nevis Universal Benevolent Association (SKNUBA), formed and registered under the Leeward Islands Friendly Societies Act in 1917. Two of its sponsors had clear ambitions to organise labour. J. Matthew Sebastian, the president, started a newspaper called *The Union Messenger* in 1921 which was printed by the SKNUBA, and J.A. Nathan, the secretary, a small shopkeeper, had acquired some familiarity with unionism when he lived in the USA. The paper aired workers' grievances and problems and frequently reported news of labour discontent in Jamaica and Trinidad throughout the 1920s. Letters and articles often shared experiences, notably of migration for work and the restrictions that were imposed on such migration after 1929.[1] In 1932 the federalist labour leaders, Albert Marryshow of Grenada and Arthur Cipriani of Trinidad, visited St Kitts, met with groups of workers and encouraged them to organise. The St Kitts Workers' League was formed that year, 'as an advocate of political and social reform in general and to promote the welfare of the working class in particular'[2], but, like the Grenada Workingmen's Association and the Trinidad Workingmen's Association, it could not legally act as a trade union.

In October 1934 the administrator of St Kitts received a letter from Rev. Newnham Davis' of St Anne's in the west of the island, saying that the biggest employer of labour in the district, Bourke's Estate of Sandy Point, because the owner had died intestate, had dismissed all labourers except those required to care for the stock. 'As a result of so many people being thrown out of employment a very great deal of distress is bound to occur', he wrote, and raised the question of whether this situation 'will not result in much unrest amongst the labouring people'.[3] The administrator passed this news on to the governor, adding that thousands of other field labourers might be thrown out of work if the planters, unable to resolve their impasse with the St Kitts (Basseterre) Sugar Factory, ceased to grow more cane. 'There is already evidence of some disquiet which may possibly develop', he reported, and he attributed the main cause of this to agitation over the 'elective principle'. Since

13 December, when the Legislative Council voted down proposals for constitutional change, several cane fires had been lit, 'indicative possibly of a growing antipathy by labourers towards planters, and this is not unlikely being encouraged by the St Kitts Workers League, Ltd., and its thoroughly pernicious organ, the *"Union Messenger"* '. Further, the fact that some planters had shared a bonus from the factory with their labourers while others had not, 'in itself led to dissatisfaction, with, of course, the inevitable suspicion in the minds of some that labourers have been exploited'. If these factors were not settled, he predicted, they 'will precipitate a difficult and serious condition involving civil commotion probably of an unprecedented kind'.[4] According to the chief colonial official on the spot, therefore, growing distress caused by unemployment and dissatisfaction with wages and the constitutional issue had been provoking unrest for several weeks before the actual rebellion occurred. Yet nothing appears to have been done about it. As trade unions were illegal and Sebastian and his associates were labelled 'pernicious', there were no labour representatives with whom the colonial officials were prepared to discuss the problems.

By 1935 sugar production had been increasing for several years. Yet while the production of sugar per acre increased, the average gross receipts for sugar per acre declined, putting pressure on wages at the same time that fewer workers were employed by the industry. The wages of field workers employed by the planters as well as the employees of the St Kitts Sugar Factory at Basseterre, the only factory which purchased all the cane grown on the island, had been reduced in preceding seasons. The rate for cutting cane, having risen to 1s. per ton when sugar prices were high, was reduced to 8d per ton, the same rate as in 1881 before the first great depression.[5] This put even more pressure than usual on the workers to obtain decent rates at the start of the crop season.

Before the start of grinding at the factory, J.A. Nathan sent a circular to the principal labourers on the various estates, such as head cutters and head cartmen, inviting them to a meeting on 20 January at Union Hall, Basseterre, 'to discuss what wages should be demanded for reaping the present crop' and to be sure that 'no labourer should start to work until he or she knows what wages they are to obtain'.[6] The editorial in *The St Kitts-Nevis Daily Bulletin*, a conservative newspaper, suggested that the low price for sugar made it an inopportune time for labour to make demands. Nathan replied that, as 'the Planter has been recently granted a minimum price for their product (sugar cane), why should we not seek to get a minimum wage for the labourer?',[7] the factory having agreed to a minimum price of 14 s. per ton for cane delivered. To this, the president of the Agricultural Society and an ex-member of the Legislative Council, E.J. Shelford, responded that it was indeed 'an inopportune time for any organisation to attempt to agitate the labouring classes to expect any higher rates for wages', given the low market price of sugar and dependency on British and Canadian government preferences. 'In fact, as sugar stands today — for agitators to endeavour to incite the labouring classes I take it as a mere manifestation of the rabidity of their rather Bolshivistic *[sic]* tendencies — agitators — some of whom in the near future perhaps — hope to become our local Legislators'.[8] To this provocative letter, Nathan replied that the St Kitts Workers' League was a political organisation, but the SKNUBA is 'strictly concerned with Labour and labour conditions in this Island... [where] the labourer (not being organised) gets the worst end of it'. He stated that they are 'organising Agricultural Labourers' and that the meeting on 20 January will be 'the first Labour Convention ever held in this Island'.[9]

At the meeting delegates decided that the SKNUBA 'should assume the responsibility of representing the Agricultural labourers interest throughout the Island, as far as wages and general working conditions are concerned... and the secretary promised to see what could be done to improve the wages paid'. Over 100 members were said to have registered by the meeting's close, and registration continued afterwards at the association's office.[10] On the eve of the crop season, 27 January, Nathan wrote in *The Union Messenger* that there was 'a little friction at Pond Estate' when labourers were threatened by management and told to remove their animals if they did not work as before.

> No definite news has reached us as to what price per ton the Planters intend paying for reaping the present crop. It is hoped that they will increase the labourers' pay at least 12 ½% We have heard that quite a few Planters are willing to do this much, but there are some die-hards who are not willing to move one inch in this direction.

Nathan added that it was up to the planters 'to relieve the community from the terrible hardship suffered last year'.[11] In the light of all these activities and demands, it seems that the strike that began on 28 January 1935, a week after the meeting and on the opening day of the crop season, was not quite as 'spontaneous and unorganised' as has been claimed.[12]

Governor Johnston, certainly, believed that some 'agitators', including Nathan, may have stirred up trouble. Before 28 January, he acknowledged, 'there had been a considerable amount of discussion among so-called labour organisations as to the prices that should be demanded by the labourers for their different varieties of work'. He thought that Nathan's comment about the labourers' pay being increased by at least 12 ½ per cent would lead 'ignorant labourers' to 'jump to the conclusion that the pay *had* been so increased, and become enraged when the planters did not do this'.[13] Whatever Nathan's precise role may have been, there is no doubt that sparks touched some very responsive tinder on 28 January.

The strike began at Buckley's Estate, just north-west of Basseterre, when the workers, probably joined by some unemployed persons from the town, demanded that their wages be restored to the rate they had been in 1932, when the planters had reduced them from 11d. to 8d. per ton of cane. The manager, E.D.B. Dobridge, ordered them to work but they downed tools and walked off to begin 'spreading the word' at other estates around the island. They went north, to the neighbouring estates of Shadwell and Monkey Hill, and convinced others to join them. At Monkey Hill, the Police Inspector, Major Duke and the Magistrate, Mr Bell, urged the crowd to disperse but the strikers went on to Douglas Estate where they collected the cane cutters' cutlasses and threw them on the manager's veranda 'with various threats'.[14] While smaller groups of strikers went north to St Peters and Stapleton, the chief crowd continued to Needs Must Estate and followed the main road around the north-eastern bend, stopping at various estates. By noon the crowd, numbering between 300 and 400 and armed with sticks, reached Brighton Estate. There the manager, Mr Yearwood, ordered them off the property. No violence was done to him, but the strikers took the mules and cattle out of the carts and cut the driving gear so they could not be used to haul cane.

Half a century after the event, a black schoolteacher who was teaching at the Cayun Village school, recalled the day of the riot and the mood of the crowd and the villagers,

> The Osbornes at the Telephone Exchange nearby had received a message that a band of rioters was coming our way, and the news spread through Cayon quickly. In a short time the main road was crowded with people, excitedly awaiting the arrival of the rioters, some curious to see them, others anxious to join them. The teachers tried to carry on school as usual, but there was little, if any, concentration on lessons. Every bit of news about the riot increased the excitement of the pupils. At about two o'clock in the afternoon, we heard the noise of pans knocking, shells blowing, and people shouting, coming up the Cayon Hill. Someone in the school shouted, 'De Riot a come!'

> The children immediately made a mad rush for the door, and in a minute the school was empty. Teachers and pupils alike could not miss this once-in-a-lifetime event. There were the rioters — hundreds of them, all in their working clothes, barefooted, with sticks, bills and other weapons in their hands, shouting: 'We strike for higher wages! Everybody mus' stap wok today!' Some gave an occasional blow on a conch shell, between their shouts. But they all seemed fairly orderly as they followed their ring-leaders across Dunn's Cottage, heading for Brighton's Estate....

> That same [more likely, the next] afternoon, Mr Clarke, our headteacher and a member of the St Kitts Defence Force, was ordered to get into uniform and report immediately for service. The children, regarding what they were seeing as nothing but fun and excitement, cheered their headteacher as they saw him, dressed in khaki shirt and shorts with bayonet at his side, rush off to town on his motor-cycle.[15]

Not all was fun and excitement, however. One of the villagers who joined the crowd, named Ralston, was arrested and sent to prison, and others remained in hiding while the police tried to pick up rioters.[16]

The crowd, still increasing in numbers, reached Lodge Estate at about 2.20 pm. The owner, Philip Todd, who like Dobridge and Yearwood was of 'European descent', ordered them off. Feeling threatened, he got a shotgun, but he was knocked down and beaten. His gun was broken and a few stones were thrown at his house servants. The crowd proceeded to other estates, 'unharnessing all cattle carts and damaging the working gear. From here onwards the leadership would appear to have been left to the labourers who constitute the working class on estates on the Northern portion of the Island'.[17] At Estridge's Estate, Major Duke and eight police, by now armed with rifles, intercepted the crowd and arrested five leaders. Other strikers went on around the northern point at Dieppe Bay to Willet's Estate, where the manager and overseer, who were of 'African descent', were threatened and carts were unharnessed, but no violence was done.

According to the chief justice, the police had not followed the crowd further because they were '12 to 13 miles from Headquarters and with hostile villages in their rear'.[18] This remark, and his comment about local leadership, contradicts the governor's assertion that the trouble was caused by agitators and 'loafers' from Basseterre who ordered the 'peaceful labourers' to strike. It suggests, rather, that there was widespread sympathy for the strikers among villagers around the island. Some people, however, were intimidated and even wounded. A labourer who refused to join the crowd at Saddler's Village was struck down with a piece of iron pipe. A jury subsequently acquitted the man charged with wounding him, though the chief justice thought he had been convincingly identified.[19] This suggests that the members of the jury, too, may have been sympathetic with the strikers, or 'partisan' as the Chief Justice expressed it.

The next day, 29 January, a smaller gang of striking workers set off in the opposite direction to reach the west of the island, where they had not spread the news before, again visiting estates to urge others to join them. Quite evidently, they were aiming to achieve a general, island-wide strike on all the estates. The governor himself started a tour that morning in the wake of the previous day's crowd, and he 'found very little work going on'.[20] As he reached Estridge's and Belleview Estates in the north, he received an urgent message asking him to return to Basseterre because there were further disturbances at Buckley's and West Farm Estates, just west of the town. At the latter, Magistrate Bell had read the Riot Act and the police fired three shots. 'Stone-throwing had been continuous on the part of the mob'.[21] As the violence escalated, the governor, on the advice of the Executive Council meeting in emergency session, sent telegrams asking Colonel Bell to bring police reinforcements from Antigua and the admiral at Bermuda to have a warship ready, if needed.

The main group of strikers, meanwhile, had marched to Sandy Point, the western point of the island, where they heard that Dobridge had employed strike-breakers to start cutting cane at Buckley's Estate. Many of them turned back and by 3 pm a crowd, estimated at 200 - 300 persons, armed with sticks, entered the estate yard and began to haul out a cart. Dobridge, accompanied by his overseer, both of whom had shotguns, ordered the crowd out. Stones were thrown at them and Dobridge fired, hitting several people with pellets and wounding two in the face and one in the shoulder. This enraged the strikers, but they retreated as Dobridge and his overseer had two revolvers and a rifle as well as the shotguns. An armed contingent of 11 police, led by Major Duke and accompanied by Magistrate Bell, arrived at about 3.45 pm and lined up in the estate yard, facing the crowd at 10 yards' distance. Some of the strikers approached Duke and Bell and demanded that they arrest Dobridge. When Duke told them to come to the police station along with the injured parties to make statements, the crowd shouted angrily, 'We want Dobridge'. People taunted the police, shouting, 'Oh, you can't shoot because you have no ammunition', 'You only have blank cartridges', and 'See me here, shoot me if you have anything in your gun'.[22]

Major Duke arranged for reinforcements, asking the governor to sign the necessary proclamations to call out the Defence Force and Defence Reserve Force, which he did about 5 pm. Conveniently, the governor happened to be having a garden party at Government House, and he commented that 'a good many of the gentlemen of these forces were present',[23] as they were predominantly white planters and their associates, under the command of Geoffrey P. Boon, a leading planter and merchant. The Defence Force consisted of largely black and coloured men, commanded by white officers and the Defence Reserve had been formed in 1919 when whites objected to serving in the Defence Force because of its growing numbers of coloured men. At 6 pm the governor telegraphed for the warship and for the extra police from Antigua because, he averred, 'the affair was assuming some seriousness'.[24] He even concluded his garden party early so the guests could return home in daylight.

Though the striking workers appear to have been quite restrained, the governor reported that soon after 6 pm the combined forces, under the command of Major Duke, 'found it impossible to control the very large mob',[25] by then numbering 400 - 500 men women, and children.[26] The magistrate read the Riot Act and urged the strikers to disperse but they continued to shout and to threaten Dobridge. When the Riot Act was read a second time, the crowd responded by throwing stones, some of which struck the police, but none was seriously injured. Major Duke ordered the police to press the crowd backwards towards St Johnston's Village. Orders were then given to fire on the crowd, though there 'were women and children in the main body of the rioters'.[27] In all, 55 shots were fired, resulting in three men being killed, J. Samuel, John Allen and James Archibald, and eight or nine wounded.[28] Many of the shots were fired at people who threw stones from behind fences in the village as well as at persons in the crowd, and the men killed were on the street in the village, some 200 yards away from the estate buildings. The chief justice concluded that the shooting was justified because the angry crowd had refused to disperse, and that it was 'a serious civil disturbance which threatened the lives and property of law-abiding citizens of the Crown as well as the peace and good order of the Colony'.[29]

Major Duke reported that all was quiet by about 9.30 pm. At 2.30 am on 30 January the *Lady Nelson* arrived from Antigua with Colonel Bell and six men and the governor was informed that HMS *Leander* was on its way. He received messages from different parts of the island that morning, on the third day of the strike, that 'large bodies of men are parading about and still trying to intimidate the peaceably inclined labourers. They had also driven off the cattle and cut the harness on a number of estates'.[30] In the circumstances, he decided not to 'scatter and dissipate' his small forces into these different localities, but to wait until *Leander* came with reinforcements. The governor commented that, contrary to his usual experience, he 'was met everywhere by sullen and sulky looks' as he drove around town. 'Small knots of people had gathered at street corners and I could see but little was needed to start off further trouble at any moment'.[31] That night several cane fires were started, six of them near the town, and one a few yards from Government House. Colonel Bell, who seems to have been easily impressed, heard a rumour that Basseterre was to be burned down and all the white people exterminated, so he kept his forces on constant patrol.

At about 1.30 am on 31 January HMS *Leander* arrived. Its searchlights were directed on the town and a party of 40 marines landed to intimidate the people. Subsequently, the marines were used to keep Basseterre secure while parties of police roamed the island searching for rioters and making arrests.

Looking at the pattern of these three days as a whole, it is apparent how little and how limited was the violence used by the strikers, despite considerable provocation, and how disproportionate was the violence employed against them. Though the workers were equipped with and accustomed to using long, razor-sharp cutlasses, no report suggests that they ever used them, even to threaten people. At one estate they threw cutlasses on to the manager's veranda and made threatening remarks, but the only 'arms' they were reported having or using were sticks and stones, and on one occasion an iron pipe. There were only three instances of physical harm committed on people by these hundreds of strikers over a three-day period. Philip Todd was knocked down and beaten, in all, five or six blows;[32] Jonathan Moore, the labourer, was struck in Saddler's Village and the left of his face partially paralysed; and some of the police, including Major Duke, were struck by stones, 'but not seriously injured'.[33] The only other violence the strikers used was demonstrative and tactical, like cutting driving gear to immobilise carts and setting fire to canefields, but it was not against persons.

The reports by colonial officials often suggest how restrained the strikers were. They state, for example, that 'no personal violence was done' or that strikers 'used threats of violence but did not take any further action'.[34] Colonel Bell described, on the morning of 30 January, near two incendiary fires,

> a rather impudent demonstration by lawbreakers. A crowd, not a disorderly one, assembled in the public street near one of these fires...composed largely of persons of the field labouring class, men and women,.... Someone in the crowd shouted out that the sugar factory was making big money and that the factory should share with planters and labourers. [35]

He heard of crowds armed with sticks 'inducing labourers willing to work to join them', yet when he received calls for protection from planters he did not feel justified to disperse the crowd because it was not violent. The Commander-in-Chief of the America and West Indies Station expressed doubt that the situation was ever sufficiently critical to justify landing a naval detachment. He pointed out that after 29 January 'the strikers appear to have confined themselves to normal strike picketing varied by occasional forcible persuasion of strike breakers to stop work and to scattered cases of cane burning, i.e. to activities which the police and local forces should be able to control and which are not appropriate to naval intervention.'[36] What these reports underscore is that this was a predominantly non-violent strike, a determined and militant labour action to stop the cane harvest until better wage rates could be obtained, not a violent riot. Yet the strikers were threatened with guns on several occasions, by the police and also by white managers and their overseers, were twice fired on, and some people wounded, even before the 'riot' of 29 January.

Of course, the strikers were vocally threatening, often angry and sometimes disorderly, but they were desperate and frustrated because they had no legal or institutional means to make their case. To understand the escalation of the violence and the tragedy of 29 January we have to consider the racial factor. The chief justice identifies in his report various protagonists as of 'European descent', 'African descent', or 'coloured'[37] but, ironically, in his covering letter he urges that such references should be omitted when the report is published because he makes them only 'to distinguish the particular types of persons' and he would not want to 'create any ignorant misapprehension that I make distinctions between races as a Judge, which I do not in Court'.[38] What his original report reveals and the published version conceals is what one would expect, namely that the 'particular types of persons' involved in this confrontation reflected the history and social structure of St Kitts over 300 years. Repeatedly, the strikers, who were overwhelmingly of African descent, encountered managers of European descent, men who were accustomed to ordering them around and were willing to threaten them with guns when they were slow to obey. And these managers and their overseers had the confidence that they would be supported by the police and, if necessary, the navy. Even after Dobridge fired on and injured some of the strikers the police protected him, rather than arresting him as the crowd justifiably demanded. Not least, the 'gentlemen' whom the governor summoned from his garden party to support the police were the white planters with whom the strikers were in dispute. The purpose of these defence forces was not to defend the island against outside powers but to maintain public order and to control labour, in short, to maintain the social order, the old social hierarchy of whites over blacks, in which they were the beneficiaries.

> The strikers at Buckley's Estate on 29 January were directly confronted with the physical embodiment of the source of their discontent. Drawn up before them, in the ranks of the Defence Reserve, were the visible representatives of the local planter class. But, in this undisguised class confrontation, the planters were armed with rifles and the plantation workers with sticks and stones.[39]

What the police and defence forces saw, from their viewpoint, was that they were greatly outnumbered by hundreds of angry black people who, far from being intimidated by this show of force, refused to do what they were told and were jeering and throwing stones. If Major Duke and Magistrate Bell had been willing to take Dobridge into custody the crowd might have dispersed, but, given their traditional roles, it was inconceivable that they would do that, nor did Chief Justice Rae seem to have considered that this was an option. Instead, he concluded that, to maintain law and order, 'the only course open to them was to maintain it by the only means open to them — that of firing on the rioters'.[40]

Glenn Richards points out that

> Existing labour legislation in the presidency made the preservation of public order indistinguishable from the maintenance of labour discipline. The armed forces at the disposal of the St Kitts administration, both local and imperial, found themselves enlisted in the task of guaranteeing the planters' control

over labour on the sugar estates of the island.... Policing in St Kitts, therefore, became essentially the management of industrial relations in the interest of the employing classes.[41]

The strikers persisted, even after the marines landed to protect Basseterre and enable police to go into the outer districts. When police made a road block, the marchers dispersed into the canefields and regrouped the other side of the police. Each time the police tried to intercept a crowd, it had dispersed before they arrived, warned on at least one occasion by a man on a motorcycle. On 1 February Colonel Bell patrolled the island to reassure planters and arrange 'armed pickets on each affected estate' to keep off the strikers. This arrangement worked, 'and the labourers gradually went back to work and molestation ceased. By Monday the 4th February all estates and the factory were working' and the marines re-embarked.[42] Though not all the ringleaders were found, more people were arrested. The strike was effectively broken, though it was evidence of the strikers' determination that the harvest had to be commenced under armed guards. By 17 February some 63 persons were in custody. Of the 24 people who were charged with rioting at Buckley's Estate, only two were convicted. In all, only four were convicted of riot and two of wounding with intent, though others were punished for disorderly conduct.[43] Among those convicted, sentences ranged from two to five years' imprisonment with hard labour.

While the governor and others believed that Nathan and Sebastian, along with a mob of 'loafers' from the town who had picked up 'bad habits' while working on the Spanish sugar islands,[44] were responsible for instigating the disturbances, they produced no evidence of this. The extent to which the SKNUBA tried to act as a trade union at the beginning of January probably encouraged the workers to make demands and to press them militantly, so Nathan's efforts should not be underestimated. But nor should they be exaggerated. From the moment the strike began it seems that only local leaders among the strikers themselves shaped the tactics and form of their action. The conservative newspaper, which had earlier criticised Nathan, reported, 'When the trouble started on Tuesday members of the St Kitts Workers' League and the "Union" did their best to pacify the people but to no avail'.[45]

Glen Richards shows that the form of the protest, labourers marching round the island, armed with sticks, calling on fellow workers to join the strike and demonstration, was the same as in the 1896 labour protest, which also lasted several days. As an editorial in *The Union Messenger* pointed out, it had long been the custom around Christmastime for bands of masqueraders to parade through the villages armed with sticks, so 'the form of industrial protest adopted by the striking labourers was instinctively derived from their working-class cultural traditions'.[46] Nevertheless, Richards' conclusion that both the 1896 and 1935 protests 'were undeniably the result of the spontaneous action of the plantation workers', while largely true, underestimates the encouragement and preparation that Nathan and Sebastian appear to have provided, whether entirely intentionally or not, in 1935.

The chief reason for the St Kitts labour rebellion, unquestionably, remains the poverty and insecurity experienced by the sugar workers and their families, along with their growing sense of injustice about their obvious exploitation.

Nobody had to point this out to them. They were also clearly aware that the sugar factory was making a lot of money and that the planters had been guaranteed a minimum price for their cane, while their own wages were less than they had been in 1932. The reduction of wages and threat to their employment, in addition to the return of many workers from Cuba and the Dominican Republic, made these poor people increasingly desperate and angry. Whether they had an expectation or only a hope of an imminent wage increase in January 1935, we cannot doubt that they believed they deserved one. And, while the labour rebellion began essentially as a strike over wages, the violent overreaction by the authorities made this a historic event in the shaping of Kittitian, and indeed West Indian, political consciousness.

On 4 February, while the workers were returning to the estates, J. Matthew Sebastian, the editor of *The Union Messenger*, published an open letter to Mark Moody Stuart, the director of the St Kitts (Basseterre) Sugar Factory. He challenged the board of directors to share their profits with the planters, thus enabling them to pay more to their workers, for the good of 'the whole community':

> It is no secret that the shareholders of the company have received handsome dividends for many years. It is also no secret that during those years the planters have, more often than not, failed to make any money, or made very little, and the position of Labour during nearly all that period, has been, to say the most of it, worse than hand to mouth.... If the shareholders of your company would be satisfied with smaller profits... would it not be possible to benefit the planter and through him the labourer? Every one concedes that the Sugar Factory is very efficiently operated. For this you and your co-Directors are mainly responsible. It should, therefore, be possible for you and them to make such re-adjustments in the distribution of profits as will result in disseminating contentment and happiness in place of the present conditions of discontent and poverty....
>
> The key to the situation lies in your hands. Will you open the door to happiness and prosperity among planters and labourers alike, or will you keep the door firmly locked and thereby help to foster class and race hatred?[47]

At a meeting between Moody and G.P. Boon, representing the planters, no concessions were made. The governor's view was that 'the Factory Company is unreasonable in refusing to meet at least some of the requests of the Planters', who threatened to cease planting cane. According to the governor, the company's shareholders made big profits at the expense of the planters. Between 1930 and 1933, in *'good* crop years', the shareholders received £80,178 and the planters lost £57,642.[48] Three months later the planters offered to buy the factory. Governor Johnston reported, 'Directors decline £200,000 offer for factory but am glad to report planters have agreed to continue operations for 1937 crop'.[49]

The workers of St Kitts gained nothing, not even recognised spokesmen, in the immediate aftermath of the 1935 labour rebellion. In March Nathan asked that the governor should appoint a 'special man' to represent the labourers' interest to the Legislative Council. 'Had the Labourers whom our Organisation represents been allowed a special Representative on the Legislative Council of the Presidency, the matter of wages which caused the recent disturbance would have been settled, and the whole trouble avoided'.[50] Meanwhile, the situation in the sugar industry persisted. In the governor's words, 'Though crops are more abundant and more is produced per acre more labour is not employed'.[51] Not surprisingly, there were reports of further restlessness among the workers, and planters expressed 'definite uneasiness'. Despite high property and income qualifications that limited the franchise to less than 5 per cent of the population, an election in 1937 resulted, for the first time, in victory for some popular candidates supported by the Workers' League, and the governor believed that 'this will have steadying influence'.[52] Nevertheless, local police feared 'the possibility of disturbances at St Kitts',[53] perhaps as a repercussion of the dramatic events in Trinidad and Barbados.

In 1938 the Masters and Servants Ordinance (1922), with its penal provisions, was repealed.[54] The governor reported that in St Kitts there were about 9,000 wage earners, of whom probably 98 per cent were 'wholly dependent on wages'. Of these, some 7,400 worked in agriculture, chiefly in sugar and cotton, and fewer than 600 in sugar manufacture; most of the remainder produced salt or worked for the government.[55] A few hundred workers still migrated to the Dominican Republic and a handful to Curacao and Aruba, the total number of whom had increased from 418 in 1936 to 706 in 1938. Though the migrants were sometimes ill-treated, 'the general attitude is maintained that it is advantageous to go to these islands to work', often in order to send or bring back money to build houses.[56] On the one hand, such labour migration served as a limited safety-valve to the unemployment problem at home, but on the other hand the returning migrants may well have contributed to the unrest in St Kitts, both because they were out of work and because they may have had some politicising experiences abroad. Richardson argues that the periodic migration of young labourers from St Kitts afflicted the incipient labour movement with 'an inherent weakness' through 'inhibiting the local, long-term coalescence of a critical mass of laborers for a truly unified political organization'[57] At any event, it was not until 1940, when the law prohibiting trade unions was rescinded, that the St Kitts-Nevis Trades and Labour Union was established, with Matthew Sebastian as president, five years after the historic strike.

Notes

1. Richardson 1983: 129-31.
2. *Ibid.*, 166.
3. Rev. N.W. Newnham Davis to D.R. Stewart, 23 Oct. 1934, enclosed in Stewart to Gov. Johnston, 2 Jan. 1935, CO 152/454/15.

4. Stewart to Johnston, 2 Jan. 1935, CO 152/454/15.
5. Richards 1987b: 1.
6. St Kitts-Nevis Daily Bulletin, 12 Jan. 1935, in CO 152/454/15.
7. *Ibid.*, 14 Jan. 1935.
8. Letter from E.J. Shelford, *St Kitts-Nevis Daily Bulletin*, 18 Jan. 1935, in CO 152/454/15.
9. Letter from Nathan, *St Kitts-Nevis Daily Bulletin*, 19 Jan. 1935, in CO 152/454/15.
10. Letter from Nathan, *The Union Messenger*, enclosed in Johnston to SS Sir Philip Cunliffe-Lister, 30 Jan. 1935, CO 152/454/12.
11. *Ibid.*
12. Hart 1988: 66.
13. Johnston to SS, 30 Jan. 1935, CO 152/454/12.
14. *Ibid.*
15. Sutton 1987: 148-49.
16. *Ibid.*, 150.
17. Chief Justice James S. Rae's report, 8 May 1935, enclosed in Johnston to SS, 13 May 1935, CO 152/454/12.
18. *Ibid.*
19. *Ibid.*
20. Johnston to SS, 30 Jan. 1935, CO 152/454/12.
21. *Ibid.*
22. Rae's report, *op. cit.*
23. Johnston to SS, 30 Jan. 1935, CO 152/454/12.
24. *Ibid.*
25. *Ibid.*
26. Rae's report, *op. cit.*
27. *Ibid.*
28. Rae's report says eight and Johnston's letter nine.
29. Rae's report, *op.cit.*.
30. Johnston to SS, 30 Jan. 1935, CO 152/454/12.
31. Johnston to SS, 31 Jan. 1935, CO 152/454/12.
32. Rae's report, *op. cit.*
33. *Ibid.*
34. *Ibid.*
35. Lt. Col. Edward Bell's report, 17 Feb. 1935, enclosed in Johnston to SS, 16 March 1935, CO 152/454/12.
36. J.S. Barnes (Admiralty) to UnderSS (CO), 17 April 1935, CO 152/454/12.
37. Rae's report, *op. cit.*
38. Rae to Johnston, 11 May 1935, CO 152/454/12.
39. Richards 1987a: 7.
40. Rae's report, *op. cit.*
41. Richards 1993: 19.
42. Bell report, *op. cit.*
43. Rae's report, *op. cit.*
44. Johnston to SS, 12 April 1935, CO 152/454/12.
45. *St Kitts-Nevis Daily Bulletin*, 2 Feb. 1935, in CO 152/454/15.
46. Richards 1987a: 9.
47. *The Union Messenger*, 4 Feb. 1935, in CO 152/454/15.
48. Johnston to SS, 15 Feb. 1935, CO 152/454/15.

49. Johnston to SS, 31 May 1935, CO 152/454/15.
50. Nathan to Cunliffe-Lister, 8 March 1935, CO 152/454/12.
51. Gov. G.J. Lethem to SS, 8 June 1937, CO 318/ 427/3.
52. Lethem to SS, 29 July 1937, CO 318/427/11.
53. Lethem to SS, 30 July 1937, CO 318/427/11.
54. Official gazette, St Kitts-Nevis, 27 Jan. 1938, CO 318/431/1.
55. Lethem to SS, 28 Oct. 1938, CO 318/434/8.
56. Lethem to SS, 15 Sept. 1939, CO 318/440/14.
57. Richardson 1983: 143.

Chapter SIX

St Vincent

If the labour rebellion in St Kitts was more of a strike than a riot, then that in St Vincent was more of a riot than a strike. The occasion that sparked the St Vincent riot was a consideration of increased customs duties by the local legislature, but it was not limited to 'a protest against rising retail prices'.[1] The facts that workers struck on two estates near Georgetown, on the other side of the island, before the riot occurred in Kingstown, and that demonstrators in the capital complained of unemployment and low wages, suggest that labour issues were also central to the disturbances. However, unlike St Kitts, retail stores were targets of the rioters and those Europeans who were subject to animosity were chiefly shopkeepers and merchants rather than planters and estate managers.

The governor of the Windward Islands, Sir Selwyn Grier, was convinced that agitators, particularly those who fomented hatred against Europeans, had organised the rebellion, but, while they may have contributed, this was surely not the underlying cause he believed it to be.[2] T.A. Marryshow of the Grenada Workingmen's Association and the Legislative Council had passed through St Vincent and given a 'provocative speech' in Kingstown on 16 October.[3] Grier claimed also that the Bishop of the Windward Islands had made an 'imprudent...farewell speech' on leaving St Vincent, in which he 'advised the St Vincentians that they must fight for what they wanted',[4] but this would hardly have provoked a riot. The problem, rather than poor people listening to such supposed agitators, was Grier's reluctance to recognise or listen to representatives of poor people about their problems until it was too late, with the result that social tension built up, particularly in the capital.

On 18 October 1935 a bill was read at a meeting of the Legislative Council of St Vincent for the first time. It proposed to reduce the scale of import duties on motor vehicles and to raise them on other items, including matches, in order to produce more revenue. Among those present were members of the St Vincent Representative Government Association, an essentially middle-class organisation, among whose leaders were Ebenezer Duncan, a teacher, and George McIntosh, a pharmacist. During the following days, before the second reading of the bill which was scheduled for 21 October, there were rumours, which may or may not have had a factual basis, that 'retail shopkeepers had increased the charges made for a variety of commodities',[5] including matches and also items that were not to be affected by the proposed taxation. The governor believed there was a 'deliberate campaign of misrepresentation' before the riot, 'undertaken for the purpose of causing discontent and ill-feeling'. According to him, 'The people were told and believed that the Government was largely increasing taxes on the necessities of life, was doubling the land tax, and was introducing increased licences on such animals as donkeys, dogs, etc. These statements though untrue were believed' and the governor acknowledged in retrospect that 'he should have taken steps' to explain the proposals better to the public in order to forestall 'the campaign of misrepresentation'.[6]

Whatever the real extent of such a campaign, the disturbances began on the morning of 21 October, when the bill was to receive its second reading in Kingstown. Workers struck on two estates near Georgetown and the owner of one estate was slightly injured by a stone later in the day, but elsewhere 'people remained at work throughout the disturbance', so there was no attempt to produce a general strike as in St Kitts. At about 11.30 am, while the taxes were being discussed in the council chamber above the court–house, a noisy crowd gathered outside. Seated among the public observers in the chamber was George McIntosh of the Representative Government Association, who was then a popular member of the town council. McIntosh, who was born on 8 March 1886 and died on 1 November 1963, was an important figure in the early struggle the working people of St Vincent.[7] The crowd was said to have gathered at his shop before moving to the court–house. He delivered a letter to the governor, asking for an interview 'as he wished to represent the views of some of the people'.[8] The governor sent a verbal reply that he would be willing to meet him at 5 pm, after the council's business had been concluded. The crowd of about 300 strong, feeling that he was putting them off, became angry and the police, who were then unarmed, could not control it. According to the governor, who went to the steps of the court–house to tell the people to disperse, they were 'in a very excited condition', many carried heavy sticks and some were drunk. They were shouting "We want work", "We want money", "We want food'" By ringing a bell, McIntosh quieted the crowd enough for the governor to make himself heard, but when he said he would speak with some representatives in the court–house there was such a rush of people that the hall was immediately filled and the noise continued. The main cry of the crowd was unemployment and that they wanted work and that they wanted money; also that the wages paid were too low'.[9] When the governor told them that 'If there was genuine unemployment among them roadwork would be found for the unemployed on the windward road within the next fortnight...some raised the cry of taxation and that prices had gone up'.[10] The governor said that he could not speak with them when a hundred were talking at the same time, and told them to go outside and to send their representatives to meet him at the library at 5 pm.

Perhaps the governor underestimated the crowd's anger at this time, or maybe he simply did not know what to do, but it seems to have been the turning point when a noisy confrontation in which there was still opportunity for some dialogue became increasingly violent. Some of those who left the court–house, presumably frustrated by the lack of results in their encounter with the governor, met a gang of prisoners with a stone cart on which was a sledge-hammer and a load of stones. The warder was driven off, the hammer was used to smash the doors of the prison behind the court–house, and the prisoners were released. Two warders were injured in the attack. Another section of the crowd advanced on the court–house itself and used the stones to smash doors and windows and to damage cars parked in front of the building. Others streamed across the market square to the dry-goods store of F.A. Corea, a leading merchant and estate owner, who was a member of the Legislative Council. They ransacked his place.

The police, meanwhile, sought reinforcements and arms from their barracks on the opposite side of the square, near the sea. Armed with rifles, a group of six police joined the governor and other officials at the court–house and the chief justice, at about 1.50 pm, read the Riot Act. Across the square some people were breaking into a rum shop and a constable had been wounded and his rifle broken. However, the 'considerable body of people in front of the court house... were in a state of growing excitement but taking no actual part in the rioting'.[11] As the crowd did not disperse, warning shots were fired in the air and then a volley was fired into Corea's store. Further firing took place and the rioters, who had suffered several casualties, streamed out of the square. One of the two women who were seriously wounded by this shooting, who subsequently died, was 'not in any way taking part in the rioting'. The police were joined by some armed members of the local Volunteer Force. One of them, described as 'a prominent merchant in Kingstown who is a Lieutenant' in the Force, when attacked by a man with a knife, shot him.[12]

When the governor's ADC tried to send a cable to Grenada to ask for naval assistance he found that the office had been broken into and the wires cut. He proceeded to the cable hut near the beach and used emergency equipment to send a telegram. On the way back his car was attacked by 'a gang of men armed with cutlasses', one of whom was wounded with a revolver. Further damage was done to downtown properties on Hillsboro Street, Upper Bay Street and Bedford Street, where shops were damaged or looted. It was estimated that the total number of actual rioters was about 200, and that 'a great deal of damage was done by small boys and women'.[13] The captain of the Volunteer Force arrived with more men to secure the government offices and other buildings around the square, and the governor with his ADC joined the administrator and chief of police of the island in the police barracks. While they were organising the Volunteers and swearing in special constables whom they could trust, some houses on the outskirts of the town were attacked and looted. After they had got a sufficient force and mobilised vehicles, patrols of armed men were sent out to get the situation under control. During the afternoon telephone wires were cut near Kingstown.

At 5pm the governor went with McIntosh to the library and met about a hundred people. 'They were in an excited condition and their one and only cry was that they wanted work and money and that wages were low'. The governor 'gave them a very severe warning regarding their future conduct' and repeated that if there was 'genuine unemployment amongst them and they were anxious to obtain work', they would create some additional road work. 'No reference to any other grievance was made by this crowd than that of lack of employment and low wages'.[14]

Kingstown and its suburbs were reported quiet by 10 pm but there was a disturbance at Georgetown when police fired shots over a crowd that was breaking windows and doors. At midnight, HMS *Challenger* arrived in St Vincent and a party of 24 men and four officers, armed with rifles, landed in Kingstown, making it possible for armed patrols to be despatched towards Georgetown. Some of the Georgetown crowd went south to Byera where they began cutting telephone poles and wires until they were stopped by an armed patrol. Several were taken prisoner, including one who was wounded in the attack.

Early in the morning of 22 October a state of emergency was proclaimed and censorship was imposed on the local press and on news cables. Before 8 am rioting broke out at Camden Park, some 3 ½ miles from Kingstown, and a house and store owned by a Portuguese shopkeeper were looted. An armed patrol of Volunteers sent out to stop this was ambushed by rioters where they could hurl stones on the truck from a steep hill alongside the road which they had 'blocked with fallen trees and telegraph posts'.[15] Two Volunteers were injured and they opened fire, killing one man and wounding four others. More demonstrations, without rioting, took place in Lownams and Chauncey Villages, north-west of Kingstown, Stubbs Village, about 5 miles east of Kingstown, and Park Hill and Grand Sable Estates near Georgetown on the east coast. Some other noisy demonstrations by young men armed with cutlasses and sticks were reported.

On 23 October the police began 'rounding up' those who had taken part in the riots. The landing party returned to HMS *Challenger* on 24 October but Governor Grier asked for the ship to remain at Kingstown until 29 October, after the Legislative Council had resumed the sitting which had been adjourned earlier. Ten Grenada police who had come on the *Challenger* remained as reinforcements until 5 November. On 12 November Grier admitted he did not intend to 'relax precautions...for it is known that small gangs of men, wanted as ringleaders in the Kingstown riot, are in the hills and some of them are reported to be armed'. He said they had threatened to retaliate by attacking 'members of the community who assisted in restoring law and order',[16] but no such attacks were reported. The officially listed casualties of the whole event consisted of six people killed, 19 detained in hospital and 18 treated as outpatients. Of those wounded, 12 were police, warders, Volunteers or special constables.[17]

The troubles continued as late as January. The administrator of St Vincent justified extending the state of emergency on the grounds of the continuing trials, the volatility of about 200 persons in Kingstown's slums, and the need to censor newspapers and news telegrams which could 'increase tension at a time of unrest'.[18] A local planter, Claude Hadley, was killed by his chauffeur, Williams, who had been dismissed after being charged with an offence connected with the riots. In Kingstown itself there were 'still signs of sullen hostility'. Don Morgan, 'one of the most notorious of the ringleaders', was shot and killed while resisting arrest, and two of his associates, Sutherland and McDowall, were arrested. Morgan had worked in Cuba and the governor believed that 'some of the worst characters' were labour migrants who had returned from the Spanish republics.[19] Morgan had led the uprising in the Camden Park district. They found it hard to arrest him because 'the hostility of many of the local inhabitants made it impossible for any enquiries to be made without warning being given to Don Morgan'. He came to be regarded as 'something of a hero' and each time a police raid failed 'his prestige increased'.[20]

On 1 February 1936, as the situation at last appeared to be satisfactory, the state of emergency was ended. Of the most serious cases, 33 had already been tried and of these 29 were convicted and sentenced and the others acquitted.[21] Altogether, of the 114 persons (91 men and 23 women) who were tried only 14 were acquitted; 45 men and 5 women were sentenced to terms in prison.[22]

Governor Grier insisted that 'the Kingstown riot was organised',[23] but this is unlikely or at least exaggerated, despite the evidence of more or less simultaneous disturbances in Kingstown and Georgetown, and the fact that more than one group cut telephone and cable wires in different places. The governor sought to place most of the blame for what he believed to be 'a deliberate campaign of misrepresentation' on George McIntosh, whom he said was 'mainly responsible for staging the whole business'.[24] McIntosh was arrested and charged with treason felony as the leader of an armed mob on 23 November. However, the charge was so ridiculous that the magistrate who heard the case dismissed it without even calling on the defense.[25] McIntosh, along with Ebenezer Duncan, was certainly critical of Crown Colony rule and their opposition to the Italian invasion of Ethiopia, which began in 1935, probably encouraged race consciousness and anticolonialism. Duncan published reports of the war in his newspaper, *The Investigator*, and McIntosh posted news and photographs about it on a bulletin board outside his Kingstown shop.[26] Others who participated in the demonstrations were also associated with advocating Ethiopia's cause. Sheriff Lewis, a working man who was said to have served as a volunteer in Ethiopia, was nicknamed 'Selassie', and Bertha Mutt, a labourer for the Agriculture Department, was known as 'Mother Selassie'. These people have been characterised as working-class leaders of the rebellion.[27] Lewis served five years of a 21-year prison sentence, the longest given to a convicted rioter.[28] However, there is no evidence that any of these people plotted or planned an uprising, or that it was organised at all. Though the government sought to portray McIntosh as the instigator of the riots, both he and Duncan soon condemned them. Duncan's editorial in *The Investigator* on 26 October described the riots as 'a blot on the history of the colony' and on 29 October McIntosh moved a resolution at a meeting of the Kingstown town board conveying its 'deep regret' about the riots and congratulating the government for 'suppressing the disorder'.[29]

As for the underlying causes, Grier argued that 'the bitter and growing feeling of resentment against the white races...continually fomented by public speakers at pro-Abyssinia meetings' had been responsible.[30] Though in his own report he states that the demonstrators complained only about unemployment, low wages and lack of money, he asserted that 'the main driving force of those who rioted was a bitter hatred of the whites'.[31] His evidence for this is quite limited, however. Amongst the threats made in the market square, the administrator heard 'we lick all you white men up tonight', and arrested rioters abused the police who had 'sided with the whites'. One 'ringleader' was said to have secured two black and two white fowls from a local merchant of Portuguese descent, and to have 'publicly decapitated the 2 white fowls with appropriate remarks'.[32] But such comments and demonstrations, particularly in such a heated moment, are better understood as the normal idiom of social tensions in a society rooted in slavery and colonialism than as evidence that race hatred, as such, was the underlying cause of the riot. Perhaps more important is the evidence that shops and houses belonging to residents of European descent were singled out for attack, but even here it is impossible to distinguish the class from the race factor. Corea's store was probably a special target because he was a rich member of the Legislative Council which was about to vote taxation measures that, it was believed, favoured people like him while making the poor pay more. Perhaps, too, the cars were attacked in market square because the council was proposing to reduce import duties on motor vehicles, used only by officials and the rich, but this was not simply 'bitter racial animosity'. On the other hand, if St Vincentians had known that Grier went so far as to say that 'If the Abyssinians achieved a similar success to that of 1896 [when Emperor Menelik II defeated an Italian army at the battle of Aduwa], the repercussions might be more dangerous than they will be if Italy succeeds in annexing Abyssinia',[33] they may have been provoked justifiably to such animosity.

Finally, Governor Grier blamed criminal gangs, including one called 'The Ranch Boys', named presumably after 'some American "gangster" film.... The connection between this gang and another directing organisation which remained in the background is the subject of investigation'.[34] However, nothing more is heard about this sinister plot, the gangs, or the unnamed 'directing organisation'. In fact, Grier seemed to get the underlying causes and the symptoms or contributory causes mixed up. He could not admit that unemployment and low wages, combined with high prices and unfair taxation, could cause such a riot in his colony, though this is clearly what the demonstrators were repeatedly telling him. Instead, he had to look for agitators and criminal gangs, sinister designs and plots, which misled the normally peaceful and loyal working people of St Vincent so as to leave his paternalistic colonial vision intact. He admitted that wages for estate labourers were low, seldom exceeding 1s. a day for men and 10d. for women, and that much of what was available for workers in town was 'casual employment as stevedores and porters and boatmen'. He also acknowledged that the 'position of estate owner is reminiscent of feudal times', yet he claimed that labour relations on the estates were 'most cordial' even when many estate owners were in 'financial difficulties'.[35]

If the underlying cause was clearly economic, as the demonstrators repeatedly said, a contributory cause was inadequate communication between the poor people and the colonial administration. Because the colonial officials contemptuously dismissed such men as George McIntosh as agitators, they cut themselves off from any popular representation of grievances, with the predictable result that poor people became increasingly frustrated and angry. Equally predictable, the governor, who was unable to acknowledge such a serious defect in the colonial system, argued for more police as he did not have 'the men available to keep in touch with the activities of local agitators who are well-known to be exercising a subversive influence', though his Volunteer Force, numbering between 50 and 60 loyal men, 'proved of great value' during the crisis.[36]

One outcome of this labour rebellion, and more particularly of the subsequent prosecution, was that George McIntosh 'emerged as unchallengeably the most popular leader of the working class'.[37] In 1936 he organised the St Vincent Workingmen's Cooperative Association, the first organisation explicitly organised for working people in the island. It was registered as a limited liability company on 2 July, as it could not legally be registered as a trade union. Another outcome was that more attention was paid to the unemployment problem. An unemployment bureau, dealing with unemployment in an area up to 10 miles from Kingstown, was established on 7 August 1936. In the absence of accurate statistical information it was estimated that, of some 11,500 workers and peasants, 1,000 were 'more or less regularly employed' on sugar estates, another 1,000 had regular employment in Kingstown in various capacities, about 300 worked for government departments 'more or less regularly', and of the 3,000 who were partially employed on the windward coast and 1,500 who had partial employment on the leeward coast, about half had access to small plots of land on which they grew food. Others made a living, or made do, by fishing or by obtaining casual employment, but 'there are one thousand persons unemployable who exist by begging or by relying on their relations and friends' and 400 persons received poor relief. Of the 189 people registered at the bureau as in search of work, 32 were skilled, 137 unskilled and 20 were domestic workers. The number of persons for whom employment was found was 'disappointing'. Seven of the skilled labourers found work in the Public Works Department, and two of the domestics and 24 of the unskilled labourers found work. 'Outdoor relief' during the last three months of 1936 provided an average of 21 persons weekly with such employment as weeding and clearing the churchyard and cemetery.[38] This report reveals the extent of underemployment as well as unemployment, and that most St Vincentians had to mix casual work with their own food production. It also shows that the response of the bureau and of relief efforts was pitifully inadequate.

At the end of July 1936, McIntosh, in his capacity as president of the new St Vincent Workingmen's Cooperative Association (SVWCA), invited Marryshow to visit. The administrator of the island, Alban Wright, agreed to address a labour rally on 3 August provided they sang 'God save the King' instead of 'Toilers' and 'The Red Flag', and that he could speak after Marryshow. He was told this 'would be regarded as betraying the Labour Cause, if they were omitted, and that they had been sung at every Labour gathering in the West Indies', but he got his way. Some 3,000 - 4,000 men and women were in the procession, carrying banners proclaiming the villages whence they came and with such slogans as 'God Save the People', 'No sticks must be carried', 'Preserve perfect quiet and order', 'We demand employment', and 'The people must have land'. The procession 'moved quietly and in perfect order' to the Anglican Cathedral and the rally in the park was also 'perfectly orderly and good-humoured throughout'. Wright thought Marryshow 'completely reasonable and in every respect moderate in his speeches and actions', and felt that the rally would help re-establish 'friendlier and more sympathetic relations' between white people and people of colour on the island.[39] These cooperative efforts, better communications and friendlier relations were achieved less than a year after the riots. In an election in 1937, under a still limited but somewhat more liberal franchise, McIntosh's Association won four of the five elected seats to the Legislative Council. At the end of that year, the 1839 Masters and Servants Act, containing penal sanctions, was repealed.[40] The SVWCA and the associated St Vincent Labour Party (SVLP), led by McIntosh and Duncan, 'laid the groundwork for the growth of political unionism' in the period before adult suffrage in 1951.[41]

Despite these gains and achievements in the two years after the labour rebellion, the endemic problems of St Vincent persisted. In 1938 Wright belatedly pointed out the obvious when he reported, 'One of the main difficulties in St Vincent is that there is no alternative employment for labourers other than agriculture which must be subject to seasonal inactivity.'[42] The SVWCA still could not register as a trade union, though it achieved some promising legislation on a minimum wage and work hours and a token land settlement scheme.[43] In 1939, W. Arthur Lewis wrote:

> In three short years the Association has become the focus of radical opinion in St Vincent, and a body of great political influence. It is not registered as a trade union, but it represents the workers in all negotiations. It has also attracted wide middle-class support, and its candidates were enthusiastically returned at the last General Election. It is one of the new organisations which is changing the orientation of West Indian politics. [44]

This organisation and McIntosh's leadership role emerged directly out of the fiery crucible of October 1935. Had the colonial administration been willing to take McIntosh and his followers seriously in the first place, to listen to their grievances rather than dismiss them as criminals and agitators, the violence and tragic deaths in that month could have been avoided. However, it may be argued also that it was precisely those events that led to a modest revaluation of the situation. Colonial officials began to see that it was better to recognise and talk to moderate leaders of working people's organisations than to risk another outright rebellion.

Notes

1. Hart 1988: 67.
2. Gov. Sir Selwyn M. Grier to SS Malcolm MacDonald, 12 Nov. 1935, CO 321/363/64320. He claimed to know that 'a Russian Jew, an accomplished linguist who professed a philanthropic interest in the slums of Kingstown and Castries [St. Lucia], where he spent much of his time, was present in these islands in 1934 and early 1935. He is also known to have visited St Kitts'. A marginal minute identified him as Nathan Leipziger and refers to 'No.10 in 7057/35 General'. That file appears in CO 378/106 (Colonies General: Register of Correspondence) as 'General suspects', but was 'destroyed under statute'.
3. *Ibid.*

4. Grier to Sir Cosmo Parkinson, 17 Nov. 1935, CO 321/363/64320.
5. Grier to MacDonald, 12 Nov. 1935, CO 321/363/64320.
6. *Ibid.*
7. Cecil Ryan and Cecil A. Blazer Williams *From Charles to Mitchell, Part 1* (St Vincent, n.d.), p.6.
8. Grier to MacDonald, 12 Nov. 1935, CO 321/363/64320.
9. *Ibid.*
10. *Ibid.*
11. *Ibid.*
12. *Ibid.*
13. Commander A. Jones, HMS *Challenger*, to C-in-C, 29 Oct. 1935, CO 321/369/64320.
14. Grier to MacDonald, 12 Nov. 1935, CO 321/363/64320.
15. Jones to C-in-C, 29 Oct. 1935, CO 321/369/64320.
16. Grier to MacDonald, 12 Nov. 1935, CO 321/363/64320.
17. *Ibid.*
18. A. Grimble to Grier, 24 Jan. 1936, CO 321/369/64320.
19. Grier to Parkinson, 20 Jan. 1936, CO 321/369/64320.
20. Lt. Comdr. C.D. Milbourne to A. Grimble, enclosed in Grimble to Grier, 22 Jan. 1936, CO 321/369/64320.
21. Grier to SS, 31 Jan. 1936, CO 321/369/64320.
22. Grier to J.H. Thomas, 28 March 1936, CO 321/369/64320.
23. Grier to MacDonald, 12 Nov. 1935, CO 321/363/64320.
24. Grier to Parkinson, 17 Nov. 1935, CO 321/363/64320.
25. Grier to Parkinson, 18 Dec. 1935, CO 321/369/64320.
26. Young 1993: 66-67.
27. Hart 1988: 69.
28. Young 1993: 68.
29. Quoted in Ralph E. Gonsalves, "The 1935 Labour Riots in St Vincent and their Political Significance", n.d., pp.13-14.
30. Grier to MacDonald, 12 Nov. 1935, CO 321/363/64320.
31. *Ibid.*
32. *Ibid.*
33. *Ibid.*
34. *Ibid.*
35. *Ibid.*
36. *Ibid.*
37. Hart 1988: 69.
38. Report by Alban Wright, Administrator, in Gov. Popham to Ormsby-Gore, 2 June 1937, CO 318/427/3.
39. Alban Wright to Gov., 2 Sept. 1936, enclosed in Act.-Gov. Edward Baynes to Ormsby-Gore, 8 Sept. 1936, CO 321/369/64354.
40. Popham to Ormsby-Gore, 29 Dec. 1937, CO 318/431/1.
41. Gonsalves, *op. cit.*, p.19.
42. Wight to MacDonald, 27 Sept. 1938, CO 318/434/8.
43. Young 1993: 69.
44. Lewis 1977:21.

Chapter SEVEN

St Lucia

On St Lucia, St Vincent's northern neighbour, most wage labour was on plantations but there was also an important business supplying ships with coal at the port and capital, Castries. Though there was a history of strikes and militant workers in this trade, no working-class organisations had been formed. By the 1930s, as ships increasingly used oil, this business was providing less employment and it was the workers in this trade who started the labour unrest in St Lucia. These workers were most likely to be in fairly close touch with events on other islands, and even international labour issues, through the sailors with whom they would have come into contact.

On 4 November 1935 about 350 - 400 workers employed in unloading a collier went on strike at 1 pm. 'The strikers dispersed quite quietly', but it was said that some members 'of the hooligan class became increasingly offensive to any of the white community who were abroad in the town'.[1] For this reason, presumably, as there had been no public disturbance and the strikers had yet to make their demands, a detachment of 28 marines was landed from HMS *Challenger* to guard the police barracks during the night. At 11 am the next morning, a deputation from the strikers visited the governor. 'The men demanded double wages; they also complained about the overloading of baskets'.[2] Governor Grier argued that, in the present state of the trade, the coaling companies could not increase the wages. In 1934 one company had shown a loss of £900, while another was in liquidation.[3] Nothing was agreed, and the strike persisted.

The governor, who had proceeded directly from St Vincent to St Lucia on 1 November, was predisposed for trouble and quickly overreacted. He commented that the principal speaker of the deputation was 'a man who had at one time been in Cuba, and who speaks at times in a manner which is reminiscent of a communist orator in England'. He reported that anonymous letters, signed 'Hail *[sic]* Selassie our King', had been sent to a St Lucia police sergeant threatening 'all those who sided with the "whites" as well as against the "whites" themselves'.[4] Grier decided promptly that the situation on St Lucia 'had become threatening[5] so he declared a state of emergency. The Volunteers were mustered and special constables enrolled to support the 61 regular policemen and the marines, even though 'no trouble or rioting was reported from the town'.[6] The Volunteers were led by a white man, Captain Wade, the Inspector of Schools.

At 1 pm on 6 November, about 50 persons, chiefly women and boys, were organised to carry on unloading the coal. 'These workers were threatened and intimidated, but suitable police protection was available. At 1800, attempts were made to molest them on their way home from the dumps. One arrest was quickly made and no further trouble was experienced throughout the night'.[7] The next day a gang of about 80 workers, 30 of whom were said to be regular coal workers, recommenced unloading the coal and no attempt was made to interfere with them. By the morning of 8 November, 'about 40% of the coaling gangs had returned to work...without any interference or disturbance'.[8] By 11 November the strike was said to be over and the situation remained quiet.

This was such a minor event that it could be argued there was no rebellion in St Lucia. The strike was a quite normal and orderly labour dispute. The only people threatened by the strikers were some strike-breakers who worked under police protection. But Governor Grier, with the St Vincent experience so fresh in his mind, reacted to this minor and reasonable labour dispute with an unnecessary show of force. Searchlights from HMS *Challenger* played over the town at night while marines patrolled the streets with the intention of disturbing and intimidating the inhabitants.[9] The police and the special forces were used by the colonial administration on behalf of the coaling companies to put down the strike. Despite this show of force, or perhaps in sympathetic reaction to it, a strike occurred among agricultural workers on Lime Estate, about 8 miles from Castries, on 12 November, but it was 'neutralised by borrowing labour from a neighbouring plantation'.[10] A committee set up by the governor subsequently reported that no wage increase for the coal haulers was possible.

Detectives were brought from Barbados to investigate sedition mongers. One of them reported that the principal speaker at a meeting of the local branch of the UNIA, 'who had the reputation of a troublemaker, urged the necessity of avoiding any trouble in view of what had taken place in Kingstown',[11] in neighbouring St Vincent. In February 1936 Grier wrote that 'the trouble makers were sufficiently frightened to remain quiet for the time being...and interest in the Abyssinian War seems to have disappeared'.[12] While his efforts to intimidate people and to silence dissent appear to have succeeded, even Grier seems to have been aware that the underlying problems were unchanged, as he commented that the economic situation in St Lucia 'is pretty bad' and the Minimum Wage Committee 'has a difficult task in front of it'.[13]

Despite prolonged investigations into the activities of those believed to be responsible 'for the dissemination of subversive propaganda', no evidence was produced which would have justified legal proceedings against anybody. Nevertheless, the governor claimed that the enquiries themselves 'had the desired effect of discouraging for the time being subversive propaganda' and several people continued to be 'closely watched'.[14] In this way, any criticism of the administration or the society came to be defined as subversive activity and subjected to official intimidation. In the same process, the absence of any public dissent was then construed as proving the effectiveness of such measures against agitators. Thus was a dangerously authoritarian pattern, subversive of the democratic process, established within the colonial regime.

At the end of 1936, a minimum wage for agricultural workers was set in St Lucia that was the same as the normal current rate, namely 1s. for men and 10d. for women for a day of not more than nine working hours.[15] Nine months later, on 5 August 1937, a strike occurred on Cul-de-Sac Estate, one of the two largest plantations in St Lucia, about 10 miles from Castries. Some 1,500 workers were involved and the administrator called out the Volunteer Force as a 'purely precautionary measure'.[16] The strike spread to Roseau Estate, where the manager said he had heard threats that the radio station would be destroyed and all the Europeans slaughtered. More believably, it was said that higher wages were demanded because the workers had heard that the governor of Trinidad had recommended them there. To counter this, the administrator impressed on the manager of the Cul-de-Sac Estate 'the necessity for a strict observance of the Minimum Wage Order.... It has been alleged that evasion is practiced by fixing task rates at such prices that it is impossible for the labourer to earn the daily minimum wage, also by the employment of juveniles at less than the full rates, and so on'.[17] The administrator expressed concern lest the owners of the two largest estates increase wages beyond the rates that small employers could afford, thereby resulting in 'a greater increase of unrest and discontent', so he kept the Volunteer Force mobilised.[18] However, if the large employers were paying below the minimum wage by cheating their workers, as he had previously suggested, then the smaller employers were surely not paying more. In effect, the so-called minimum wage was really a maximum, but one that many workers did not receive.

Governor Popham commented that several communities in the Windward Islands had been 'keyed up' in 1937 by the recent events in Trinidad and Barbados, and that the administrator of St Lucia had to 'allay the fears of the law-abiding elements and restore confidence'.[19] But there was no rioting in St Lucia where, once again, special forces were called out as soon as a strike occurred, in anticipation of disorder. Lewis commented that even the government's own nominees in the Legislative Council criticised 'the waste of public funds entailed by unnecessary mobilisation'.[20] It seems that the real function of these auxiliary police forces was to intimidate strikers and keep the labour situation favourable to employers.

On 6 December 1938 an ordinance repealing the penal sanctions in the old Masters and Servants law was passed in the St Lucia Legislative Council and it received the governor's assent on 14 December.[21] Early the next year, 1939, the first St Lucian trade union was formed, organising urban and agricultural workers. [22]

Note

1. Jones to C-in-C, 9 Nov. 1935, CO 321/369/64320.
2. *Ibid.*
3. *Ibid.*
4. Grier to MacDonald, 12 Nov. 1935, CO 321/363/64320.
5. *Ibid.*
6. *Jones to C-in-C, 9 Nov. 1935, CO 321/369/64320.*
7. *Ibid.*
8. *Ibid.*
9. Lewis 1977: p.21.
10. Letter of proceedings of HMS *Dundee*, 25 Nov. 1935, CO 321/369/64320.
11. Grier to Parkinson, 20 Jan. 1936, CO 321/367/63796.
12. Grier to Parkinson, 27 Feb. 1936, CO 321/367/63796.
13. Grier to Parkinson, 15 March 1936, CO 321/367/63796.
14. Grier to J.H. Thomas, 6 May 1936, CO 321/367/63796.
15. St Lucia Rules and Orders, No. 55, 26 Nov. 1936, enclosed in Grier to Ormsby-Gore, 5 Jan. 1937, CO 321/368/63834.
16. *St Lucia Gazette*, 6 Aug. 1937.
17. Edward Baynes, Administrator, to Gov. Popham, 6 Aug. 1937, enclosed in Popham to Ormsby-Gore, 12 Aug. 1937, CO 318/427/11.
18. Baynes to Popham, 7 Aug. 1937, enclosed in Popham to Ormsby-Gore, 12 Aug. 1937, CO 318/427/11.
19 Popham to Ormsby-Gore, 12 Aug. 1937, CO 318/427/11.
20. Lewis 1977: 22.
21. Popham to MacDonald, 24 Dec. 1938, CO 318/437/13.
22. Lewis 1977: 22.

Chapter EIGHT

Trinidad

The working people of Trinidad were agitating and mobilising long before their great labour rebellion in 1937. As in Belize, returning soldiers from the West India Regiment in 1919 participated in a rash of strikes that began on the Port of Spain waterfront and spread around the island and to Tobago. 'The situation in December 1919 was the nearest thing to a general strike the colony had yet seen'.[1] There followed a period of repression. Some of the earliest organisations oriented toward the needs of working people in the British Caribbean were created in Trinidad but, as elsewhere, legal restrictions on trade unionism blunted and frustrated these efforts. By the mid-1930s a more radical new leadership had developed, reflecting the degree of proletarianisation and urbanisation of the working people of Trinidad and their desperation in the depression years. Politically motivated militant groups began to agitate and organise workers and the unemployed in 1934 and 1935, but the rapid expansion of trade unionism occurred after the labour rebellion in June 1937. By the end of 1939 13 trade unions had been registered in Trinidad and Tobago,[2] and the labour movement was well on the way to becoming institutionalised.

Trinidad, along with Belize and Guyana, is one of the most racially diverse parts of the British Caribbean. This diversity has been evident in a segmented labour force that corresponds to a large degree to a sharply bifurcated economy. The salience of race and class, and their relationship to the structure and fluctuating fortunes of the economy, were central to the emergence of the labour movement in Trinidad. Three primary groups of trade unions emerged, among workers in the sugar industry, the oil industry and the urban workers such as those on the docks and in public works. The oil industry since the early twentieth century had come to dominate Trinidad's exports by the 1930s, but it was a capital-intensive industry and far more people were employed in agriculture. While crude oil and its by-products accounted for about 60 per cent of the value of exports and sugar, rum, molasses and cocoa for about 33 per cent, the sugar and cocoa industries employed over 68,000 people compared with only about 8,000 employees in the oil industry. From the point of view of labour, therefore, plantation agriculture remained the dominant sector, but from the point of view of imperial officials the oil industry was critical, especially in terms of defence policy. The fact that Trinidad had become the British empire's largest producer of oil 'was an important determinant of imperial policy towards the labour disturbances'. [3]

By the early 1930s the Trinidad Workingmen's Association (TWA), which was founded in 1897 and had been revived after the war, had become 'a less effective and united organization than it had been in the 1920s'.[4] Between 1919 and 1934 the TWA was a pioneering and progressive political force, but Captain Cipriani's reformist leadership, which was committed exclusively to legal and constitutional methods, became challenged by younger and more militant leaders. As early as 1929 a rival organisation, the Trinidad and Tobago Trade Union Centre, was formed and it claimed some 2,000 members, mostly in transport in 1930.[5] However, trade unions were illegal until the Trade Union Ordinance of 1932 empowered the colonial government to register them, thereby making them legal, or not, as it chose. But the law did not legalise peaceful picketing, nor protect unions from legal actions for damages arising out of strike actions, as was the case in Britain. In these circumstances, after seeking advice from the British TUC, Cipriani decided not to register his organisation as a union. Instead, he decided in 1934 to rename it the Trinidad Labour Party (TLP).

Cipriani's intolerance of criticism within his party and his refusal to challenge the limitations of the Trade Union Ordinance made his organisation increasingly marginal during the labour struggles of the next few years.

> It may be that Cipriani believed that the political strategy was more important than the development of trade unionism, or that he viewed the emergence of new leaders and new labour unions as a threat to his leadership of the workers, or simply that he had faith in the TUC's advice. In any case, there was increasing dissatisfaction within the TWA/TLP over Cipriani's authoritarian leadership.[6]

As other, younger labour leaders quickly developed new tactics and expressed the working people's demands more militantly, Cipriani and his TLP were overtaken and became an obstacle to the further development of the labour movement.

In the early 1930s a group of intellectuals developed a radical critique that helped shape a new political culture in Trinidad. C.L.R. James and Alfred Mendes started a literary journal called *Trinidad*, which appeared at Christmas 1929 and Easter 1930. Its portrayal of slum life was considered scandalous by middle-class society. This was the precursor of *The Beacon*, 28 issues of which appeared between 1931 and 1933. Financed and edited by Albert Gomes, who had recently returned from the USA, this magazine challenged conventions about culture and politics in exploring issues of West Indian identity, race consciousness, socialism and communism. James's biographer writes that James

> insists that the magazine and the milieu around it dominated literary life, not only in Trinidad, where it had no competition, but in the English-speaking Caribbean, where it had next to none. And not only literary life, but also the maturing sensibility of the Caribbean's historical place within the century and the world. [7]

Whatever influence this journal may have had upon the younger labour activists and cultural nationalists, James left before the real action started. In 1932 he migrated to Britain, carrying his manuscript of *Minty Alley*, a social realist novel written in the 1920s but not published until 1936, and his study of Cipriani and the movement towards self-government, *The Life of Captain Cipriani: An Account of British Government in the West Indies* (1932), revised as *The Case for West Indian Self Government* (1933). These intellectuals were imagining a new West Indian world that was soon to be actually initiated by the working people's movement. By the time James returned to Trinidad in 1958 the colony's politics had been transformed.

A series of hunger marches and demonstrations, beginning in 1933 and accelerating in the following two years, moved beyond reformist politics and intellectual critique to the mass politics of the street. Several new organisations emerged, chief among them the National Unemployed Movement (NUM), the Trinidad Citizens League (TCL) and the Negro Welfare Cultural and Social Association (NWCSA). They attacked Cipriani's leadership of the labour movement, mobilised workers and initiated new, radical labour politics. Several of the leaders of these organisations had formerly participated in the TWA/TLP and had broken with Cipriani. A hunger march to the governor in the Red House, the seat of colonial government in Port of Spain, on 19 June 1933, took place against Cipriani's advice. The demonstrators demanded the reintroduction of rent control and relief work for the unemployed. The next year, a core of working people, Elma Francois, Jim Barrette and Jim Headley, formed the National Unemployed Movement. Francois was born in St Vincent in 1897 and migrated to Trinidad in 1919, where she worked as a domestic servant, became a member of the TWA and started to speak at public meetings. Jim Barrette was her companion. Jim Headley, as a ship's cook, had been active in the National Maritime Union and the Young Communist League in the USA, where he had been in touch with George Padmore, the Trinidadian revolutionary who was then a leading member of the International Trade Union Committee of Negro Workers of the Comintern. Headley, like Francois, had been a member of the TWA. They were joined by Dudley Mahon, a cook at the Port of Spain Colonial Hospital. The NUM organised demonstrations in 1934, the 'idea spread like wildfire throughout the country and "Hunger Marches" were organised by other groups'.[8]

As economic conditions worsened and increased mechanisation threatened employment, strikes and demonstrations occurred on the sugar estates, chiefly in central Trinidad.[9] The NUM contacted the sugar workers, who were predominantly Indian. A militant Indian sugar worker, Poolbasie, informed the NUM members of living and working conditions on the estates. She said that a severe drought was making the earth particularly hard to work and that exploitative drivers were not only checking more frequently on the completion of tasks but were also taking young girls to their houses on pretexts. In addition to the inherent abuses of this situation, the sugar companies passed on the problems caused by the depression to their workers. 'High unemployment and high rents for barrack accommodation were combined with unilateral increases in the size of tasks',[10] and the workers still had no legally recognised representatives, organisations or negotiating processes.

The demonstrations began on 6 July 1934 among some 800 workers at the Brechin Castle and Esperanza estates. When violence erupted and the police were attacked, 12 persons were arrested. Mass demonstrations were staged in Couva, Chaguanas, Tunapuna and San Fernando, involving some 15,000 estate workers in the sugar belt.

> Overseers, managers and policemen were attacked, company buildings set on fire, shops looted; it was the spontaneous violence of desperate men close to starvation. The disturbances were not organized, and no leaders were publicly identified. [11]

Though no people were killed by the police, many were arrested and fined or imprisoned. Basdeo concludes that the repressive activities of the police, including firing into the air and random arrests, 'helped to infuriate demonstrators'.[12] A commission of enquiry stated that the sugar workers had legitimate grievances, but its recommendations were 'commonplace, simplistic and conservative, lacking in any fundamental provisions to remedy the situation'.[13] The governor pointed out that 'callous retrenchment and overtasking by the sugar companies were the major causes of the riots, yet the only positive steps he could recommend were the distribution of the princely sum of £150 in relief for destitute workers and the irrigation of rice lands to enable them to plant rice'.[14] On 20 July 1934 a march from the Caroni area to Port-of-Spain was planned, to unite the Indian sugar workers with the predominantly African hunger marchers of the NUM, but a cordon of police stopped it. The important participation of Indians in these marches and the growing unity between rural Indian and urban African workers were remarkable features of these demonstrations, which were among the earliest in the growing labour rebellions of the 1930s in the British Caribbean.

The NUM organised a register of unemployed and collected 1,200 names within two weeks in 1934 in Port of Spain. In addition to organising the marches, they held public meetings at which they spoke about economic and labour issues. By the end of 1934 Headley had returned to his job as a seaman but the others, though harassed by the police, persisted. One of the leaders of the NUM, who were progressive in their attitude to gender equality, was Elma Francois. Speaking at a meeting in Woodford Square early in 1935, she impressed Bertie Percival, an oilfield worker from Fyzabad, who subsequently joined the group. Other leaders included Clement Payne, who became a major figure in the Barbados labour rebellion in 1937, Christina King, who worked as a writer and undercover agent in the NUM, and Rupert Gittens, who had been deported back to Trinidad for his activities with the French Communist Party in Marseilles. Gittens had previously worked for several years in the USA, where he was influenced by Communist ideas and by radical black nationalism. Under his influence, 'the NUM was exposed much more to socialist thinking at an international level and became convinced of the limitations of "unemployment" as a political issue'.[15] By 1935 the NUM had transformed itself into an organisation with more broadly defined goals but a narrower social base, the Negro Welfare Cultural and Social Association (NWCSA).

In March 1935 the workers at Apex Oilfields, which was the largest of the oil companies that in 1936 produced 29 per cent of the total oil output of Trinidad,[16] went on strike. Apex refused to redress the workers' grievances, which included 'low wages, long hours, wage deductions for late-coming and poor conditions',[17] so the Fyzabad branch of the TLP asked Cipriani for help. When Cipriani refused to sanction strike action, the workers went ahead anyway and two members of the Fyzabad TLP executive, Tubal Uriah 'Buzz' Butler and John Rojas, organised a hunger march to Port of Spain, openly challenging Cipriani's leadership in the oil belt. Cipriani responded by enjoining the police to stop the march. He promised the demonstrators that he would arrange for a delegation to meet the governor to discuss their grievances, but 'no redress was forthcoming'.[18] Though the strike petered out and the workers settled for a meagre 2 per cent increase in wages, this event marked the start of Butler's rise as a labour leader in the oilfields of southern Trinidad.

Butler, born on 21 January 1897 in Grenada, had enlisted in the West Indian regiment at the age of 17 in the the First World War. An immigrant to Trinidad in 1921, he had worked as a pipe fitter until forced to retire as an oil worker in 1929 because of an industrial accident that had left him with a permanent limp. From 1931 he was the chief pastor of the 'Butlerite Moravian Baptist Church', and he joined the TWA about the same time.[19] Working as a preacher around Fyzabad, where there were many other Grenadian immigrants, Butler became increasingly politicised as he witnessed the problems of his flock. Always flamboyant, he succeeded in dramatising the grievances of the oil workers and made them a national issue. 'Combining rhetoric culled from socialist vocabulary, with biblical phrases and images, and appeals to African race consciousness, Butler by early June, 1937, had become the catalyst that was needed for industrial action in the oil districts'.[20]

Links were established between Butler and the NWCSA. Bertie Percival worked with Butler during the 1935 strike at Apex and lost his job in the oilfields as a result. Butler stayed at the home of Percival and Christina King when he visited Port of Spain. They were all increasingly critical of Cipriani who, as mayor of Port of Spain, sought to prevent the NWCSA from using Woodford Square for their meetings. At a May Day meeting in 1935, Francois criticised Cipriani, calling him 'Britain's best policeman in the colonies',[21] and the NWCSA won over many former members of the TWA/TLP with its more radical ideology and militant activities.

The NWCSA played a major role in agitation against the Italian invasion of Ethiopia and this became, in Trinidad as elsewhere, a key aspect of raising race and political consciousness. Dockers refused to unload Italian ships and the owner of a Port of Spain store was forced to take down the sign for an Italian shipping line of which he was the agent.[22] The NWCSA organised protest meetings and contributed articles, leaflets and letters to newspapers on the issue. They handed in a petition to the Italian consul after a large demonstration. The climax of these activities was a meeting on 10 October 1935, at which speakers denounced Britain for refusing to sell arms to Ethiopia, condemned 'Italian Fascist Imperialism', and 'criticised the prohibition of meetings and marches as a direct attack upon the political rights of the working class by a government incompetent to solve the unemployment crisis'.[23] In this way the NWCSA linked local and international political issues, showing the connection between human rights and oppressive systems at home and abroad. The NWCSA continued its agitation through 1936, with a Friends of Ethiopia meeting on 9 May and a mass meeting in Woodford Square on 29 May, at which Elma Francois was the chief speaker. [24]

By this time of the NWCSA extended its activities all over northern Trinidad and it cooperated with Butler and his southern-based movement. In 1936 the NWCSA took up the question of the cost of living and created the Condensed Milk Association to criticise the price of this commodity and the importers' advertising which encouraged women to buy expensive brands for their babies. They did research on the cost of living, nutrition, health services, pensions and school meals and discussed the issues with other labour activists, including the Clerks' Union, which was founded by the TLP in 1933 but not registered as a union, and the Amalgamated Building and Woodworkers' Union, which was the first organisation to register as a trade union, on 30 March 1936. They went together with Butler to speak with the governor, Sir Murchison Fletcher, on 8 November 1936, but before the NWCSA members, many of whom were women, could deliver their memorandum, Butler fell to his knees, kissed Fletcher's hand, and begged for his assistance. Elma François like others was angered by Butler's behaviour as she was the designated leader of the delegation and Jim Barrette had stepped aside in favour of Butler in order to promote unity and broader representativeness. [25] François disagreed with Butler on the questions of loyalty to the British monarchy and empire, and the relation of religion to the political struggle. Despite these disagreements, however, the NWCSA continued to work with Butler.

Another issue espoused by the NWCSA that showed their concern for the everyday problems of working people was the Shop Hours (Closing and Opening) Bill, introduced in June 1936. This bill was promoted by the larger merchants, represented by the chamber of commerce, to stop the small shopkeepers from opening for longer hours. The 1921 Shop Hours Ordinance gave a 45-hour week to many clerks and shop assistants by limiting opening hours to between 8 am and 4 pm on five days and 8 am and 1 pm on the sixth, but in 1929 small stores, defined as those in which one proprietor and not more than two other persons worked, were allowed to stay open from 7 am to 7 pm on weekdays and up to 8 pm on Saturdays. The NWCSA opposed the new bill on behalf of the small shopkeepers and their predominantly working-class customers. On 25 June 1936 some 600 people passed a resolution against the new bill at a meeting in Woodford Square, but in July Cipriani refused to allow the NWCSA to hold another meeting there. [26]

The NWCSA's influence peaked in 1936. Though governor Fletcher later testified that it was the NWCSA that first drew his attention to the poor people's condition and the colonial secretary, Howard Nankivell, is said to have 'maintained clandestine relations' with them, [27] they were frequently harassed by the police. The leaders, like the people they were organising, were all 'miserably poor', according to Albert Gomes, who said that he had served his 'political apprenticeship' with the NWCSA. [28] They faced great hardship, even hunger, as well as insecurity and imprisonment. Though these dedicated working-class intellectuals of the NWCSA 'never had the mass appeal that

Butler developed',[29] their persistent work 'did much to prepare the way for the 1937 riots'.[30]

Another organisation that helped prepare the way was the Trinidad Citizens' League (TCL), founded in 1935 by Adrian Cola Rienzi, another former TWA/TLP activist who had become disillusioned with Cipriani. Rienzi, born in San Fernando in 1905, changed his name from Krishna Deonarine in 1929. He had been involved with the TWA since 1925 and, as president of the San Fernando branch, developed it into an active base for local organisation. Always to the left of Cipriani, Rienzi had gradually withdrawn from TWA activities as he became more enthusiastic about Indian nationalism and world socialism. He was elected general secretary of the Indian National Party in Trinidad in 1928 and campaigned for a shelter for destitute and homeless Indians. At this time, even as such a young man, the governor considered him 'notoriously seditious' and refused to acknowledge his petitions or receive any deputation from his party. He left to study law in Dublin in 1930. When in England between 1931 and 1934 he associated with socialist, anti-imperialist and Indian nationalist groups, and he remained under British surveillance. He returned to Trinidad in 1934 as a qualified lawyer but the attorney general refused to allow him to practise at the bar because of his political views. Only after Sir Stafford Cripps, the eminent Labour Party politician, intervened with the Colonial Office on his behalf was his petition to practise granted.[31]

Rienzi started the TCL in December 1935 with Butler and Rojas. The TCL, several of whose core members were of working-class status, 'immediately addressed itself to the more pressing problems of oppressive working-class conditions, maladministration and financial corruption' and petitioned for an inquiry into 'the general state of the colony'.[32] The TCL soon became a serious rival to the TLP in the south, but on 27 July 1936 Butler seized the initiative by launching his own political organisation, the British Empire Workers and Citizens Home Rule Party (BEWCHRP), declaring himself the 'Chief Servant'. Rienzi was temporarily outmanoeuvred by Butler, but his professional skills were important and Kelvin Singh argues that his 'role in the labour movement, especially in the crucial years 1937-40, was not only critical but perhaps indispensable for the establishment and survival of trade unionism in Trinidad'.[33] Whereas Butler's loyalty to Britain and his desire to see the rights of British citizens extended to the colonies is reflected in the name of his party, Rienzi's TCL, though it did not last long, helped politicise people in terms of nationalism and self-government. The explosion of June 1937 cast Butler and Rienzi into new roles and a difficult relationship in the labour movement.

While Francois, Butler, Rienzi and others played a part in politicising and organising working people in Trinidad for several years before the labour rebellion exploded, the fundamental cause of the 1937 riots was not their agitation so much as the continuing deterioration of the conditions of the majority of people through the economic crisis. Masses of evidence, including that given to the Forster Commission in 1937 and the Moyne Commission in 1938-39, shows that 'for the labouring population, mere subsistence was increasingly problematic'.[34] However, it was not the absolute misery of the working people alone that provoked the rebellion. There was also 'the presence of an oil industry whose advanced structure and profitability brought into high relief the contradictions between capital and labour'.[35] The labour leaders succeeded in politicising these class contradictions in connection with frustration about racial oppression so as to heighten dissatisfaction and produce the *'peculiar* vibrancy of Trinidad's experience in the 1930s'.[36] It was the combination of all these factors that produced the great labour rebellion.

As the price of sugar collapsed in the depression, the small cane farmers in Trinidad could not get a profitable price for their cane at the factories, so pressure on wages and employment was felt by all the sugar workers, whether they worked for the small farmers or the larger estates. The lowest rates of daily wages in the sugar industry fell from 1s. 8d. in 1930 to 10d. in 1933 and rose to only 1s. 5 1/2d. in 1936, with women receiving less. This was for a nine hour day, from 7 am to 5 pm with an hour for lunch, six days a week. Skilled estate workers at the top end of the scale earned around 3s. per day and worked a 54-hour week.[37] These wage rates would result in annual incomes of £23–47 only if the workers were employed through the year, but of course most were not. Consequently, most workers received an annual income of £20–30, and some considerably less. Ten workers, selected randomly at Orange Grove Estate, earned between them only £113 for a total of 1,218 man-days in the 1936-37 season, an average of 9d. per day. The two who worked the longest, for 237 and 202 days, received annual incomes of less than £22 pounds and £19 respectively, in a context where an annual income of £158 was estimated to be required for the minimum needs of a family of five.[38]

Workers in the oil industry fared somewhat better if only because this capital-intensive and highly profitable industry with a relatively low wage bill could easily afford to pay its workers more. Although many sugar workers received only 35 cents per day and worked up to 54 hours a week, oil industry workers received 72 cents per day for a 48-hour week.[39] Nevertheless, prices were high in the oil belt and they rose by at least 11 per cent and perhaps as much as 17 per cent, between 1935 and 1937.[40] Even discounting inflation, 'wages were never restored to pre-Depression levels',[41] when the companies had reduced their labour costs. Moreover, the rate of profit had risen rapidly for the oil companies in the 1930s, resulting in total dividends of 25 - 35 per cent to the British shareholders[42] and smugness among the company directors. The chairman of Apex Oilfields, the largest oil company, reported a total dividend for 1937 of 45 per cent (52.25 per cent of gross), after some £2 million had been written off in depreciation and amortisation. He said just six months after the labour riots, 'I have no doubt you will agree that there is good reason to be satisfied with the position disclosed in our balance sheet'.[43] An assessment of the profits being made in the oil industry in the 1930s concludes that five of the six leading companies, together accounting for some 90 per cent of output, enjoyed great prosperity, particularly after 1933, a conclusion that concurs substantially with that reached at the time by the trade union leaders and W. Arthur Lewis.[44] The workers' awareness of the high profits that coincided with their low wages, at a time when prices were rising but the taxes and royalties paid by the oil companies remained low, was a cause of intense resentment. As Brereton writes, 'The rising cost of living while wages were not adjusted, in an industry known to be prosperous, was the major grievance of the oil workers, who had no recognised machinery of collective bargaining to articulate their demands or discuss conditions'.[45] The oil workers, concentrated together in the oilfields, were more easily mobilised than agricultural workers, though the pay and conditions of the latter were even worse.

The most intensely felt grievances of the oil workers, that were especially conducive to their politicisation, were the result of racial discrimination and victimisation. The black workers were well aware of the visible inequalities in standards of living of the white managers and employees and themselves. They objected particularly to their treatment by some white South Africans employed by Trinidad Leaseholds. The black workers objected to the use of racial epithets and insulting modes of address, such as 'boy', and the companies' practice of giving preference in the form of higher wages and promotions to whites who were no more and sometimes less qualified or experienced. They objected, too, to the notorious red books, the records of service that companies shared with each other, the problem of job insecurity, the arbitrary fines imposed by companies and the absence of compensation for injuries sustained at work. Workers were fined for being late or misplacing tools, and could be dismissed without any compensation after years of service and then blackballed by other companies. They received little or no compensation for overtime or work on Sundays or public holidays and no pensions or gratuities on retirement. They felt that, white employees were favoured, they had to suffer from chronic insecurity and low status.[46] In the wake of the publicity and agitation over the Italian war in Ethiopia, the oil workers' growing race consciousness coincided with class issues in a most compelling fashion.

The experience of the Apex Oilfields strike and march in 1935 was still fresh in many people's minds early in 1937 and Butler made sure it was not forgotten in the southern oilfields where he held public meetings, appealing to the workers' race feelings as well as their labour grievances. From 1935 he was the oil workers' leader and his messianic style and Biblical rhetoric caught fire in the oil belt, where many Grenadian and other 'small island' immigrants like himself were concentrated. In many ways, however, Butler was a traditional rather than revolutionary leader. Far from espousing the socialist and anti-imperialist ideas of Rienzi and the NWCSA, Butler said he was conducting 'a heroic struggle for British justice for British Blacks in a British country'.[47] While his radical tactics may be seen as pushing the apparent promises of imperial ideology beyond the limits the imperialists were prepared to permit, he nevertheless displayed a loyalty to the empire and its symbols of authority that inhibited any long-term goal or strategy of liberation. Partly for this reason, he seems to have been unprepared in terms of how to respond to the labour rebellion and the massive use of force with which it was crushed, though he himself had done more than any other individual to provoke it. Singh writes, 'Butler suffered the fatal weakness of popular agitators: he had no strategy for dealing with the crisis that would inevitably develop in the event of a popular confrontation with the establishment'.[48] In the crisis after 19 June Butler gained popular status as a martyred leader while he was in hiding and in jail, but it was E.R. Blades, Rienzi and the members of the NWCSA who provided leadership, direction and organisation for the emergence of trade unions.

In June 1937 it was the police, not Butler, who triggered the widespread rioting and violence. Butler struggled to deal with the oil companies at a time when there was no trade union and the government viewed him as an irresponsible if not actually crazy agitator. When he turned to strike action, however, 'he envisaged a peaceful sit-down strike; he cautioned against demonstrations, looting or violence',[49] and against encouraging strikes in other industries. The strike was planned to begin on 22 June but when the oil workers learned that the companies and the police intended to frustrate them they brought the date forward to 18 June. At midnight oil workers sat down on their jobs at Trinidad Leaseholds, in Forest Reserve and Fyzabad. This tactic of a peaceful 'sit-in' or 'sit-down' was quite new, having been used effectively by rubber workers in Akron, Ohio and in the creation of the United Automobile Workers' Union in Detroit in 1935 and 1936.[50] The employers and government in Trinidad, like those in the USA, were prepared to use force against this peaceful tactic.

The oil companies pressed for Butler's arrest and police were deployed in the oilfields and reinforcements were sent to San Fernando. A warrant was issued in the afternoon of 19 June to arrest him on charges of using violent language and inciting breaches of the peace. While he was addressing a meeting of 400 - 500 workers in Fyzabad at about 6 pm, the police tried to arrest him but 'the crowd exploded in anger, rushed the police and hustled Butler out of their grasp'.[51] In the confusion and violence that followed, Corporal Charlie King was beaten, soaked with paraffin and burned to death.[52] Even though the telephone lines between Fyzabad and San Fernando had been cut, police reinforcements arrived. They were stoned and fired on, and Sub-Inspector Bradburn was killed. The police were forced to retreat without having captured Butler or having recovered King's body. At 8.55 pm, when the governor was informed of the situation, it was decided to mobilise the Trinidad Light Horse, a mechanised volunteer unit, and to send for naval forces. The determination of the government and oil companies to crush the strike and arrest Butler triggered further violence, which soon escalated into an island-wide rebellion. Before long, as Bridget Brereton writes, 'The unrest cut across race lines, and affected every sector of the economy'.[53]

An armed police platoon and a detachment of the Trinidad Light Horse entered Fyzabad on the morning of 20 June and recovered King's body. In making a house-to-house search for suspects and arms, they 'encountered no opposition'.[54] Nevertheless, HMS *Ajax* was ordered to Trinidad and press censorship was introduced. Governor Fletcher and the Inspector-General of Constabulary visited the troubled areas, but when Timothy Roodal, a local businessman, member of the TLP and a friend of Butler, addressed a crowd he unintentionally inflamed them. Though the disturbances had occurred so far only in the south, more detachments were deployed in an increasing show of force in the oilfields and also on sugar estates. On 21 June the strikes spread, with action in Fyzabad, Point Fortin, San Fernando, Penal and Ste Madeleine, and a second cruiser was requested. At Point Fortin workers blocked the road to prevent access to the refinery and in San Fernando a crowd roamed the business section, closing shops and holding up traffic. Meanwhile, a group set off for the sugar factory at Ste Madeleine where they stopped the cane trains, called the workers out of the fields and the factory, assaulted company managers and closed down the water supply and lighting plant. In response, the first and second battalions of the Trinidad Light Infantry Volunteers, an almost exclusively white force armed with machine-guns, was mobilised. Some were sent to San Fernando, where rioters armed with axes, cutlasses, sticks and stones had cut telephone lines to the power station and driven out its staff. When they attacked the telephone exchange, the first battalion of the Volunteers fired on them, killing two and wounding eight. Later, a police patrol was fired on in Penal and a Volunteer was wounded.[55]

On 22 June the resistance spread to Port of Spain and to more sugar estates. Several hundred people, armed with sticks and agricultural implements, invaded the Waterloo Estate and closed it down. They moved on to Wyaby Estate, which was also stopped, and then Woodford Lodge Estate where they tried to break through a police cordon to close the factory. The police opened fire, killing one man and wounding two. More trouble broke out that morning at Tabaquite and Rio Claro. At the latter, the strikers stopped work on adjacent estates and took over the railway station but the police repulsed them, killing five men and wounding 20 more.[56] In Port of Spain members of the NWCSA, who had planned but then postponed a mass meeting on 18 June, had been taken by surprise. Francois spent 20 June in Fyzabad, 'investigating everything', before returning to Port of Spain to urge her comrades into action.[57] A strike among workers on the new Treasury Building was supported by a group from the NWCSA. A crowd demonstrated in the city, closing down stores and calling out workers at the Trinidad Trading Company and Harbour Scheme Works. By 22 June, according to the *Trinidad Guardian*, 'All Stores [were] closed in Port of Spain', but a raid on a train sending arms to San Fernando was repulsed when the police opened fire on the demonstrators. The strikes spread to Belmont, St James and Woodbrook and schools and shops were closed. The *Port-of-Spain Gazette* noted on 22 June in its Editorial that Trinidad was experiencing a general strike the proportions of which were 'previously unknown in the history of labour agitation' in the colony.

The general strike continued to gain momentum around the island, as workers went on strike on the Caroni sugar estate on 23 June and on several estates near Arima (O'Meara, Carapo, Esperanza, La Reunion, San Raphael and Golden Grove). Workers at the government farm and experimental station at St Augustine went on strike, as well as workers on the Port of Spain waterfront. Strikes spread among the employees of the Port of Spain city council and the Public Works Department, then at the Bamboo Paper Pulp factory in Champs Fleurs, at Trinidad Clay Products, at Aranguez Estates, San Juan, and Black Estate in Flanagin Town. Under the headline, 'Strike Moves Fast', the *Guardian* reported, 'Men, young and old, women and children brandishing sticks, cutlasses and other weapons walked from factory to factory in the district, inflicting workers with the strike fever'.[58] Bus drivers went on strike and schools and post offices were closed. By 26 June the strikes reached Mayaro, affecting the Beaumont, St Anns and Lagoon Doux Estates. On 27 June bus drivers struck at Arima and Tunapuna, as well as workers at Caigual and Fishing Pond and on the Non Pareil and St Lawrence estates. Though there was no coordinating revolutionary leadership, this spontaneous series of actions had evolved into a prolonged general strike, combining mass demonstrations with a few sporadic armed confrontations.

Butler remained in hiding and the workers without any effective coordination, lacked a clear sense of direction. On 20 June and 22 June Butler smuggled brief notes to Rienzi, asking him to defend him and his followers against the legal charges brought by the police.[59] Rienzi soon found himself thrust into a more active role as the workers perceived him to be a sympathetic lawyer. A 'strike action committee' of oil workers wrote to him on 24 June asking him to visit Fyzabad, preferably with other independent observers, to witness the military occupation and intimidation occurring there. While Cipriani still opposed the formation of unions and Butler was not in a situation to organise them, Rienzi became drawn into a leadership role.

> It was in these circumstances that Rienzi now re-emerged to make his most decisive contribution to the labour movement...when Cipriani and the TLP were expressing undisguised hostility. Rienzi moved to salvage the gains that could still be made for the workers out of a situation in which the sheer military superiority of the ruling class could easily lead to the restoration of the *status quo ante.*[60]

On 26 June Rienzi sought a meeting with the governor, but it was not until 30 June that the Executive Council's Mediation Committee met him in San Fernando.

In the meantime, the arrival of HMS *Ajax* and HMS *Exeter* on 22 and 23 June, respectively, changed the balance of force in the government's favour. Altogether, some 2,200 officers and men were mobilised. Most of the officers were white and many were expatriates. Of the 21 police officers, 13 were from England and two from Ireland and the 933 constables were predominantly black.[61] The marines and sailors not only bolstered the tiring local forces but they also helped restore the confidence of the ruling class and intimidated many workers. The governor who, as Brereton points out, had a double policy of 'conciliation' and 'repression',[62] announced on 24 June that he would seek a settlement 'which will be fair to employers and employees alike', while he deployed more troops and persistently sought to arrest Butler. A state of emergency was declared on 26 June,[63] and a committee of the Executive Council, including the colonial secretary, Howard Nankivell, was appointed to hear the workers' grievances and seek reconciliation between them and their employers. Given the critical nature of the oil industry to the empire and the danger of an expanding general strike, it was important 'for both the state and the capitalists...to get the workers to return to work as quickly as possible'.[64] Governor Fletcher knew that it would be hard to arrest Butler, who was believed to have an armed escort of 80 - 100 men with him at all times, so he sought to regain the initiative from the strikers by making offers to government workers and encouraging the oil companies to make similar offers to their workers. On 28 June when several NWCSA leaders, including Elma Francois, Jim Barrette and Bertie Percival, were arrested and held in jail, Fletcher complained,

> The Government's efforts to negotiate a settlement are seriously impeded by the lack of trade union or recognised leader of the oil workers and by the fact that the oil company managements are in London, out of touch with the local situation, with the result that prompt decisions which are so imperative cannot be taken.[65]

The problem, of course, was partly of Fletcher's own making, as he refused to recognise or deal with the workers' leaders, preferring to jail them. He proposed to offer new wage rates to government workers, since he believed that the wages of unskilled labour were too low throughout the colony. Government workers' wages were to be increased to 72 cents per day for men and 60 cents for women in Port of Spain, and 60 cents for men and 36 cents for women outside the city, with the working week reduced from 54 to 45 hours. Fletcher's double policy was a way to enhance the paternalistic role of the state, by granting limited wage concessions while jailing the workers' leaders, but in so doing it unavoidably made the colonial administration more clearly political.

Butler, who was still in hiding, wrote to Rienzi on 1 July, saying he found himself in the perhaps unhappy position of not being able to call off the strike which has caused so much hurt to the Colony and its inhabitants as a whole. 'The workers, I am told, are in the main prepared to put up a "last-ditch" fight to secure at least a general all-round increase in their wages as a prerequisite to going back to work.... I respectfully beg that you communicate this information to His Excellency the Governor'.[66] Governor Fletcher, who may have seen this as a confession of weakness, pressed his two-pronged policy. On the one hand, he reported on 2 July, 'With the cordial agreement of the Legislative Council, I have taken the opportunity of this unrest to fix a minimum wage only a fraction higher than that of pre-depression', while refusing to agree to a claim for a 25 per cent increase by the dock workers or to bargain with 'known agitators'. On the other hand, and on the very same day, three platoons were deployed throughout Fyzabad, the centre of the militancy, to 'comb out' the troublemakers, as it was put. Beginning at 6 am, the troops and police searched houses, seized arms and arrested 22 people, three of whom had been on the list of ten men Butler had nominated as workers' negotiators. Three more communities were 'combed out' in dawn operations on 4 July and, though a few rigmen remained on strike at Forest Reserve and Fyzabad until 8 July, the strike was essentially broken. The *Trinidad Guardian*, 'organ of capitalist interests in the colony',[67] triumphantly exclaimed on 6 July, 'The strikes are now dead; only their ghosts remain to be buried'. The use of the press and press censorship had contributed to breaking the strike and rebellion, often by deliberately spreading lies and confusion. In an effort by the press to turn other poor people against them, the dock workers, one of the most militant sections, were accused of trying to raise food prices and starve the colony.[68] The NWCSA created a Workers' Defence Organisation consisting of three groups, the Defence Fund Committee, the Propaganda Committee and the Public Communication Committee. The last organised small groups of activists who travelled at night through the island, speaking unannounced in towns and villages in order to avoid the police.[69] Despite their efforts, most workers were prevented from having accurate information about the strikes and the actions of the armed forces.

The strike may have been broken, but when HMS *Exeter* left on 5 July, only government workers and dock workers had actually negotiated terms of work, while all others were left with only offers and promises. That 'the situation remained explosive'[70] is suggested by the fact that the senior police officers wanted a warship stationed in the Gulf of Paria, to be available if required. Many people remained active. The NWCSA members, Percival, Barrette, Ashby and Francois, were eventually acquitted and continued to organise meetings to collect defence funds and protest against the prosecution of strikers. Along with members of Butler's BEWCHRP, they formed a Workers' Defence Committee and held meetings in Fyzabad, Point Fortin, Siparia and elsewhere. Butler himself, meanwhile, was not caught, which is a reflection of the loyalty of his supporters. He was arrested on 27 September 1937, when he came out of hiding to give evidence to the Labour Disturbances Commission.

On 9 July Fletcher and Nankivell spoke to the Legislative Council, castigating the oil and sugar companies for paying starvation wages, oppressing labour and repatriating profits. Craig has suggested this was a tactic to 'play for popular support', mere rhetoric aiming 'to appease with words while repressing with deeds',[71] but there is reason to believe that they were sincere as they wrote in similar fashion in confidential despatches to the Colonial Office. Their speeches were not merely a public posture but arose from their conviction that the low wages and general poverty were largely to blame for the widespread unrest. On the other hand, this did not make them 'champions of the working class', as Brereton, Ryan, and Basdeo claim,[72] although the infuriated business community saw them that way. Fletcher cabled Ormsby-Gore on 28 June, saying he was 'satisfied that the oilfield workers have legitimate grievances' and that 'the wages of unskilled labour throughout the Colony are admittedly too low'.[73] He reported on 5 July 1937: 'The roots of this colony-wide unrest go very deep. Labour has lived in conditions of extreme poverty and squalor, and the colour line has kept employer and employed at a long arm's length apart'.[74] To the Legislative Council, Fletcher acknowledged that government shared the blame for not implementing a minimum wage and pressed the employers to make concessions in the interests of peace. He warned, 'I am certain that the white employer class in Trinidad will find in tact and sympathy a shield far more sure than any forest of bayonets to be planted here'.[75] At the same time, of course, he showed that he was willing to use the bayonets and he dismissed Butler as a misguided agitator.

Nankivell, the colonial secretary who was working on the council's mediation committee, was even more outspoken. Recalling that the Wages Advisory Board had received data the previous year about the workers' conditions and grievances, he pointed out that the cost of living had continued to rise and government revenue had increased while industry prospered, yet the workers' situation had clearly deteriorated. 'In the past', reproached Nankivell, 'we have had to salve our consciences with humbug and we have had to satisfy labour with platitudes. Those days have gone by....' He accused employers of treating 'the human element' worse than their machinery, of keeping people employed 'in conditions of economic slavery', and of branding workers as communist agitators as soon as they expressed their grievances. He went so far as to say that 'an industry has no right to pay dividends at all until it pays a fair wage to labour and gives the labourer decent conditions'. He concluded that it would be 'entirely in the interests of the colony' if the profits of the oil industry were transferred from the pockets of British shareholders to those of the workers, thereby stimulating consumption in Trinidad among 'our own people'.[76]

Rather than characterising these colonial officials as either champions of the working class or deceitful hypocrites, they are best understood as genuine liberals, suffering from the contradictions of liberalism in a polarising situation.

As the two senior representatives of British colonialism in Trinidad, they did take their 'trusteeship role seriously',[77] but that meant that they would ruthlessly suppress disorder while at the same time seeking to reform the situation that they understood to have given rise to it. The difference between the views of the capitalists and the colonial officials is that, whereas the former were selfishly interested in their own particular profits, the latter had to be concerned about maintaining general industrial peace and the social order as a whole. The rage of the capitalists, in Trinidad and England, over what they perceived to be the intemperate speeches of these officials does not support the view that Fletcher and Nankivell set out to appease the workers for their benefit. The capitalists obstructed the mediation efforts, refused to make any substantial concessions to the workers and petitioned the Colonial Office to suspend the mediation committee. The Duke of Montrose, chairman of a Trinidad oil company, opined in the House of Lords that 'the trouble had nothing to do with wages and living costs, but was purely the result of communistic propaganda – the work of Communists who had been touring the islands stirring up racial conflict and urging the natives to grab all the wealth'. This was absurd. The chairman of Caroni was equally intemperate, claiming that the disturbances were 'an attempt at revolution by a minority of extremists. There was no question of unemployment, underpay, or undernourishment'.[78] These men, who sounded rather like slave owners who claimed that their contented slaves were only led to rebellion by outsiders, wanted an overwhelming show of force and protection for their colonial properties without any diminution of their profits. Kelvin Singh correctly concludes that 'both Fletcher and Nankivell, while not wishing for any fundamental re-ordering of worker-management relations, nevertheless took a far more humane view of the plight of workers in Trinidad than did the representatives of corporate management'.[79] Whether or not their view was more humane, however, as the chief colonial officials on the spot they were responsible for suppressing the labour rebellion, and they did just that. By the time the combined armed forces had crushed the resistance, 14 people had been killed (two of them policemen), 59 wounded and hundreds arrested.

A commission of inquiry into the disturbances, chaired by John Forster, began its work on 6 September. Although the representatives of capital, who maintained an unrelenting lobby on the commissioners,[80] welcomed the report for supporting their contention that government had failed to promptly suppress the disorders at the outset, the commission was outspoken about the appalling conditions that working people suffered in Trinidad. The report stated that the condition of most agricultural workers 'justifies the view that many managements display a surprising indifference to the welfare of their labour', and that housing was very poor also in the oil belt and in Port of Spain. Fyzabad, they wrote, was 'a village which has grown up on the edge of the oilfields without any apparent regulation or control or observance of elementary rules as to structure, space, or sanitation', and they saw barracks in the capital that were 'indescribable in their lack of elementary needs of decency', yet charged rents at 12–15 s. per month.[81] Though the commission agreed with Fletcher that low wages and poor working conditions had been the basic cause of unrest, it made no recommendations about these issues.

The commission did recommend the creation of a labour department and the appointment of a labour officer to act as a mediator and arbitrator between employees and employers, the establishment of an industrial court and that the workers' compensation law should henceforth include agricultural labourers. To encourage industrial peace, the commission supported the development of unions, while saying that government should have the power to refuse recognition to unions whenever they viewed their leaders as unsatisfactory. The report rejected Cipriani's suggestion that a large measure of self-government was desirable. Most shockingly, the commissioners criticised the police for hesitating to fire on the crowd in Fyzabad on the evening of 19 June. The representatives of capital welcomed these conclusions when the Forster Report was published in February 1938, calling it a 'Law and Order Report'.[82]

Governor Fletcher was forced to resign even before the Forster Commission's report was published. As the winds began to turn, Fletcher had abandoned Nankivell, informing Ormsby-Gore that he 'has shown a bias towards labour',[83] and he called for more troops and riot control equipment in October. Imperial troops arrived in Trinidad in mid-November, but the business community remained opposed to him. Fletcher had strengthened the sedition laws and sought to restrain public meetings and public speakers. The Summary Jurisdiction Ordinance (1937) made it illegal for more than ten persons to assemble in public. Fletcher's liberalism had crumbled under pressure, and he felt 'impelled to the conclusion that a small permanent garrison is inevitable', as the balance between capital and labour was fraught with difficulty and risk.[84] On 10 November, the day after Forster had returned to England and reported to Ormsby-Gore, Fletcher was recalled to London. He was forced to resign, supposedly on the grounds of ill health, in December 1937. The Colonial Office had concluded that he lacked 'independent capacity of decision, stability of character and constancy of purpose',[85] and that the 'possibility of achieving the desired industrial peace in Trinidad was endangered by Fletcher's erratic behaviour'.[86] Sahadeo Basdeo concludes that Fletcher's recall 'was a warning to labour in Trinidad that capital had still not lost its traditional allies in Downing Street. The dismissal of Fletcher was the work of the Colonial Office at its worst'.[87] Fletcher was replaced by Sir Hubert Young, a choice that was believed to have been influenced by the absentee interests in London because he had crushed a strike in the copper mines in Northern Rhodesia in 1935.[88] Howard Nankivell, removed from office a few months after Fletcher, killed himself in France in January 1939.

Cross, referring to the manoeuvring by the capitalists against the colonial officials, concludes that 'the rift within the ruling elite of Trinidad galvanised support for class-based movements'.[89] While this support had been building for some time before the rift appeared, as we have shown, it is probable that the awareness of these divisions encouraged the labour organisers. Certainly, the speed and effectiveness with which trade unions were organised in the months after the labour rebellion is astonishing.

The Oilfield Workers' Trade Union (OWTU), in particular, was formed extraordinarily quickly in July 1937, in the immediate wake of the labour rebellion. According to the union's official history, some informal and even clandestine meetings took place in Fyzabad in mid-July, prior to the more formal conference, at which representatives from most of the oilfields attended, that launched the union on 25 July.[90] The speed with which the OWTU was formed was made possible because it was based on an extant organisation of workers that had been started two years earlier. According to a memorandum by Elbert Redvers Blades, the first general secretary of the OWTU, a small group of workers got together at Forest Reserve, Fyzabad, around the middle of 1935, to form a 'sort of cooperative movement whereby they could buy and sell to and from themselves'.[91] Their efforts were prompted by the fact that the cost of living was rising while their wages remained the same. The cost of food in the oil districts was exceptionally high, so some people even found it more economical to shop every two weeks or so in Port of Spain, over 50 miles away. Some workers approached the manager of Trinidad Leaseholds and asked him to use his influence to get the company to open a commissary for the workers, similar to one that supplied the staff with goods more cheaply than the workers could purchase them outside, but he replied that it was not the company's policy to make such a provision. In 1936, after this rebuff, a committee of the workers organised meetings in several oil districts and organised local subcommittees, each with a chairman and secretary, in order to start a business of their own. The organisation was called the United Workers Trading Association (UWTA). Blades, who was elected secretary of the main committee at Fyzabad, travelled frequently to different districts, 'making new contacts and setting up new groups'. This association was about to be registered in 1937, but 'the strike broke out and all activities ceased'.

When a mediation committee was formed during the strike, Blades, who was employed as a mechanic by Trinidad Leaseholds, was elected by his co-workers to represent the garage and transport departments, and to state their grievances. Later he spoke to Governor Fletcher, who urged him to 'tell the workers to form a Trade Union, and make it strong and powerfull [sic]'. Blades promptly addressed the workers and called for a meeting two days later. At that meeting he was elected provisional secretary and given the task of organising a meeting with representatives from other oilfields. The next day he had some handbills printed and circulated these around the district committees of the UWTA, inviting its members to attend 'a monster meeting' in San Fernando on 25 July in order to formally create the OWTU. The UWTA members 'devoted all of their time to the formation of the Union', so the meeting was well attended and 'a great success'. Blades wrote that he asked Rienzi for some legal advice and also invited him to the meeting. 'He said if I gave him a written invitation he would attend. I wrote one in his office and handed it to him....Mr. Rienzi attended and after giving a brilliant speech was elected President while I was confirmed in the post of Provisional Secretary'. Blades' memorandum not only suggests that the invitation to Rienzi was an afterthought and that Rienzi's speech was the immediate cause of his election as the first OWTU president, but also that the union was created and grew so rapidly because of the work of the district groups of the UWTA. Many leaders of the UWTA groups 'became union organisers and some became officers'. In addition to Blades himself, Alexander McNish, chairman of the UWTA, and Frederick White, secretary of the Guapo branch of the UWTA, became president and secretary of the Cochrane Branch of the OWTU; Bertie Aberdeen, chairman of the Parrylands group of the UWTA became president of the Parrylands Branch of the union; and James Hall (or Halls), who represented a Fyzabad group of the UWTA, became a treasurer and trustee of the union.

When the UWTA was registered as a limited liability company in November 1938, with 48,000 shares selling at $1 each, about 97 per cent of its shareholders were members of the OWTU. A year later, when the company had sold about 16,000 shares, it opened a grocery, called the United Workers' Grocery, which 'was well patronised by the workers'. It is not clear whether the formation of the UWTA had anything to do with the hunger marches and demonstrations of 1934-35, but it was responding to the same issues. It is clear, however, that the OWTU sprang into being so swiftly in July 1937 because it was based on this already extant workers' organisation and that Blades was the central organiser of both. The UWTA folded in 1940 and Blades was forced to resign his position in the OWTU in 1941, but they had played an important role in the early formation of Trinidad's greatest union.[92]

By the end of 1937 six unions had been registered: the Amalgamated Building and Woodworkers' Union (ABWU), already established in 1936, the Federated Workers' Trade Union (FWTU), registered on 27 August 1937, the Oilfield Workers' Trade Union (OWTU), formed in July and registered on 15 September, the Seamen and Waterfront Workers' Trade Union (SWWTU), registered on 19 November, the All Trinidad Sugar Estates and Factory Workers' Trade Union (ATSEFWTU), registered on 24 November, and the Public Works and Public Service Workers' Trade Union (PWPSWTU), registered on 26 November.[93] Three of these unions, the ABWU, SWWTU and PWPSWTU, were based in Port of Spain and oriented toward the urban workers there, but the other three, which were led by Rienzi, were chiefly in the south.

While Butler was still in hiding, Rienzi, acting as his agent, met with Nankivell and the mediation committee and insisted that they recognise and meet the OWTU executive. The employers' union, the Petroleum Association, was determined to prevent the workers' unionisation, however, and manoeuvred to get the mediation committee suspended. Rienzi and a group of labour leaders, including John Rojas, MacDonald Moses, E.R. Blades and Ralph Mentor, persisted in their unionisation drive, and held meetings with oil and sugar workers. Rienzi became the president-general of both the OWTU and the ATSEFWTU in the south, while the FWTU, which he served in an advisory capacity, organised railway and construction workers. Clement Payne of the NWCSA, who had played a prominent role in the Barbados labour rebellion between his arrival there on 26 March 1937 and his deportation on 26 July, was a founding member and organiser of the FWTU. During the last months of 1937, Sir Arthur Pugh, a member of the Forster Commission and general secretary of the Iron and Steel Trades Confederation, addressed several union meetings, advising the organisers of unions to register under the 1932 Trade Union Ordinance.[94] Undoubtedly, the rapid rise of trade unionism was the most important result of the labour rebellion and Rienzi played a leading role in the process, creating and consolidating organisations in the vanguard sectors of oil and sugar.

While Butler was the more charismatic labour leader and was widely seen as a heroic figure, Rienzi was the more competent builder of lasting organisations. The problem of their compatibility arose in 1939. Rienzi had to work carefully because he was categorised as a Communist by the authorities. On 20 July 1937 his home was raided, ostensibly in a search for arms but clearly in order to intimidate him, and he was under continual police surveillance.[95] Despite the limitations of the 1932 ordinance, Rienzi thought that the registration of unions would 'strengthen the hands of a sympathetic government'[96] and, in turn, recognition by that government would help the workers in their struggles with the oil and sugar companies. Registration and official recognition of the new unions did not lead the employers to recognise them at once. However, Rienzi and other union leaders gave evidence before the Forster Commission on behalf of the workers and this reinforced their standing. Rienzi's prestige among the oil and sugar workers rose and he won the support of *The People*, an influential labour-oriented paper edited by L.F. Walcott, who called Rienzi the 'idol of the South' and urged unity between Africans and Indians.[97] This paper reported that Rienzi had told workers in San Fernando in September 1937 that Indian and African Trinidadians should unite as theirs was a 'class struggle' in which the standard of living of each could best be promoted by mutual support. In January 1938 there was a joint demonstration of oil and sugar workers in San Fernando, and the marchers, many in uniform, extended for over a mile and a half.[98] While Cipriani's support was on the wane, Rienzi attracted sufficient middle-class support to be elected to the San Fernando Borough Council in late 1937 and then to the Legislative Council in early 1938, winning by 2,003 votes to 547 as representative of Victoria. According to *The People*, the workers saw this as giving trade unionism a voice in the Legislative Council, as a 'tribune of the people', replacing Cipriani in this role.[99]

The governor and the Colonial Office recognised that if the development of trade unions occurred under what they considered to be 'responsible' leadership, it could help prevent further disorders, but the employers still opposed unionisation. The conviction that properly guided trade unions, avoiding extremists and extremism, would contribute to the industrial peace became part of a general shift in policy throughout the British West Indies in order to protect British property from further labour rebellions, but it was seen as particularly important in Trinidad because of the strategic role of the oil industry in the empire. In November 1937, as the possibility of war loomed larger, the British oil board produced a memorandum at Ormsby-Gore's request, stating that the maintenance of supplies from Trinidad, which was responsible for almost 40 per cent of the empire's production, was of 'paramount importance'. Consequently, it was deemed 'essential that all possible defence precautions should be taken to safeguard the refineries and oil shipping facilities',[100] including maintaining peaceful labour relations. The oil companies still seemed to prefer to rely on force and intimidation, however, even though such an approach might have risked retaliatory sabotage. Since the employers consider Rienzi to be a dangerous communist, they 'resisted the unions in every way possible, and the early organizers faced relentless victimization and persecution'.[101] Even local government officials and the police do not seem to have got the message from the Colonial Office, as they still treated trade unionism as seditious, scrutinised and harassed union organisers and often prohibited labour demonstrations. A British writer, Arthur Calder-Marshall, who visited Trinidad in 1938, described how the OWTU leaders were constantly shadowed by police spies and pointed out how absurd this was 'when it was official government policy to foster trade unionism'.[102]

In early March 1938, Rienzi, faced with continuing police harassment and employer intransigence, urged both the oil and sugar workers to organise strike committees in case they should be needed. He made it clear that he preferred to reach a negotiated settlement through peaceful collective bargaining and advised against any violence or confrontation with police that might provoke further repression and endanger the young trade union movement, but he wanted to be ready for a strike.[103] Faced with this organised militancy, the Petroleum Association of Trinidad at last agreed to engage in direct negotiations with the OWTU, so the union won effective recognition. However, in the negotiations, chaired by the new labour officer, A.G.V. Lindon, a British official from the Ministry of Labour, the oil workers gained very little. Since June 1937 they had been demanding a general wage increase of 6 cents per hour, time and a half for overtime beyond a standard 8 hour day and double pay for work on Sundays and public holidays, as well as two weeks of annual vacation with pay and other minor concessions in their working conditions. But the employers conceded only an upgrading of the hourly rate to the minimum of 9 cents per hour, the rate that Public Works Department employees received from the government in Port-of-Spain, which would have benefited few workers, and time and a half for all overtime work, including that on Sundays and public holidays.[104]

The OWTU executive, faced with a deadlock, agreed to accept Lindon's proposal to refer the dispute to an arbitration tribunal, under the terms of the recently enacted Trade Disputes (Arbitration and Inquiry) Ordinance of 1938, a law which Rienzi had helped to draft. Strategically, 'the acceptance of arbitration by the Petroleum Association represented a further gain in the struggle to legitimise the union'.[105] Given the fact that the OWTU was still organising and had few resources, resorting to a strike at that stage might well have provoked further exercise of the state's armed forces and endangered the still weak trade union movement as a whole. When the award was finally made, on 21 January 1939, it provided for a wage increase of only one cent per hour retrospective from 1 February 1938 and an additional cent an hour from 1 February 1939, along with one week's annual vacation with full pay for workers who had completed a year of continuous service.[106] The oil workers reacted to this with 'considerable dissatisfaction' but Rienzi pointed out that this, the first instance in which arbitration procedure had given an award to labour in the West Indies, further established the legitimacy of trade unions. He urged the OWTU to continue its membership drive so they would be able 'to exert the right degree of pressure at the right moment'.[107]

The sugar workers, meanwhile, faced with a similarly intransigent attitude by their employers in the Sugar Manufacturers' Association (SMA), had tried to use the strike weapon, but without success. In February 1938, the acting governor reported that there was an 'undercurrent of unrest among labour on sugar estates'. Some 'sporadic strikes of a minor character' had been settled without difficulty, with the Usine Ste Madeleine experiencing more strikes than other estates. The union asked for an all-round increase of 50 per cent in wage rates but the SMA would not negotiate. 'The leaders of the Union appear to favour the calling of strikes in specified areas only rather than a general strike', because of lack of funds and, presumably, because they were better organised in some places than others. However, 'the demand for a general strike by a substantial number of the members of the Union remains insistent' and the union leaders, though opposed to such action, would give their support 'in the event of their hands being forced by the members.... While there has been some improvement in relations between labourers and employers in recent months, distrust still prevails'.[108]

The sugar workers, led by those at Ste Madeleine, tried to force the situation by going on strike. They demanded an all-round increase of 10 cents per day for field workers and 15 - 20 cents for factory workers. In early April 1938 Rienzi had been ready to seek arbitration but when the workers struck, the ATSEFWTU executive felt obliged to concur with the action in order to retain its legitimacy among its militant members. The union could not financially support the strike, however, and it collapsed in 16 days, leaving the Sugar Manufacturers Association in the position of being able to refuse any renewed effort to have the dispute settled by arbitration. The fact that the SMA did not agree to a negotiated settlement with the union until 1945 suggests that Rienzi's tactic with the OWTU and the Petroleum Association had been the right one in the circumstances.[109]

The Colonial Office and the British TUC, and especially Sir Walter Citrine, encouraged Trinidadian unionists 'to model their unions on "sound", constitutional, British lines...to avoid politics or extremism and to work closely with the industrial advisor and the local government'.[110] Lindon, who arrived in Trinidad in March 1938, helped arbitrate disputes and encouraged peaceful collective bargaining. Orde Browne credited him with the fact that trade unionism was more advanced, along British lines, in Trinidad in 1939 than in any other colony. However, Calder-Marshall, who interviewed Lindon, wrote that he represented himself as an instructor of ignorant trade unionists who did not even know what they wanted, so it is not surprising that the union leaders mistrusted him.[111] Clearly, credit for the rapid development of trade unionism in Trinidad should lie, not with Lindon or any other colonial official, but with the militant workers and their skilful and determined leaders, even when they decided tactically to work with Lindon in order to deal with recalcitrant employers.

While Rienzi was preoccupied with union developments in the south, in the oil and sugar sectors, the trade union movement was emerging in the north where his role was minimal. Many of theNWCSA organisers were persecuted. In October 1937 several NWCSA leaders were again arrested and tried, this time for distributing allegedly seditious literature in the oil belt in September, specifically pamphlets that called for Butler's release and an end to plans to deport militant workers. Percival, who had earlier been convicted for disorderly behaviour and using violent language, was convicted again in October and put on $100 bond for good behaviour for a year. Barrette was convicted and given a four-month suspended sentence, though he later won an appeal. The NWCSA people were linking local labour and human rights issues with British colonialism and international imperialism, so the government gave them its special attention. In February Percival and François, along with Darlington Marshall, who was not a member of the NWCSA, were tried for 'uttering words having a seditious intention'. François and Percival had spoken at a public meeting of about 150 persons on 13 October, the purpose of which was to get Butler released. According to the police informant, François had said that Barrette and Percival had been tried on

> framed up charges of Colonial Imperialism to strike terrorism into the hearts of the Negro and East Indian workers. The more prosecutions, the more jail sentences, the more ill-treatment of the workers by the police is the more hatred the workers will have for a British Colonial Imperialism. In the West Indies, the moment you say strike you get jail sentences because you are Negro and East Indian workers....

> In Trinidad when the workers ask for bread they get bullets and jail-sentences.[112]

Francois defended herself aggressively, saying that the subject of her speech that night was 'World Imperialism and the Colonial Toilers' and her intent was to link up world and local conditions, referring to Kenya, Nigeria, Germany and Russia, as well as the homeless, poverty-stricken workers of Trinidad. When asked by the court to define 'World Imperialism', she 'described the relationship between the ruling classes of the world and the exploited workers of the colonies'. Asked why she persisted in 'causing disaffection', she boldly replied, 'I don't know that my speeches create disaffection, I know that my speeches create a fire in the minds of the people so as to change the conditions which now exist'.[113] The jury found her not guilty and she was discharged, but Barrette was convicted and imprisoned for nine months. Francois, far from being intimidated, continued to organise the struggle against the Shop Hours Bill, along with Clement Payne, Bertie Percival and other NWCSA members, while at the same time seeking defence funds for Barrette's appeal.

The northern trade unions were formed in the tense atmosphere created by harassment and the sedition trials. While the main focus of the NWCSA was not on unionisation, several members, including Clement Payne, Dudley Mahon, Gaskynd Granger and Christopher Harper, did work with the unions and as workers themselves they shared the unionists' struggles. Jim Barrette was the first president of the SWWTU in 1937, and Clement Payne and other NWCSA members were active in the formation of the FWTU. Rupert Gittens, along with Quintin O'Connor and Albert Gomes, were leaders of the Trinidad and Tobago Union of Shop Assistants and Clerks (TTUSAC), registered on 30 August 1938. Granger was an organiser and acting treasurer of the PWPSWTU. When the May Day United Front Committee was formed in 1938, therefore, it included members of the NWCSA, the PWPSWTU, FWTU and SWWTU. A resolution by the Workers' Defense Committee on May Day 1938 stated, 'We realise the burning need for the 8 hour day, 44 hour week in every Industry and undertaking in the Colony', with an increase in pay, first-aid kits in all working places, and seats for women.[114] At a meeting in the SWWTU Hall in

Port-of-Spain to celebrate Butler's Day, the first anniversary of 19 June 1937, representatives of these unions were joined by NWCSA speakers Francois, Payne, and Percival, amongst others. Francois was reported to have 'delivered a most interesting address, giving a thrilling experience of her activities in South Trinidad during the strike and the disturbances that followed'.[115] On 9 October 1938 the NWCSA joined members of the Chinese community of Trinidad in a demonstration in solidarity with the people of China in their struggle against the Japanese invasion. When a boat of refugees from the Spanish Civil War landed in Trinidad the NWCSA mobilised to welcome them as fellow socialists with food and clothes.[116] We can see how, in the course of trade union formation, a new and radical political culture was shaping the labour movement, in northern as well as central and southern Trinidad.

By the end of 1938, ten unions had been registered in Trinidad and Tobago. In addition to those already mentioned, there were the All Trinidad Transport and General Workers' Trade Union (ATTGWTU), organised by John Rojas with Rienzi's assistance and registered on 8 June 1938, the Railway Workers' Trade Union (RWTU), registered on 25 July, and the Printers' Industrial Trade Union (PITU), registered on 11 October. Three more were registered the next year: the Civil Service Association (CSA), on 23 March 1939, the Tobago Industrial Trade Union (TITU), on 3 September, and the Tailors' Industrial Union (TIU), on 10 October. There was more strike activity by workers seeking better wages and working conditions.

In July 1939 Clement Payne, writing as the secretary of the Workers' United Front Committee to Arthur Creech-Jones, referred to a strike by women in the garment industry who demanded 'living wages' and 'better working conditions'.[117] This strike began at the Renown shirt factory on 20 June 1939 after negotiations between the owner and the TTUSAC broke down. There were at this date four small garment factories, each employing 50 - 100 workers, predominantly women.[118] After a week, workers in the other factories came out in a sympathy strike and the union declared they were 'determined to hold out to the bitter end'.[119] The Industrial Adviser's efforts at conciliation failed and by 8 July other trade unions had pledged assistance and supported a boycott of all stores displaying Renown-made garments. Despite the employers' attempts to break the strike, by using strike breakers protected by the police, the women won. They gained a 12 per cent wage increase, an eight hour day, two weeks' annual holiday after one year, protective clothing for pressers, and a system of shop-floor representation. Quintin O'Connor, who lost his job as a hardware clerk for having been on the picket line, merged the TTUSAC with the FWTU, which subsequently represented the majority of garment workers. As Rhoda Reddock points out, the reports of this strike name several of the men who supported it, but none of the women who were at the heart of the struggle.[120]

The rapid proliferation of union organisations in Trinidad between 1937 and 1939 was unique in the British Caribbean. In order to develop some coordination in the labour movement, Rienzi established the Committee of Industrial Organisation (CIO) in March 1938, and the ATTGWTU was intended to be a general union that would help link the northern and southern workers in different industries.[121] The CIO was precursor to the Trinidad and Tobago Trades Union Council (TTTUC), which was formed in March 1939 on Sir

Walter Citrine's advice and modelled on the British TUC.[122] In July 1938 Rienzi and Mentor represented the OWTU at the Second Guianese and West Indian Labour Conference in British Guiana where they supported the efforts towards regional labour organisation and the improvement of conditions of the West Indian working class in general.[123] In 1939 Rupert Gittens, who had been corresponding with the British TUC, received one of the two scholarships awarded by that organisation to enable West Indian trade unionists to study at Ruskin College, Oxford.[124] At the same time that some labour leaders were being harassed and imprisoned, therefore, others were being chosen by the British TUC, working in close association with the Colonial Office, for training in 'responsibility'. Rienzi, who had presided over the public meeting at which Citrine urged the establishment of the TTTUC, became its first elected president.[125]

On 6 May 1939 Butler was released from prison and greeted with spontaneous mass demonstrations. That Butler saw himself as the messianic leader of Trinidad is illustrated by the manifesto he issued on 8 May, in which he said,

> To win out in the struggle, we must maintain the June (1937) leadership at all cost. The Holy Spirit of our Infallible Leadership so clearly and definitely manifested in June must be obeyed and maintained. That is easily done by following the example of your servant, Butler...[126]

Though Butler acknowledged the contributions made by Rienzi in forming the OWTU, he did so in such a way as to leave no doubt that he saw himself, and he expected to be seen, as the supreme moral leader of the labour movement: 'You praise and honour me for what I have done, but I assure you you owe more praise to Bonnie Prince, the Honourable Adrian Cola Rienzi, your president and leader, who risked his profession, his life, in building a solid structure on the foundation which I so humbly laid'. While calling for support for the OWTU executive, he declared himself the 'Servant of the Living God' and, on asking for a show of hands from those who were 'on the Lord's side', he was acclaimed by hundreds of raised hands.[127] The problem for the OWTU was 'how to integrate the charismatic leadership of Butler with the organizational leadership of Rienzi'.[128] While both styles could be valuable, and were not in conflict when they appeared in sequence, there was a potential for conflict when they appeared simultaneously. With this in mind, a meeting of the OWTU executive with Butler and representatives of his BECWHRP decided to name him general organiser of the union, with a monthly salary.

Within months the accommodation broke down and, Kelvin Singh has suggested, 'Butler deliberately provoked the conflict'.[129] However, E.R. Blades, who was general secretary of the OWTU at the time, wrote in 1943 that the vice-presidents, Moses and Rojas, were anxious about their own positions after Butler was released, and so incited Rienzi

> to give Mr. Butler plenty of latitude and Mr. Butler, like a fool grasped at a shadow, possessed the idea that he should be the leader of the Union and worked in opposition to the officials.

I am not saying that Mr. Butler was right, he was totally wrong in his calculations, but men with the brains of Messrs Rianzi *[sic]*, Mentor, Moses and Rojas could have curbed him if they wanted, but instead they infuriated him by suddenly throwing him out.[130]

Certainly, the circumstances illustrate the nature of the difference between these kinds of authority and leadership.[131]

When a dispute arose on 26 July 1939 between the workers and management of the Lake Asphalt Company over the dismissal of an employee, the OWTU executive felt they could not support the strike. Some of the workers were OWTU members and others, including the dismissed worker, belonged to the FWTU. The OWTU had an agreement with the company which specified procedures that should be followed in such disputes and the executive thought they would be discredited if they did not follow these procedures. Both the OWTU and the FWTU advised the workers to return to work pending negotiations between the FWTU and the company. Butler, however, addressed workers at the La Brea branch of the OWTU and urged them to strike. Ignoring the executive's request for a meeting, he continued to identify with an *ad hoc* strike committee. The OWTU executive, faced with this open defiance of its authority and fearing that its leadership would be dubbed irresponsible, decided to expel Butler on 4 August. *The People*, 'hitherto an ardent supporter of Butler',[132] argued that the movement was more important than any individual and most branches supported the executive's decision. The La Brea workers campaigned for Butler, however, and even threatened Rienzi and others with violence. Butler formed a rival union. According to Blades, the executive's 'blunder' of expelling Butler, which was made against his advice, cost the OWTU a lot of support in the oilfields and some $7,000 in contributions that were not made by disaffected workers.[133] By November, when Butler was gaining considerable support, the governor felt that he could not risk further unrest in the oil industry during the war. Butler was arrested on 28 November and he remained imprisoned until 1945.
Kelvin Singh concludes that

> Rienzi and the OWTU executive almost certainly viewed Butler's removal from the labour scene once more with considerable relief. For apart from the threat he posed to their control over the oil workers, Butler represented not a revolutionary force... but an egotistical and apocalyptic force that was bound to alienate all those committed to secular organisation, sobriety and responsibility. [134]

It could also be argued, of course, that Rienzi's was the kind of union organisation with which the British preferred to deal. While Rienzi continued to mobilise the oil and sugar workers, and others worked to organise many other unions, it was clear by 1939, even before the outbreak of war and Butler's imprisonment, that the next phase of the labour movement in Trinidad would emphasise the institutionalisation of trade unions. Indeed, Trinidad and Tobago was already further along this path before the war than any other West Indian colony. In just five years, the unorganised 'barefooted men' whom Cipriani had sought to lead had become a more class-conscious and organised proletariat, led by Trinidadians of African and Indian descent.

Notes

1. Basdeo 1983: 28.
2. Of these unions, only the Public Works and Public Service Workers' Union, registered on 26 November 1937, and the Tobago Industrial Trade Union, registered on 3 September 1939, were organising in Tobago, where the Public Works Department was the chief employer of wage labour outside agriculture. A more self-sufficient peasantry and less dependence on wage labour in Tobago made that island less fertile ground for trade unions. As no strike occurred there in 1937, this account deals solely with Trinidad. (See Craig 1988: 8-12.)
3. Johnson 1975: 29.
4. Brereton 1981: 170.
5. Lewis 1977: 27.
6. Brereton 1981: 170-71.
7. Buhle 1988: 27.
8. Reddock 1988: 12-14.
9. Basdeo 1983: 109-23).
10. Reddock 1988: 14.
11. Brereton 1981: 171.
12. Basdeo 1983: 114.
13. *Ibid.*, 119.
14. Brereton 1981: 171.
15. Reddock 1988: 16.
16. Thomas 1987: 196.
17. Brereton 1981: 172.
18. Ryan 1972: 40.
19. Jacobs 1982: 32-35.
20. Singh 1982: 61-62.
21. Cited in Reddock 1988: 22.
22. Brereton 1981: 174.
23. Reddock 1988: 19-20.
24. *Ibid.*, 21.
25. *Ibid.*, 24-25.
26. *Ibid.*, 26-27.
27. *Ibid.*, 24.
28. Cited in Brereton 1988: 173.
29. Reddock 1988: 27.
30. Brereton 1981: 174.
31. Singh 1982: 11-16.

32. *Ibid.*, 17.

33. *Ibid.*, 11.

34. Brereton 1981: 177.

35. Cross 1988: 287.

36. *Ibid.*

37. Memoranda on labour conditions, 23 Feb. 1938, CO 318/432/6.

38. Evidence to the Moyne Commission, cited by Cross 1988: 287.

39. Memoranda on labour conditions, 23 Feb. 1938, CO 318/432/6. Singh's figures of 40 cents and 91.5 cents per day in 1936, though slightly higher, show a similar 1:2 ratio (Singh 1987: 59).

40. Basdeo 1983: 149.

41. Cross 1988: 289.

42. Singh 1987: 58.

43. *Financial News*, 13 Jan. 1938, cited in Cross 1988: 288-89.

44. Thomas 1987: 211.

45. Brereton 1981: 179.

46. Gov. Sir M. Fletcher to W. Ormsby-Gore, 5 July 1937, CO 295/599/70297.

47. Quoted in Brereton 1988: 180.

48. Singh 1982: 18.

49. Brereton 1981: 180.

50. There were 170 sit-downs in General Motors plants between March and June 1937; see Brecher 1972: 251.

51. Singh 1987: 62-63.

52. King may have had a bad reputation among working people. He sought to stop a NWCSA demonstration on behalf of the poor in 1936; see Rennie 1973: 75.

53. Brereton 1981: 181.

54. Singh 1987: 63.

55. See "Trinidad and Tobago Disturbances, 1937: Report of the Commission", Cmd. 5641, 1938 (hereafter Forster report), and Singh 1987: 64-65.

56. Forster report.

57. Reddock 1988: 29.

58. *Trinidad Guardian*, 25 June 1937, quoted in Reddock 1988: 30.

59. Singh 1982: 18.

60. *Ibid.*, 18-19.

61. Basdeo 1983: 150.

62. Brereton 1981: 183.

63. Fletcher to Ormsby-Gore, 26 June 1937, CO 295/599.

64. Craig 1988: 28.

65. Quoted in Craig 1988: 29.

66. Quoted in Craig 1988: 31.

67. Singh 1982: 19.

68. Craig 1988: 32.

69. Rennie 1973: 96-100.

70. Craig 1988: 33.

71. *Ibid.*, 34.

72. Brereton 1981: 182. Ryan calls Fletcher 'the champion of the interests of the worker' (1972: 55), and Basdeo writes that they 'took their trusteeship role seriously and emerged, if only for a short while, as the champion [sic] of the interests of the working class' (1983: 153).

73. CO 295/599/70297.

74. CO 295/599/70297.

75. Legislative Council Debates, 9 July 1937.
76. *Ibid.*
77. Ryan 1972: 55.
78. Quoted in Brereton 1981: 182.
79. Singh 1987: 67.
80. Sir Alexander Roger, managing director of Trinidad Leasehold's parent company, travelled to Trinidad with the three British commissioners in August and on his return to England dined with the Secretary of State for the Colonies, on 16 December. He convinced Ormsby-Gore that Fletcher was a "vacillating" person and that he "must *go*". A few days later, Fletcher was forced to resign. See Johnson 1975: 46.
81. Brereton 1981: 177-78.
82. *West India Committee Circular*, 10 Feb. 1938, cited in Singh 1987: 71.
83. 22 Oct. 1937, CO 295/600/70307.
84. Fletcher to Ormsby-Gore, 31 Oct. 1937, CO 295/600/70307, quoted in Craig 1988: 40.
85. Notes, 28 Feb. 1938, CO 295/606/70307, quoted in Craig 1988: 45.
86. Johnson 1975: 44.
87. Basdeo 1983: 168.
88. Ryan 1972: 60.
89. Cross 1988: 293.
90. Oilfield Workers' Trade Union, *50 Years of Progress, 1937-1987* (San Fernando, Vanguard Publications, 1988), p.11.
91. Elbert Redvers Blades to Sir Walter Citrine, 21 April 1943, OWTU Library, San Fernando. Subsequent quotations are from this document.
92. My copy of Kelvin Singh's recent study (1994) of the struggle in Trinidad from 1917 to 1945 arrived too late to be examined with the care it deserves. He makes no mention of the UWTA and mentions the origins of the OWTU only briefly: 'the oilworkers announced that they had formed a trade union with Adrian Cola Rienzi as their president' (p. 175). He refers to Earl [sic] Blades only with regard to his later contributions, along with John Rojas, Ralph Mentor and MacDonald Moses, to organising oil and sugar workers (p. 203).
93. Ramdin 1982: 143.
94. Basdeo 1983: 163.
95. Singh 1982: 20.
96. Report of his address to oil workers, *The People*, 4 Sept. 1937, quoted in Singh 1982: 20.
97. Singh 1982: 22-23.
98. *The People*, 4 Sept. 1937 and 22 Jan. 1938, cited in Singh 1982: 23.
99. *The People*, 15 and 29 Jan. 1938, cited in Singh 1982: 23.
100. Johnson 1975: 44.
101. Brereton 1981: 186.
102. *Ibid.*
103. *The People*, 5 March 1938, cited in Singh 1982: 24.
104. Singh 1982: 24.
105. *Ibid.*, 25.
106. *Council Paper No. 25 of 1941: Industrial Advisor's Report for the Years 1938-40*, p.8, cited in Singh 1982: 26.
107. *The People*, 4 Feb. 1939, quoted in Singh 1982: 26.
108. Act.-Gov. Mark Young to Ormsby-Gore, 22 Feb. 1938, CO 318/430/5.
109. Brereton 1981: 187.
110. *Ibid.*, 188.
111. *Ibid.*, 187.
112. *Trinidad Guardian*, 15 Feb. 1938, quoted in Reddock 1988: 35.

113.Quoted in Rennie 1973: 112.

114.Signed by D. Isaac, Printers Industrial Workers Union, Gaskynd Granger, Public Works Workers Union, Sylvestre L. Patrick, Federation of Workers of Trinidad Union, and John Broomes, Workers' Defence Committee; Arthur Creech-Jones papers, Rhodes House Library, Oxford, hereafter RH, MSS Brit. Emp. S332, Box 25, file 4.

115.*The People*, 2 July 1938, quoted in Reddock 1988: 48.

116.Rennie 1973: 124-26.

117.Payne to Creech-Jones, 10 July 1939, RH MSS Brit. Emp. S332, 25/4.

118.Reddock 1993: 253.

119.*The People,* 1 July 1939, quoted in Reddock 1993: 254.

120.Reddock 1993: 255.

121.Ramdin 1982: 144.

122.Nicholson 1986: 234.

123.Basdeo 1983: 183-85.

124.Ramdin 1982: 145.

125.Singh 1982: 28.

126.Quoted in Singh 1982: 28.

127.*The People*, 13 May 1939, in Singh 1982: 28-29.

128.Singh 1982: 29.

129.*Ibid.*

130.Blades to Citrine, 21 April 1943, OWTU Library.

131.See Braithwaite 1987: 15, on the use of Weber's discussion of types of authority for analysing trade union leadership in Trinidad and Tobago.

132.Singh 1982: 30.

133.Blades to Citrine, 21 April 1943, OWTU Library.

134.Singh 1982: 30-31.

Chapter NINE

Barbados

Barbados has a reputation for being orderly and conservative, yet in July 1937 a massive riot and several strikes broke out in Bridgetown and the disorders spread islandwide and persisted for three days. The situation on the island was explosive. Unemployment and poverty were widespread, frustration was increasing, and workers at the Central Foundry had come out on strike three weeks before the disturbances. The spark that set off the riot was the deportation of Clement Payne, who had been speaking to and trying to organise Barbadian workers since March. The governor's actions against Payne provoked his supporters and sympathisers into instigating the labour rebellion that became a turning point in Barbados history. Bonham Richardson writes,

> the 1937 flashpoint had been reached by a conflict between old and new. The white plantocracy of Barbados had attempted to maintain control over their black laborers in the 1930s as they had during the nineteenth century by keeping them tied to particular estates and by doling out tiny wages. But times had changed. A quasi-feudal system of labour control and the impersonal, monetized economy that the Barbadian emigrants had brought home from Panama were incompatible. And it had taken the desperation of the depression decade, combined with rising black expectations that had been awakened with Panama money, to bring the inherent conflicts between old and new to a head.[1]

Some progress in modernising labour relations was being made in Barbados in 1937, but at a snail's pace. A bill to abolish the penal sanctions in the Masters and Servants law was introduced in 1936, but the governor feared that 'its effect on the relations between estate owners and agricultural labourers who are their tenants may be detrimental to the labourers' interest',[2] so a new bill was introduced in 1937. This bill, which was passed on 5 June 1937, removed the penal sanctions:

> against servants other than domestic servants for (a) neglect to perform stipulated work, (b) improper or negligent performance of work, and (c) injury to employer's property entrusted to their care, by negligence or improper conduct...and against employers for breach of duty under the contract, or for injury to the person or property of the servant.[3]

Although this ordinance brought some aspects of Barbados' labour relations into the twentieth century, labour conditions and unemployment remained a severe problem.

Governor Young's memorandum on unemployment, sent shortly before the riots, acknowledged that the problem 'is likely to assume grave proportions at any time when production is either curtailed by unfavourable weather or rendered uneconomical by low market prices'. He drew attention to the absence of opportunities abroad, in such places as Panama, Cuba, the United States and other West Indian islands, where many Barbadian migrants had found work previously, and that the 'closing of these avenues of emigration...had reduced the employment of Barbadian seamen' on shipping lines. Assistance for the unemployed was inadequate. Small grants had been made in two parishes to provide relief work on road repairs and an employment agency had helped find work for less than a quarter of the 4,109 persons who had registered as seeking employment. According to official figures, most of the young people leaving school went into agriculture, trades or domestic service, but over a quarter of them were unemployed.[4] Evidence that some people had been desperate for several years came out at the hearings of the commission of enquiry into the disturbances. An unemployed ex-policeman, Alphonso Ishmael, testified,

> Somewhere in 1935 or thereabouts potato fields were raided at Crab Hill in St Lucy [the impoverished northern parish]. I think that if Government had seen fit to investigate the cause of those raids then they would have realised how bad things are in this island, and things would not have gone so far as to develop into riots. Those Crab Hill raids went to show that people were starving since that time.[5]

The price paid for Barbadian sugar in the London market fell from 26s. per hundredweight in 1923 to 9s. in 1929, then plunged to less than 5s. in 1934, staying at that level for three years.[6] Together with emigration restrictions in the 1920s and 1930s, this produced great pressure on wages and employment in Barbados. Wage rates were about the average in the West Indies, but the 'daily wage of most labourers remained below the 1s. mark, hardly an improvement since the mid-nineteenth century'.[7]

The Barbados Democratic League and the Barbados Workingmen's Association, founded in 1924 and 1926 respectively, and led by Charles Duncan O'Neale, a Fabian socialist doctor, had laid a basis for a labour movement, but O'Neale died in November 1936 and the league disintegrated. About four months before the disturbances, between 100 and 120 bakers, mostly employed by the larger firms, tried to form a union in order to increase their wages and shorten their working hours,[8] but trade unions were still illegal. Branches of the Universal Negro Improvement Association remained active, and a variety of friendly societies and lodges also provided some 'community politicisation'[9] before Clement Osbourne Payne's arrival in Barbados, but his activities and the government's response to him accelerated the process.

Payne was born in Trinidad of Barbadian parents[10] and had first come to Barbados when he was four years old. He had later migrated to Trinidad, where he lived for ten years and associated with Uriah Butler and other radical former members of the Trinidad Workingmen's Association in the National Unemployment Movement (NUM) and the Negro Welfare Cultural and Social Association (NWCSA).[11] When Payne arrived back in Barbados on 26 March 1937, aged 33, he began holding public meetings with the intention of organising a trade union. He was joined by Fitzgerald Chase, Ulric McDonald Grant, Mortimer Skeete, Darnley Alleyne and Israel Lovell, a Garveyite. A series of some 17 public meetings at Golden Square, in a poor area of Bridgetown, attracted between 400 and 1,500 persons. A member of the Barbados Political Association testified, 'Payne's methods were different from ours.... We have been placing our ills in the hands of our representatives. Payne wanted to place them in the hands of the people directly'.[12] According to Beckles, 'He did not confine his speeches to the labour question, but spoke of race relations, black cultural suppression, the pan-American nature of Garveyism, and Italian aggression towards Ethiopia'. Payne drew attention to the agitation and strikes taking place in other parts of the West Indies 'as evidence of the rising consciousness of black West Indians'.[13]

Police accounts of some of Ulric Grant's speeches, even if unreliable, give some idea of the content and tone of these meetings. Grant, and presumably Payne as well, combined an analysis of social oppression and economic exploitation in terms of race and class with a militant tone, and urged people to organise. A strike at Central Foundry failed, Grant said on 15 July, 'because the masses failed to organise against the capitalistic element. We must start a form of organisation that will capsize the capitalistic element who is oppressing us.... Poor masses, we are mistreated. Let us seek our rights'.[14]

As Payne's support grew, so did the colonial government's anxiety. In July, Payne was prosecuted for having wilfully made a false statement to the immigration authorities that he was born in Barbados, though he may well have believed that he was. His father testified that he might not have known where he was born, and Payne said he had always thought himself to be Barbadian. It was clear to all concerned that this was simply a pretence to get rid of him. On 22 July he was convicted and sentenced to a fine of £10 or 3 months' imprisonment. He appealed and while out on bail led a protest march to Government House. He carefully 'advised his followers that the procession should be conducted in an orderly manner and that no one should take offensive weapons'.[15] On this occasion Grant is reported to have said,

> The white man has no feelings for the poor negroes and if unrest starts in Barbados the capitalistic element will be responsible for it. We have to fight for what we want, not with sticks, except we are forced to. If we don't fight we will get nowhere, for it is a shame and disgrace to know that slavery still exists in Barbados. Organisation is essential to any people, so let us combine and get in mass formation. The capitalistic element is doing its best to get Payne out of Barbados. Payne and I will die for you. The sooner we get organised the better for the community. One of these days the capitalists will wake up and find things in a drastic way. The decision of Payne's case had me inflamed. I would rather die by the sword than by the famine. We must fight back at these people. Things in Barbados are going to be very serious. We are being educated and in the near future will demand our rights. Let us tell the powers

that be that their time will come sooner or later. Let us assist Mr. Payne to pay the fine. We will pay now but when the time comes for the others to pay they may have to jump in the sea.

The administration of justice today was done in a fraudish highhanded way. Before Payne entered the Court he was convicted. He had only tried to educate his people politically and the capitalistic element has started war against him. They have everything for themselves and are yet trying to exploit the poor masses. [16]

Grant referred to Garvey as a 'wonderful man' and urged people to 'remember your mother country which is Africa'.

The protesters were not allowed to see the governor and when the crowd refused to disperse, Payne and several others were arrested. For three nights, from 23 to 25 July, large protesting crowds gathered in Golden Square, Carrington's Village and the Lower Green, and threatened that they would release Payne from the police. With Payne in jail, Grant, Chase, Skeete, Lovell and others, unintimidated, addressed another crowd on 23 July in Golden Square. Grant criticised the police specifically:

Tonight is a serious night and we are here fighting a just cause. The Constabulary has acted outrageously. Today Payne has been handled like a criminal. The capitalistic element has been trying long ago to get him out of the way. The white men are all for themselves and depriving us of bread and butter. Payne has made history in Barbados today.... The Police of this Island are only practising the capitalistic element and they have no sympathy for the masses. How long are we going to stand this? Don't let us be fools all the time but let us fight the good fight in spite of all their oppositions. I am saying that the Constabulary acted outrageously; however, they will not be able to get off as cheaply as they think. This is just the smoke, the fire is at hand.... We are going to make officers and organise them so that we can strike back and heavy too. Some of the Policemen are good but some of them are very brutal. [17]

While Payne was in custody, the court of appeal reversed his conviction, as it could not be proven that he knew he had not been born in Barbados or that he had intended to deceive. Payne's supporters, who had collected enough money to pay the fee requested for the appeal by the lawyer, Grantley Adams, gathered outside the court, but Payne was not released. On 26 July the police smuggled him on to a ship and deported him to Trinidad, where he was promptly arrested for possessing forbidden literature. [18] At about 8 pm that night, the crowd, not realising that Payne had already been deported, gathered at the wharf to prevent his embarkation. When they discovered that they had been tricked, they responded in fury, spreading through the town, smashing cars and street lights. The police who tried to stop them were attacked with 'showers of stones and bottles', [19] and several were injured. Armed only with batons, the police were unable to make a single arrest.

The next morning large crowds again gathered in Golden Square. Incensed by a rumour that a child of one of Payne's followers had been killed by the police, people poured along Probyn and Bay streets, armed with sticks and stones. They smashed cars and garage show windows and pushed some cars into the sea. Proceeding by Chamberlain Bridge and Trafalgar Square to Broad Street and the commercial district, they damaged more cars and shops and attacked the police, forcing them back to the central police station. One section of the crowd prepared to burn down the building of the Barbados Mutual Life Assurance Society, into which the occupants had barricaded themselves, until they were driven off by armed police. The commercial district, home to the profiteering merchants, was obviously a prime target for poor people who were hurt by rising prices, and the Mutual building 'symbolized economic and social apartheid in Barbados during the 1930s'.[20] The police were by then armed with rifles and fixed bayonets, and, 'as the town was now dominated by the mob, the Riot Act was read and steps taken to restore order'.[21] In other words, they fired on the crowd.

Several groups of workers went on strike. According to the evidence and the opinions of the commissioners who enquired into the event,[22] these were serious strikes and they contributed to the disturbances. It is important to emphasise this, as the Barbados labour rebellion is often portrayed merely as a riot. To the workers at Central Foundry, who were already on strike, were added the waterfront workers and bus drivers and conductors, who went on strike on 28 July.[23] The foundry workers had made written demands on 6 July for a wage increase of 2 cents per hour, for overtime payment after an eight hour day and for guaranteed employment throughout the year. On 7 July 30 workers walked out. They were dismissed the next morning when the manager refused to recognise their action as a strike. Six more walked out on 9 July. They were still out on 26 July when they wrote to the manager, asking that 'the dismissals be made null and void without division'. These workers were still on strike, fighting for wage increases, recognition and reinstatement, the day that Payne was deported. The commissioners blamed the manager for treating the walkout as a breach of shop regulations instead of a strike, and for deferring consideration of their grievances. The requests for wage increases and overtime pay 'demanded attention' and the commissioners expressed the opinion that it was such 'unsympathetic action' by employers that drove the workers to 'extremes'. [24]

The commissioners also treated the waterfront workers' strike seriously. 'One of the principal centres of unrest during the disturbances was among the workers on the waterfront', who struck for higher wages on 28 July. The commissioners believed that 'the men had genuine grievances against which they were justified in making a strong protest'. As Barbados lacked a deep-water pier, all cargo had to be loaded and discharged by longshoremen who worked aboard the ships and lightermen who handled the cargo between the ships and shore. The longshoremen were hired by and worked under stevedores, labour contractors who worked for the steamship agents and employed the labourers directly. The agents paid the stevedores at agreed rates, which they had to recover from the shipowners, and the stevedores generally paid the gross amount for the labourers' wages to their foremen. The men were paid as daily workers at the rate of $1.50 per day, and $2.25 for Sundays or public holidays, with overtime at 18–20 cents per hour. The ordinary working day began at 7 am and overtime began after 6 pm. The longshoremen complained that the stevedores' profits were excessive, that they should receive a greater share of the payment, and that the method of indirect payment led to many abuses. The commissioners agreed, calling the stevedores' profits 'abnormal and excessive' and pointing out that men often had to pay the foremen part of their own wages in order to secure work. They also blamed the steamship agents, 'who are not ignorant of the conditions', and who benefit by transferring all responsibility for damage to cargo or injury to employees to the stevedores. They recommended that the system of independent stevedores be eliminated, that an adequate scale of wages should be adhered to, paid directly from the steamship agents to the workers, and that overtime rates should begin after 5 pm. In other words, the commissioners' recommendations went even further than the longshoremen's demands. The lightermen demanded an increase in wages of $1 per trip and a working day fixed from 6 am to 5 pm. As the captains of lighters often deducted sums from the lightermen's wages, the commissioners recommended that all lightermen, also, should be paid directly.

The bus drivers and conductors had been paid from $5–7 per week before 1931 but then the scale was reduced to $4–6, paid as daily employees rather than weekly as before. They worked an average of 11 hours per day with no fixed time off for meals.[25] When a bus broke down the drivers and conductors had to stand by without remuneration. The commissioners recommended that 'drivers and conductors should not be in charge of a motor bus for a period exceeding nine consecutive hours', one of which should be for unrestricted rest and nourishment. It is quite likely that some of these bus drivers and conductors spread news of the Bridgetown protests in the country parishes before they went on strike.

The rebellion quickly spread through the island as some protesters and strikers commandeered buses and cars to spread the news, though 'there is no evidence to show that there was any concerted plan to have simultaneous outbreaks in the parishes.... Gangs were quickly organized for shopbreaking and raiding of potato fields and for the stoning of motor cars along the public highways'.[26] The commissioners' report concludes that hunger rather than 'racial hatred' was responsible for these actions, as 'the number of persons who suffered injury at the hands of the lawless was insignificant and that the attacks were made against the property of persons of every colour without discrimination'.[27]

The commissioners, unlike the governor of the Windward Islands in 1935, were convinced that 'the real cause of the disturbances was in fact economic', that the 'Payne incident' was merely a 'detonator', and, further, that the explosive conditions 'which rendered this culmination possible still exist and demand immediate treatment'.[28] At the commission hearings, which began on 13 August 1937, considerable convincing evidence was given about the high levels of poverty and dissatisfaction throughout Barbados. The commissioners were certainly convinced that this was the underlying cause of the disturbances and their criticisms were explicit. Though they believed the 'root cause of many, if not all, of the economic ills' to be overpopulation and its 'inevitable concomitant', namely unemployment, they drew attention to many aspects of the economic situation and of traditional labour relations that were unjustifiable in so far as they resulted from the greed of the employers.

They recognised that the crisis in the sugar trade, along with the modernisation of sugar factories and the mechanisation of transport, had increased unemployment in agriculture and also in several subsidiary occupations. They heard 'abundant evidence that a considerable part of the population is permanently without employment, while an even larger proportion suffers from periods of unemployment of varying duration'. They attributed 'the growth of the class of idle and lawless vagrants who were chiefly responsible for the damage to property in Bridgetown' to this unemployment and to 'the effect of prolonged unemployment on the minds and characters of those who are forced to be idle', especially on those young adults who 'leave school to find themselves without occupation and without any prospect of steady and remunerative employment for years'.

Recognising the tendency in this situation for wages to decline, 'when for every place a man is eagerly waiting to supplant its holder', the commissioners nevertheless believed the wages to be so shockingly and unnecessarily low that they resulted in discontent and feelings of injustice as well as material hardship. Wages paid to unskilled manual workers, clerks and shop assistants were 'definitely inadequate to provide the bare necessities of existence', while agricultural labourers who received no more than 30 cents per day, or a weekly wage of $1.78, were 'living from hand to mouth without reserves for times of scarcity and illness'. The commissioners expressed the opinion that 'in many cases the wages paid are inadequate and cannot be justified having regard to the prosperity of the businesses which employ these workers'. They pointed to 'the striking disparity' between wages paid to manual and clerical workers, on the one hand, and managerial staff, on the other. In one firm eight employees received salaries totalling $1,243 per month while the 73 clerical workers received a total of $1,750, averaging $155 and $24 per employee respectively.

Impressed by the 'high dividends' and 'comfortable salaries and bonuses' earned by some and the low wages paid to many, the commissioners urged:

> a reconsideration of the fundamental conditions and organization of industry....
> A fundamental change in the division of earnings between the employer and
> his employees is essential if hatred and bitterness are to be removed from the
> minds of the majority of employees.... It is clearly no less the duty of a
> Government to maintain a fair balance between capital and labour than to
> provide for the security of life and property.

The commissioners, commenting that 'the improvement of the condition of the agricultural labourer...brooks no delay', recommended wages should be immediately increased by 20 per cent, to a minimum of 24 cents per nine–hour day for women and 36 cents for adult men, even though this 'is still below what we regard as a reasonable subsistence level', having calculated a 'working man's weekly budget' at $1.97, not counting any recreations or margins for illness or misfortune. 'If the labourer has to provide for a partner in life and a family of three children...expenditure will be a minimum of forty–six and a half cents per day'. (We should note that if a husband and wife both worked and received the recommended wages, they would together earn only 60 cents per day, while a single mother working to support two or three children would be hopelessly poor.) Moreover, the commissioners acknowledged that their calculation of the cost of living did not take into account the recent 'sudden and abnormal rise in the price of the basic foodstuffs in use by peasants, artisans and labourers', such as the 50–60 per cent rise in the cost of flour. This rise in the price of imported foodstuffs, which had effectively reduced the labourers' pay by around 25 per cent, 'coincided with a scarcity of locally grown provisions, and the resultant hardship quite naturally helped to swell the volume of dissatisfaction', much of it attributed to local merchants and shopkeepers.

The commissioners also drew attention to the poor housing and absence of recreational facilities for working people. They recommended that the government should provide playing fields, initiate slum clearance and build houses for working people in Bridgetown. They visited slum areas and commented that they were 'a standing reproach to local apathy and inertia'. Coincidentally, the commissioner of police complained of the difficulty of patrolling areas such as Golden Square where the police could be attacked in narrow unlit alleys. As house rents were often 'exorbitant and a major factor in poor people's budgets, the commissioners urged the government to 'plan boldly and on generous lines' in building houses and relieving the congestion. In addition to initiating public works schemes, the government 'should foster the development of new industries', such as dairy farming and soap manufacture, as well as supporting the local production of vegetables.

The commissioners commented that 'Barbados is singularly backward in the organization of labour' and they recommended the appointment of a labour officer 'before whom workers with a grievance may lay their demands', and who would act as 'a liaison officer between employers and workers. Finally, they drew attention to the need for the police to be given 'adequate power for the control of public meetings'. This should include the authority to prohibit meetings, more powers to search premises for 'suspected seditious literature', and widening the law on sedition, 'making it an indictable offence punishable by fine and/or imprisonment to make use in public speech or writing of language of such a nature as is likely to provoke public disorder or influence others to acts of violence by provoking class or racial antagonism or in any other way'. They even recommended that the police should be able to enter 'any private premises on which a meeting of more than ten persons is being held' at which they suspected such 'inflammatory or seditious language' was being used. In other words, while acknowledging that the causes of the rebellion were essentially economic and recommending some reforms to address these problems, the commissioners also supported strengthening the police powers of the colonial state to make it 'almost impossible for a campaign of inflammatory propaganda to be carried out'.[29]

The class factor in this rebellion is quite clear. On the one hand, many working people went on strike, and poor people sought food or attacked the property of the rich, particularly cars and stores in the business district, while on the other hand, planters enlisted armed special constables and other volunteers to restrain workers and assist the police in protecting their properties. [30]

By the morning of 30 July these various armed forces had put down the rebellion. The police and Volunteers fired 811 rounds of ammunition in quelling the protests, killing 14 people and wounding 47.[31] Some 666 persons were charged with over 700 offences, including shop-breaking, larceny, robbery, malicious damage, wounding, riotous assembly and sedition. Hundreds were convicted and imprisoned.[32] Alleyne and Lovell were sentenced to five years and Skeete to 10 in prison. Grant, found guilty of sedition on four counts, was sentenced to five years' imprisonment on each count, two to run concurrently with the other two, making a total term of ten years.[33] Payne was not allowed back to Barbados to testify to the commission. He stayed in Trinidad where he became chairman of the NWCSA, a founding member and organiser of the Federated Workers' Trade Union, registered on 27 August 1937, and a member of the radical Workers United Front Committee in 1938. He collapsed while speaking at a meeting on 7 April 1947, and died soon after.[34]

Grantley Adams, who had been Payne's lawyer at the Court of Appeal, was the first witness to give evidence to the commission on 13 August 1937, and this began his rapid rise to power. At these hearings Adams was careful to situate himself as a spokesman for the poor and disenfranchised, whilst sharply distinguishing himself from radicals like Payne, Grant and Lovell. Payne, Adams claimed, was 'not sincere' and was 'willing to take money from either side', but he offered no evidence to support either accusation. It was during this period, in the months following the labour rebellion, that Adams' position was established in 'the reformist leadership which dominated the labour movement for the next two decades or so'.[35] In November 1936 Adams had roundly criticised the power of Barbados' plutocracy and advocated a political solution to the island's economic problems. He wrote in the *Observer*:

> Power in this colony rests in the hands of a narrow, bigoted, selfish, grasping plutocracy. To financial pressure is added political overlordship and the powerful alliance of a state Church and various brands of religion whose ministrations help to delude the multitude. The remedy is, like the evil, primarily political. When the political fight is won, economic evils will disappear.[36]

However, after the labour rebellion Adams spoke to the commissioners in a less radical and more conciliatory manner. He said that the key problems were unemployment, low wages and rising prices: 'When we get down to bed rock we find it is a question of food prices, poverty, starvation'.[37] People's dissatisfaction was enhanced by news of the Abyssinian War, which 'has accentuated the colour question', and of the riots and strikes in Trinidad and St Vincent, but not by 'Communist agitators', charges of which were 'sheer moonshine as far as Barbados is concerned'.[38]

Adams's message to the commissioners was essentially that people need representatives in labour organisations and in the House of Assembly to whom they can express their grievances.

> There are no labour organizations in Barbados, no Trade Unions, by means of which our people can air their grievances... Many...people clerks, shop

assistants and others are afraid to come before this Commission and express their grievances with regard to wages. They are afraid that if they do so they will be fired by their employers who will have no difficulty in getting others to take their places. That is why grievances are bottled up.[39]

While voters can complain to their representatives, Adams pointed out, the average labourer 'knows practically nothing about making representations to members of the House, first of all, because, not being a voter, he does not come into contact with the members of the House. And so their grievances, whatever they may be, can find no means of expression, and become bottled up'.[40] The implication is that, without representatives to whom dissatisfied people can express their grievances, the eventual result will be riots. Of course, the kind of constitutional reforms Adams had in mind would provide people like himself with a broader base of support in the House of Assembly for their struggle with the 'plutocracy', and this became Adams's strategy.

Adams's concern about Payne was likewise legalistic and constitutional. Distrusting his aims and methods, Adams would have nothing to do with him until he was hired in his legal capacity to appeal against his conviction. On 27 July Adams tried, apparently, 'to pacify the irate mob', but, as he told the crowd that the Solicitor General who prosecuted Payne had only been doing his duty, he was unlikely to succeed. It was, according to Adams' biographer, the 'legality of the whole proceedings' that continued to worry him and he suggested to the governor that Payne should be brought back into custody. He believed that the people 'would be pacified if they were informed that Payne was to return and that the question of his domicile would be determined in a court of law in Barbados'.[41] If Adams really thought that this would pacify people, he was out of touch with their mood. Despite his carefully legalistic stance, however, there were people who believed Adams was more closely connected with Payne and even involved in the disturbances. Some Barbadians were so opposed to any changes that they viewed even Adams as a threat. Adams and his family felt insecure and he mounted an armed guard at his house and fitted the grounds with lights so that the place could be floodlit at any sign of danger. 'Above all, there was the fear, ever present in the minds of his followers, that Adams would be arrested and tried for sedition along with the hundreds who were already in prison',[42] though there was never any real danger of that. Adams's friends collected money to enable him to go to England for a while, ostensibly to present a petition to the secretary of state. He left Barbados at the beginning of September and stayed away until the end of the year.

While in England, Adams became acquainted with Arthur Creech Jones and other members of the Fabian wing of the Labour Party and he won the favour of W. Ormsby-Gore, the colonial secretary. His reputation as a reliable reformer became 'of critical importance in understanding the remaining years of Adams' career.... He was considered the kind of man the Colonial Office wanted to lead the ethos of reform... Adams enjoyed the status of a Colonial Office favourite from then until the 1950s.'[43] The crucial political outcome of the labour rebellion in Barbados, therefore, was the elimination through deportation and imprisonment of the radical nationalists and the strengthening of the reformist progressives, with Adams soon to become their chief. The Barbados Labour

Party was started in March 1938 by Hope R. Stevens, a native of Tortola and resident of New York City, who had organised the St Kitts Workers Defence Committee to support the people who had been arrested there in 1935. While Adams was off the island, he met with C.A. Brathwaite, J.A. Martineau, Dr H.G. Cummins, Dr Philip Payne, Wynter A. Crawford and C.E. Talma.[44] The party's name was soon changed to the Barbados Progressive League (BPL) and it was officially launched in October 1938. Brathwaite, a black businessman who had formerly been in the Democratic League, became president and Adams was vice-president. Herbert Seale, a radical Garveyite, soon became general secretary. Within a few months Adams came to dominate the BPL, as he did in the next decade the labour movement in Barbados, and he became a leader of the West Indian federal movement.

The labour situation and the plight of the working people in Barbados did not improve immediately after the rebellion. Despite the recommendations of the commission, which were surprisingly far-reaching, the government was slow to respond. A Colonial Office meeting was convened on 13 May 1938 to consider the question of the provision of labour officers to Barbados and other West Indian colonies[45] and an act providing for a labour officer was passed in Barbados on 3 August 1938. His duties would include receiving and investigating all representations, whether of employers or workers, in order to settle disputes and grievances, 'especially regarding hours and conditions of work and regulation of wages'.[46] He would also prepare cost of living indices, statistics of earnings, of employment and unemployment, and would advise on arbitration machinery and the establishment of industrial courts. He would register trade boards and trade unions, though the latter were not yet legal.

When a memorandum was sent to the secretary of state on 29 March 1939, reporting on the progress made concerning the commission's recommendations, no labour officer had yet been appointed. In fact, though bills, studies and committees were being considered, no progress had been made in any area. No land had been acquired for providing playing fields, the question of wages for manual workers in Bridgetown was still being investigated, a bill to create machinery for establishing a minimum price for peasants' canes was being drafted, no steps had been taken to make the government responsible for social work and welfare, and proposals for the centralisation of health services were still being considered. No action had been taken on minimum wages, and the possibility of a building programme was still being examined. The tone of bureaucratic procrastination is conveyed in the comment on housing, the provision of which the commissioners described in 1937 as the 'most urgent need': 'Consideration is being given to the possibility of making a large scale survey of Bridgetown with the object of providing data for the drawing up of a plan for slum clearance'.[47]

In the light of the colonial government's continuing inactivity, it is not surprising that there was widespread labour unrest, including another round of major strikes, in 1939. On 10 February Governor Waddington reported numerous strikes for higher wages on sugar estates, many of them accompanied by cane fires. Workers who swept the Bridgetown streets and labourers employed by a shipping firm went on strike briefly and obtained a promise of an increase in wages.[48] On 16 February the staff of the largest hotel went on strike, their wages were promptly doubled and they returned to work; but the next day workers at other hotels went on strike and some were still out a week later. Strikes among the dock workers were settled when they received 'considerable increases' but 'these concessions will be followed by further demands by labourers'. Waddington concluded, 'the position is far from satisfactory. Labour has become much more organised and I think that the leaders are anxious to avoid disturbances but I am doubtful of their ability to control their followers in an emergency'.[49] A week later he reported, 'Strikes and cane fires continue on many estates'.[50] As this was in the middle of the crop season, it was an urgent matter to settle the disputes and complete the harvest. On 21 February dock workers went on strike against 'the expressed advice' of Adams who, Waddington feared, 'may be losing control'. The next day many of the dock workers resumed work but Waddington was worried about 'an attempt to organise a general strike'.[51]

Governor Waddington, in a secret report sent on 23 February 1939, commented that the West India Royal Commission, which was in Barbados between 14 January and 3 February, had inadvertently stirred up the unrest. He was careful to deny that 'the present state of unrest would not have occurred but for that visit', though many workers apparently believed that the commissioners had promised and brought benefits which the government was denying them. He thought that:

> the combination of unemployment, low rate of wages for agricultural labourers and the probability of a record sugar crop made discontent and strikes inevitable at this time, and that the Commission's visit created an atmosphere wherein the workers began to see the possibilities for them that lay in organised demands. This realisation has caused many workers to get the impression that they can dictate the terms of their employment and may lead to serious unrest unless they are controlled by leaders who can relate their aspirations to the economic facts. [52]

In the absence of legally constituted trade unions, 'a number of associations of workers at various trades' were forming in relation to the BPL, which Waddington thought 'expedient to recognise' in order 'to guide its activities along constitutional lines'. He believed Adams to be 'a Liberal and opposed to any form of communistic or other subversive activity'. After several discussions with the colonial secretary, Adams had undertaken 'to use all his powers to restrain his followers', and particularly to see that no members of the BPL would use expressions 'calculated to cause racial animosity'.[53] Nevertheless, 'cane fires and strikes of cane cutters increased daily' and Adams was warned about the 'inflammatory' speeches of W.H. Seale and John Hinds at League meetings in private rooms and houses, as reported by police spies. Waddington, believing that some increase in wages was 'reasonable in view of the heavy crop', urged the planters to deal promptly with the incipient labour organisation, lest it become controlled by 'extremists', at the same time that he warned Adams that 'any outbreak of disorder would necessitate prompt intervention by Government'. [54]

Waddington thought that some strikers had been 'fomented by the independent and unauthorised activities of the less responsible and less reputable members of the League', such as Herbert Seale, the secretary, and Sidney Skinner, who had been sentenced to nine months' imprisonment in 1937. He believed Adams 'took a firm line with his associates' against a general strike but he was not confident that he could continue to control the radical members of the BPL if discontent increased. Waddington concluded, 'I am not apprehensive that a general strike, if it is organised, would be protracted, for there would be many ready, provided that they were assured of protection, to take the places of the strikers, and the funds of the Barbados Progressive League are limited'. He felt there was a danger of clashes between those who wanted to work and strikers who sought to prevent them, but he was prepared to use 'forcible measures' to prevent disorder.[55]

On 28 February some bus drivers and conductors went on strike but, repudiated by leaders of the BPL, they applied for reinstatement on 1 March. Most cane cutters and dock workers were by then back at work and a 'goodwill committee', which included Adams, was reviewing the wages of manual workers. The House of Assembly heard the Trade Union Bill for the first time on 28 February and the next day Adams and other members of the BPL addressed a large meeting in Bridgetown to explain the working of trade unions, pay tribute to the government and appeal for 'patience and good behaviour'.[56] The colonial secretary made it clear to Adams and Brathwaite, the 'responsible' League leaders, that Waddington saw the BPL as 'an instrument and symbol of unity' that the government would work with, 'so long as the leaders continued to fulfil their undertakings, and to advocate settlement of all labour disputes by constitutional methods of negotiation'.[57]

It was in this heated context of labour unrest and pressure from the colonial administration that Adams purged the BPL of its radical members and followed up by taking almost sole control of it. Former members of the defunct Democratic League shared the view of the Deane Commission and the colonial government that Payne's followers in the labour movement had to be isolated and kept from power. During the visit of the Moyne Commission, Morgan Jones and Sir Walter Citrine, the two Labour members, 'gave the organisers of the League invaluable advice as to how they should build up the political and industrial sections of the working-class movement in Barbados',[58] in the British fashion, by keeping them distinct. The BPL 'was essentially a middle-class-led organisation vying for a mass base in order to confront and eventually reduce the oligarchical political power of the consolidated merchant-planter elite',[59] and in order to play with the colonial government it had to agree to abide by its rules. Within a few months the leadership was in conflict, with Adams leading the right and Seale on the left. Though Seale had support among Garveyites and some of the more radical urban workers, such as those on the docks, Adams had the backing of the colonial officials. In Barbados in the late 1930s there could be little doubt that the radical would lose to the reformer.

Adams, pushed by the colonial officials, criticised Seale's radicalism, though the latter was one of the BPL's most effective organisers during the five months he was secretary. In his key speech on 1 March 1939 Adams claimed, we have the government willing to assist us, we have an influential body of merchants willing to go thoroughly into the facts and figures connected with workers in Bridgetown. We give them the assurance that we as your officers of the Progressive League will keep the workers in check, and will tell them how stupid apart from being criminal it is to strike when negotiations are the correct way to improve conditions. [60]

Adams condemned the strikes that were taking place in the city and dissociated the BPL from such actions, thereby isolating Seale. He reminded people of the advice Citrine had offered, namely that a strike was a weapon of last resort, and claimed that without a trade union act strikes were probably illegal in Barbados. He pointed out that the last time a procession had gone to Government House it had resulted in a riot, so 'instead of forming a procession to Government House...let the procession be that of the Progressive League to a seat at a conference table'.[61] In short, Adams told the crowd to abandon their militant leaders and militant actions and to rely henceforth on his advocacy. The *Barbados Advocate* approved, lending 'its wholehearted support to all those who are resolved to give labour such responsible guidance'.

Within a few days Hinds was expelled and Seale forced to resign his post as secretary, where he was replaced by Adams's supporter, C.E. Talma. In April, when members of the BPL Committee of Management voted to give Seale a $50 honorarium for his services to the organisation, Adams absented himself from the meeting and tendered his resignation as vice-president. This was a calculated power play, as Talma promptly suggested that Adams should be made president. F.A. Hoyos concludes: 'It seems clear that he chose to make the Seale issue the occasion to impose his will on the Committee of Management and to make a bid for the summit of power in the workers' movement'.[62] Adams went secretly to the acting governor behind Brathwaite's back, and explained why there was a power struggle in the BPL.[63] Adams then went for public support and Brathwaite and other members of the committee were heckled and harassed. They answered Adams in the press, charging that he was filled with 'an overmastering lust for power and overweening sense of his own importance'.[64] On 1 July Brathwaite and Martineau, in a desperate effort, asked the acting governor to take control of the BPL's funds to keep them from Adams, but he refused.[65] Soon after, the executive committee resigned and Adams acquired the free hand he wanted. He was nominated by Talma for president-general and he proposed a slate of his supporters for the executive committee. The election gave 12,332 votes for Adams and his committee and seven against.[66] Adams's bid for power was complete.

In the two years following the labour rebellion, little advantage had accrued to the working people of Barbados and Adams's control of the labour movement was achieved at great price. Some workers had obtained wage increases and the Deane Commission had made a reasonable assessment of some of the problems and needs of the island, but it was not until August 1939 that the first labour officer was appointed and the Trade Union Act did not come into force until 1 August 1940. Of those who were imprisoned in 1937, Israel Lovell, aged almost 60, was pardoned and released on 19 August 1939, but others remained in jail. Several individuals and organisations petitioned for their release, including the National Council for Civil Liberties,[67] the League of Coloured Peoples,[68] Arthur Creech Jones, who called Grant's case 'an outrageous travesty of justice...a case of prejudiced victimisation for trade union activity',[69] and Sir Walter Citrine, who thought the sentences passed on Grant and Lovell 'quite excessive' and 'altogether unjust'.[70] Alleyne was released in July 1940 and Grant, the last prisoner of the 1937 labour rebellion, was freed on 20 December 1941.[71]

If little concrete was achieved in the years immediately following the rebellion, Barbados was nevertheless transformed. George Lamming, whose first novel, *In the Castle of My Skin* (1953), reflects the emerging cultural nationalism of the period, has commented on how he perceived the shattering of illusions about his colonial society.

> I remember as a boy, a very young boy, Barbados being thought of as a very ordered, very conventional, very conservative society. But in July 1937 nobody on the island could have had those illusions when those barefooted men marched on Government House with the demand to see the Governor. And in the town, whites fleeing, cars overturned into the harbour, stores being smashed....
>
> There were very very violent moments, but more important than the violence was the creation of a confidence in very ordinary people that they could and should be heard by those who were called authority.[72]

Notes

1. Richardson 1985: 242-43.
2. Gov. Mark Young to Ormsby-Gore, 5 April 1937, CO 318/426/10.
3. Young to Ormsby-Gore, 5 April and 21 June 1937, CO 318/426/10.
4. Young to Ormsby-Gore, 5 July 1937, CO 318/427/3.
5. Deane Commission hearings, 16 Aug. 1937, CO 28/319/9.
6. Deerr 1949: 531.
7. Beckles 1990: 163.
8. Report of the Commission appointed to enquire into the Disturbances, 2 Nov. 1937 [henceforth the Deane report], CO 28/319/8.
9. Beckles 1990: 161.
10. Reddock says he had a Barbadian father and a Trinidadian mother (1988: 32).
11. Ramdin 1982: 86; Reddock 1988: 31-32.
12. Deane report, CO 28/319/8.

13. Beckles 1990: 164-65.
14. Account of Grant's trial, 12 Nov. 1937, enclosed in Act.-Gov. W.H. Flinn to Ormsby-Gore, 14 March 1938, CO 28/321/12.
15. Deane report, CO 28/319/8.
16. In Flinn to Ormsby-Gore, 14 March 1938, CO 28/321/12.
17. *Ibid.*
18. Hart 1988: 71.
19. Deane report, CO 28/319/8.
20. Beckles 1989: 42.
21. Deane report, CO 28/319/8.
22. The Commission of Inquiry consisted of Sir George C. Deane (chairman), Matthew A. Murphy and Erskine R.L. Ward.
23. Hilton Augustus Vaughan's evidence to Commission, 16 Aug. 1937, CO 28/319/9; Deane report, CO 28/319/8.
24. Deane report, CO 28/319/8.
25. Orde Browne later remarked, 'Major Flinn [the Acting Governor] has obviously never had the unnerving experience of passing buses driven by a Barbadian chauffeur fatigued to the verge of sleep at the wheel. Whether from the point of view of the menace to the public, or from consideration for the drivers, the hours ought to be reduced.' Minute by Orde Browne, 7 June 1939, CO 28/324/11.
26. Deane report, CO 28/319/8.
27. *Ibid.*
28. *Ibid.*
29. *Ibid.*
30. Beckles 1990: 167.
31. Deane report, CO 28/319/8.
32. Young to Ormsby-Gore, 2 Oct. 1937 and 1 Dec. 1937, CO 28/319/8.
33. Flinn to Ormsby-Gore, 14 March 1938, CO 28/321/12.
34. Hart 1988: 72.
35. Beckles 1990: 168.
36. *Barbados Observer*, 14 Nov. 1936.
37. Adams's evidence to the Commission, 13 Aug. 1937, CO 28/319/9.
38. *Ibid.*
39. *Ibid.*
40. *Ibid.*
41. Hoyos 1974: 62-64.
42. *Ibid.*, 65.
43. Beckles 1990: 168-69.
44. Hoyos 1974: 81-82.
45. Note of meeting convened by Lord Dufferin, 13 May 1938, CO 28/322/3.
46. Gov. E. Waddington to MacDonald, 26 Aug. 1938, CO 28/322/3.
47. Flinn to MacDonald, 29 March 1939, CO 28/324/11.
48. Waddington to MacDonald, 23 Feb. 1939, CO 28/324/11.
49. Waddington to SS, 10 Feb. 1939, CO 28/324/11.
50. Waddington to SS, 18 Feb. 1939, CO 28/324/11.
51. Waddington to SS, 22 Feb. 1939, CO 28/324/11.
52. Waddington to MacDonald, 23 Feb. 1939, CO 28/324/11.
53. *Ibid.*
54. *Ibid.*

55. *Ibid.*
56. Waddington to MacDonald, 14 March 1939, CO 28/324/11.
57. *Ibid.*
58. Hoyos 1974: 89.
59. Beckles 1990: 170..
60. Quoted in Beckles 1990: 173.
61. Quoted in Hoyos 1974: 91.
62. Hoyos 1974: 91-92.
63. Flinn to MacDonald, 3 July 1939, CO 28/324/11.
64. Quoted in Hoyos 1974: 92.
65. Flinn to MacDonald, 3 July 1939, CO 28/324/11.
66. Hoyos 1974: 93.
67. Resolution passed at a meeting on 4 March 1938, enclosed in Flinn to Ormsby-Gore, 3 May 1938, CO 28/321/12.
68. Harold A. Moody to MacDonald, 16 June 1938, CO 28/321/12.
69. Arthur Creech Jones to George H. Hall, 24 April 1941, CO 28/328/2.
70. Walter Citrine to Lord Moyne, 29 Sept. 1941, CO 28/328/2.
71. Waddington to Sir Alan Burns, 27 June 1941; Gov. Sir G. Bushe to SS, 18 Dec. 1941, CO 28/328/2.
72. Drayton and Andaiye 1992: 266.

Chapter TEN

The Bahamas

The Bahamas, like the rest of the British West Indies, suffered from the depression and from the closure of immigration possibilities to the United States and elsewhere. Many Bahamians who had migrated earlier returned home in the 1930s to face unemployment and poverty. Some of the same factors that produced labour rebellions throughout the British Caribbean were present in the Bahamas, but 'protest and change were generally slow in coming to the Bahamas'.[1] Relatively isolated from the rest of the West Indies and with its small population dispersed throughout an extensive archipelago, communication within the Bahamas and between the Bahamas and other British colonies was difficult. Nevertheless, shortly after the Trinidad and Barbados labour rebellions, a disturbance occurred at Matthew Town in Great Inagua, a remote island in the southern Bahamas, 65 miles north of Cuba. This incident has become known as the 'Inagua Riot' of 1937.[2]

The Bahamian economy, threatened by the decline in sponge and sisal prices, had benefited from proximity to the United States when the US Congress passed the Volstead Act in 1919 prohibiting intoxicating liquors in the United States. This led to large-scale 'bootlegging' in the Bahamas and, until the repeal of the Eighteenth Amendment in 1933, provided a windfall in profits not only for the bootleggers but also for the Bahamian government which, far from cooperating with the US Excise Service, obtained a fantastic increase in revenue from imported liquor. Craton says that 'to a limited extent, the whole of the Bahamas profited from the Prohibition goldrush', as construction and dock work increased and wages rose. However, as he says, 'one of the least happy aspects of the Prohibition boom was that it produced an even deeper separation between the 'haves' and the 'have-nots'. The result was that when prohibition was repealed there was a 'savage depression' as 'wages fell to starvation levels even where work was available',[3] and racial tensions increased between the poor black majority and the affluent white merchants, known as the Bay Street Boys, who dominated the colony politically and socially as well as economically. These were the social tensions, derived from the predominant class and race relations, that lay in the background. However, the Inagua Riot was not a labour rebellion comparable with those that occurred elsewhere.

Inagua had a successful salt industry in the nineteenth century which collapsed in the early 1900s. By the 1930s the population had declined as the islanders went to Nassau or the United States in a desperate search for work. In the early 1930s Inagua was dominated by Arthur L. Symonette, a coloured merchant who, as an agent for the Royal Netherlands Steamship Company, employed stevedores and kept them indebted by making their families purchase supplies at his store.[4] 'There was a great deal of dissatisfaction among the stevedores as to the method whereby such stevedores were selected, the manner of making payments to them and...the exorbitant rates charged for foodstuffs that they were compelled to purchase for the truck system was rampant'.[5] Symonette also engaged in a small way in the salt industry, paying his workers 1s. per day and compelling them to buy goods at his store. In 1934 there was a strike over wages by workers in the salt pans. A fledgling labour union was organised by Theodore Farquharson, who had spent 15 years in the United States before returning to the island to take over his father's general store. This union was said to be 'one of the sources of trouble in Inagua'.[6]

In 1935 some Crown lands were sold 'at a very low price'[7] to an American family, the brothers Josiah, Douglas and Wentworth Erickson. In January 1936 the Ericksons established the West Indian Chemical Company, employing about 50 men and a few women, to revive the salt industry in Inagua. Though this offered employment at wages of 2s. per day for men and 1s.6d. for women, it was seen by Symonette and some other local families as a threat to their traditional monopoly as employers. Consequently, when strikes for higher wages occurred in December 1936 and early 1937, they were said to be 'instigated by several of the leaders in the town'.[8]

When the Ericksons imported strike-breakers from other islands, particularly Acklins Island, and took over the steamship agency from Symonette, 'an atmosphere of considerable hostility towards the Americans and these intruders rapidly developed'.[9] There was also an element of racial tension involved, as some Inaguans who had experienced discrimination in the United States resented white Americans taking superior positions in their own country. The Ericksons even threatened the acting colonial secretary that they would 'import a number of ex-Marines to the Island and run it as it ought to be run',[10] and they used an armour-plated car on the island. On 19 December 1936 a fight broke out between Charles Kaddy, a white American truck driver for the Ericksons, and George and Willis Duvalier, Bahamian brothers who had lived in the United States and were supporters of Symonette. Kaddy drove his truck into the side of Symonette's store, whereupon a brawl developed between the Duvaliers and their supporters, known as the Band of Inagua Terrors, and the white staff of the West Indian Chemical Company. Commissioner Fields, a coloured Trinidadian doctor, subsequently fined the combatants £2 each side for disturbing the peace, but it appears that the Duvaliers 'continued to harbour a grudge against the Ericksons'.[11]

In July 1937 Dr Fields ordered two other members of the Band of Inagua Terrors to stand trial in Nassau for burning down a house. On 19 August George Duvalier was arrested for assaulting a witness in the arson case but he escaped from the courtroom. The policeman who pursued him was wounded by Willis Duvalier, who also threatened Commissioner Fields with his knife.

George obtained a gun and confronted Dr Fields at the wireless station where he had gone to telegraph for help. Duvalier shot and wounded Fields, then ran to the Ericksons' and attacked Josiah Erickson. Josiah escaped with his brother Douglas and arming themselves and accompanied by two of their American employees, including Kaddy, they went to the wireless station. They brought Fields out but were attacked, and three of them wounded, by Willis Duvalier. While they spent the night in fear at the Ericksons' house, the Duvaliers went on a rampage. They shot and killed John Munroe, a black employee of the West Indian Chemical Company whom they considered to be the Ericksons' informer, and then set fire to the commissioner's residence, the wireless station, the Ericksons' store and the Company's salt house.

The next morning, the Ericksons, along with three of their employees, Dr Fields and the wounded policeman, fled from Inagua in their motor-boat. The Duvaliers, left in control of Matthew Town, 'terrorized the inhabitants'[12] for two days, 'though causing little further harm',[13] and left in a sailing boat on 22 August. They were later arrested in Haiti, brought to Nassau for trial, found guilty of murder and executed. According to Saunders this incident was 'blown out of proportion by the press within and outside the Bahamas',[14] because of the recent labour rebellions in Trinidad and Barbados. Certainly, there was no actual riot, nor was this a labour rebellion, as such. Yet to dismiss it as merely a 'local brawl', as did a report of the West Indian Department of the Colonial Office,[15] misses its significance.

There is little doubt that conditions similar to those that caused the labour rebellions in the rest of the British Caribbean gave rise to this incident, as there was 'a state of unrest' in Inagua, according to the commissioner, that was provoked by both labour and racial issues. The persistent use of the truck system to get employees indebted, and the Ericksons' use of strike-breakers, created resentment among Inagua's workers. Dr Fields concluded, 'While the rest of the inhabitants exhibited no willingness to help the Duvaliers, they equally made no effort and signified no willingness to stop them'.[16] This suggests that the majority of people may have sympathised with the Duvaliers, and not simply have been terrorised by them, and that there may have been mixed feelings about the Ericksons and Fields being chased off the island. The industry the Ericksons had brought offered some employment, but it also disturbed the established paternalistic relations of this little community. A Colonial Office minute commented that: 'The impact of modern business methods on a community used to, and set in, old fashioned ways (however inefficient and corrupt) is liable to produce an explosion'.[17]

Perhaps this incident is best understood, then, not merely as a clash of personalities, but as a microcosm of social change and social tensions, and that the conflict broke out between these particular people because they embodied those tensions. The conflict did not spread, however, because of Inagua's isolation and also because the feelings of resentment against the Ericksons for employing strike-breakers, bringing in white American employees and taking over the stevedoring trade, were not universal, even on Inagua. So, as Saunders points out, the Inagua disturbance 'occurred in a potentially explosive atmosphere but failed to develop into a political or labour riot'.[18]

In 1939 labour organisation and labour reform in the Bahamas lagged behind the rest of the British Caribbean. Orde Browne reported that, while penal sanctions had been abolished, there was no measure for workingmen's compensation and that trade union organisation was still 'in an embryo form, being registered under friendly society regulations'.[19] The Bahamian 'labour rebellion' occurred, not in Inagua in 1937, but in Nassau in 1942.[20]

Notes

1.   Saunders 1990: 25.
2.   Saunders 1990: 49-75. This section draws largely on this article.
3.   Craton 1986: 253, 255.
4.   Johnson 1986.
5.   Report by Commissioner J.A. Hughes on "Inagua disturbance and present conditions", 23 Feb. 1938, enclosed in Gov. to Ormsby-Gore, 19 March 1938, CO 23/638.
6.   Report by Att. Gen. G.W. McL. Henderson, 7 Feb. 1936, enclosed in Gov. Charles Dundas to Ormsby-Gore, 21 Feb. 1938, CO 23/638.
7.   Report by K.E. Robinson on "The disturbances in Inagua", n.d., CO 23/618.
8.   Saunders 1990: 55.
9.   Robinson's report, *op. cit.*, CO 23/618.
10. Report of Act. Col. Sec. Charles P. Bethel re Inagua disturbance, 6 Sept. 1937, enclosed in Administrator J.H. Jarrett to Ormsby-Gore, 17 Sept. 1937, CO 23/618.
11. Saunders 1990: 57.
12. Robinson's report, *op. cit.*, CO 23/618.
13. Saunders 1990: 60.
14. *Ibid.*, 61.
15. 20 May 1938, CO 318/433/1.
16. *Votes of Legislative Council*, 1937-38: pp.42-3, quoted in Saunders 1990: 65.
17. Minute by H. Beckett, 4 June 1938, CO 23/638.
18. Saunders 1990: 68.
19. Orde Browne's report, 4 April 1939, CO 23/682.
20. Saunders 1985-86.

Chapter ELEVEN

Jamaica

During the first 30 years of this century there was a good deal of labour organising in Jamaica, but no actual lasting organisations resulted. The law legalising trade unions in Jamaica, which was passed on 25 October 1919, did not confer immunity from liability for tort or breach of contract, or legalise peaceful picketing.[1] The most persistent of the early unions, the Jamaica Trades and Labour Union (JTLU), had an erratic existence. Founded in 1907, it ceased to function in 1909 but was revived in 1918, sponsored meetings in 1929 at which Otto Huiswood, the Communist from Surinam, spoke, and was said to have about 600 members in 1930. Marcus Garvey cooperated briefly with the Jamaica Workers and Labourers Association, in which S.M. DeLeon played a major role, but he would not work with Huiswood.[2] None of the early unions survived into the mid-1930s.

In Jamaica, as elsewhere in the British Caribbean, labour unrest in the 1930s was provoked by poverty and unemployment, the return of migrant workers from overseas, frustration over the lack of labour reform and absence of political rights, and rage over the invasion of Ethiopia. Amongst other, more particular social, economic and ideological preconditions of the Jamaican labour rebellion were the crisis in banana production and changes in the sugar industry, the rapid urbanisation and immiseration of Kingston, the radicalisation of waterfront workers and the influence of Marcus Garvey. These factors and their mutual influences from the early to mid-1930s created an explosive mixture of race and class feeling in a colony that has had a long tradition of often violent resistance to slavery and colonialism.[3]

Beginning in 1935, the Jamaican labour rebellion peaked in 1938 with widespread strikes, riots, demonstrations and other disturbances throughout the island. In the period between 1936 and 1939 organising resulted in lasting trade unions, the most important of which was the Bustamante Industrial Trades Union (BITU), which grew directly out of the rebellion. In this key period the early labour organisers played a role in the great labour rebellion of 1938 and that rebellion, in turn, mobilised the foundations of the first mass organisation of labour throughout the island. By 1939 the labour and political organisations and leaders that were critically important in shaping postwar Jamaica had already been established. In retrospect, this was the climax of the series of labour rebellions that spread through the British Caribbean after 1934.

In 1935 the population of Jamaica was 1,121,823. Though accurate employment statistics were not available, it was estimated in 1938 that of some 404,000 wage-earners, 231,000 were 'wholly dependent on wages'. These were located in various sectors: 100,000 in bananas (43 per cent), 41,000 in sugar (18 per cent), 29,000 in road and construction work (13 per cent) and 6,000 on the waterfront (3 per cent). The remaining 55,000 were miscellaneous labourers and unemployed (23 per cent).[4] In many cases wage rates had remained the same since the First World War, and sometimes since the nineteenth century, but the problem of low wages was made more critical by the erratic nature of employment. As Major Orde Browne perceived, Manifestly a daily wage may be satisfactory in itself but quite inadequate if the possibility of earning it is restricted to two or three days a week'.[5] It was the combination of low wages and casual employment that created such dire poverty and insecurity. Thus, if a man earned 1s. 6d. per day for six days a week he would be poor, but if he could only get work for two days his weekly income would be a pitiful 3s. There was much variation in actual wages received, as distinct from wage rates, therefore, from week to week, as well as from season to season, and between different industries, as a few examples illustrate.

On sugar estates during the crop season in 1935-36, some 22,200 men and 8,800 women were employed, but out of crop this number fell to 13,600 men and 6,000 women, a reduction of 12,400.[6] Thus, not only was there greater hardship during the six months of the cropover season but there was also much movement of people migrating in the annual search for temporary jobs. Even among those who were 'permanently' employed during the crop season there was great variation in wages received. One man fortunate enough to work regularly during the harvest at Caymanas Estate earned an average of 21s. 4d. per week for 17 weeks, whereas a woman on the same estate earned an average of 6s. 1d. per week over 10 weeks. Many people could not find such regular work so, even if they were paid at the same wage rate, they received less income. One young woman at Caymanas, for example, earned a total of 7s. 9d. for working over a period of three weeks.[7]

Though many sugar workers had access to a bit of land, this was often on the estate where they were employed, and hence was a means of keeping them in the casual labour system, rather than an independent source of income. Not surprisingly, therefore, in these conditions, many workers desired more access to land, and this became one of their major demands, along with higher wages and more secure employment. A rural survey by Jamaica Welfare Ltd. reported, 'The wish for land or more land, or more productive land, is almost universal.... Almost everyone thinks of a money crop in this connection'.[8] Such were the problems of small farming in Jamaica, however, that the conditions of peasant growers were no better than those of rural wage-earners.[9]

One of the chief problems was that Panama disease was destroying bananas, the main money crop of small farmers. While the United Fruit Company was abandoning some of its own estates in the 1930s, many small farmers, far from being able to take advantage of market opportunities, were themselves being driven into failure and then wage labour. Some peasants joined local associations, but the Jamaica Agricultural Society and the Jamaica Banana Producers' Association tended to represent and be controlled by the richer growers and 'never mobilised the peasants into an active, self-conscious and assertive force'.[10]

One consequence of the plight of the peasantry and rural wage-earners (two overlapping categories) was the growth of migration. As the opportunities overseas were curtailed, migration to the towns, particularly the capital, increased. In the 1920s and 1930s Kingston and the partially urbanised parish of St Andrew which surrounds it, grew rapidly, receiving a net inflow of almost 70,000 people between 1921 and 1943.[11] By the mid-1930s, when thousands of Jamaican emigrants were repatriated, often bringing with them children who had been born abroad, the urban population of Jamaica swelled. Thousands of peasants who were being forced off the land, because rural employment opportunities were inadequate, joined some 30,000 emigrants who were repatriated between 1930 and 1934. This swelled the urban pool of unemployed and intermittently employed and the expanding shanty towns of the Kingston-St Andrew area. Between 1921 and 1943 the combined population of Kingston and St Andrew increased by 102 per cent, from 117,000 to 237,000 people.[12] Wages in Kingston, though higher than rural wages, were low in relation to the urban cost of living, at 3s. per day for men and 1s. 6d. for women, compared with an average rate of 1s. 9d. and 11d., respectively, in private employment in the rural parishes.[13] The wage differential added to the attractions of the urban area, but the massive influx of workers kept the wages low. The Kingston metropolitan area grew most rapidly, but the population of smaller towns also increased as thousands of Jamaicans sought relief from rural poverty.

This concentration of poor people, many of whom had experience of work and politics abroad, had a major impact on the development of class and race consciousness. The growth of Garveyism, the influence of Marxism and the emergence of Rastafarianism in the 1930s all played a part in the process within which the urban working class, and the waterfront workers in particular, pioneered powerful and lasting labour organisations.

Garvey, who had been an officer in the short lived printers' union in 1907, was deported from the USA to Jamaica in December 1927 and was given a hero's welcome in Kingston. He quickly established UNIA branches throughout the island, held mass meetings and organised membership drives. The UNIA's Sixth International Convention, held in Kingston in 1929, drew thousands of people. Garvey and his organisation were an inspiration and provided a rare opportunity for many working people to develop skills as speakers and organisers. Though the restrictive franchise limited Garvey's participation in the formal political processes, 'the UNIA played a vital role in politicizing the masses, especially between 1928 and 1935'.[14] In 1929 Garvey was elected a councillor of the Kingston and St Andrew Corporation but his attempt to win a seat on the Legislative Council the next year failed and his efforts to launch a political party and a workers' association were abortive. Nevertheless, through Garvey's powerful message and inspirational leadership, 'black Jamaicans had not only been made aware of themselves as a race and the place they occupied in the Jamaican scheme of things, but had been given an institutionalized forum for talking about their problems, hopes, and aspirations'.[15]

When Garvey left Jamaica for the last time in 1935, Ethiopianism was becoming a significant force in the island. Garvey had encouraged a general reorientation towards Africa, but it was the coronation of Ras Tafari as the Emperor Haile Selassie in November 1930 and the Italian invasion of Ethiopia in 1935 that sparked the specific religion of Rastafarianism. Leonard Howell, amongst others, had preached the divinity of Haile Selassie in the early 1930s and by the time of his arrest and trial for sedition in 1934 he had established a considerable following. When the wave of sympathy for Ethiopia swept Jamaica in 1935, Rastafarianism was only one part of a 'much broader front' of a pro-Ethiopia and anticolonial movement,[16] similar to that in Trinidad. A Garveyite weekly newspaper, *Plain Talk*, edited by Alfred Mendes, 'succeeded in giving its readers a feeling of participation in defending Africa against this latest example of oppression by the white man'.[17] By the mid-1930s, then, more and more Jamaicans were 'coming to see themselves as part of a scattered and exploited but nevertheless "chosen" people...[and] to see white people increasingly clearly as their oppressors and the white (or near-white) establishment as "Babylon"'.[18] Though Garvey himself denounced Haile Selassie and his policies in 1936 from his exile in London, a mix of Garveyism, Ethiopianism and Rastafarianism had become by then an important part of the political culture of resistance in Jamaica.[19]

In this turbulent context of economic deprivation, social volatility and politicisation, labour protests took place in 1935 on the north coast. These were early warnings of the great labour rebellion three years later, especially since they involved banana workers and dock workers, who became the most militant rebels in 1938. The first issue of *Plain Talk*, on 18 May 1935, reported that banana workers in Oracabessa in the parish of St Mary had rioted five days before. A big grower had imported labourers from neighbouring Port Maria in order to increase competition and reduce wages. When the workers blocked roads and cut power lines, armed police were sent from Kingston to quell the disturbance.[20] A few days later, on 20 May, a more serious incident started at Falmouth in Trelawny, where the threat of using strike-breakers during a strike by dock workers provoked violence. At about 8 am on 20 May, Clinton Delgado of Delgado Bros reported to the Falmouth police inspector that the dock workers whom he wanted to load sugar onto a ship had gone on strike, demanding 4s. for a nine hour day instead of the usual 2s. 6d. The inspector visited the wharf and found about 30 workers, who were 'quiet, peaceful and were laughing and joking among themselves',[21] but were determined not to work for less than 4s. per day.

During the course of the day the strikers' numbers increased and at about 1.30 pm they heard that workers were being brought to Falmouth from outside to load the ship. When they threatened 'to beat the persons so brought in and run them out of town', the inspector told them he would give the strike-breakers 'every protection and see that the ship was loaded'. The inspector accompanied three strikers to discuss the matter with the Delgados, but 'after some argument, no agreement could be reached and the conference broke up'. Though the crowd 'marched down the streets singing and waving sticks', there was no disorder. Nevertheless, the inspector obtained reinforcements from Montego Bay, as he must have anticipated that his actions would provoke the strikers. When the police advised the men 'to behave' and warned of 'the consequences of any disorder', there was still 'no antagonism towards the

Police who were treated with respect', but the strikers remained determined that no outside labour would be brought in. As darkness fell the crowd had increased to about 500 or 600, many of them with sticks and iron bars, and some piled up stones at the side of the road. The strikers stopped vehicles entering the town and searched them for strike-breakers. One car bringing police was damaged, but no arrests were made. More police reinforcements arrived from St Ann at 10 pm, and by about 2.30 am most of the crowd had peacefully dispersed to their homes.

At 4.45 am on 21 May, 40 armed police were posted to secure Delgados' wharf and to block all approaches from strikers. Two hours later Donat Delgado tried to hire labourers at 2s. 6d. per day and the few who accepted were escorted to the wharf by police. The strikers then became angry and shouted at Delgado. One man, Percival Brown, armed with an iron pipe, was said to shout, 'Lick him to rass, kill him to rass', and the crowd surged toward the wharf. When the police arrested Brown, who 'put up a tremendous fight... several hundred men and women spread out facing the Police and commenced to throw stones, bricks, bottles and conch shells', pressing forward and injuring several policemen. The police shouted warnings and fired some revolver shots over the crowd but this had no effect. The crowd jeered at the police and continued stoning them. The police then fired into the crowd, killing Sidney Black, a 37-year-old man who was shot in the face, and wounding another with a bullet in the thigh. The police took Brown to their lock-up, re-formed with reinforcements outside the court house, and then charged with fixed bayonets through the streets of the town 'until the crowd was entirely dispersed', whereupon they 'scoured the town' to arrest those whom they considered to be ringleaders. Forty more police arrived in the afternoon and by 3 pm the next day 33 people had been arrested. The boat was subsequently loaded under police protection and left on 22 May.

According to the custos' report, the strike had been prepared. A meeting had been held on 15 May to discuss what should be done and on 19 May two or three young men 'of the radical element' were seen riding bicycles around town, 'stopping and speaking to people', and messengers had gone to neighbouring villages, such as Perth Town, Granville and Martha Brae, from which labourers were often recruited. The custos claimed that they referred to the Rev. J.W. Maxwell, a Baptist member of the Permanent Jamaica Development Convention, created at the UNIA convention in September 1934, who, when a candidate in the Legislative Council election in January 1935, had urged that:

> no man should work for less than a dollar [4s.] a day; that the estate owner and upper classes generally are grinding the population down and that he would enable the employer of labour to pay the dollar a day minimum wage by increasing the price of their produce; that the economic depression was entirely due to the upper classes etc. etc.[22]

Maxwell was a supporter of J.A.G. Smith, a black barrister and member of the Legislative Council from 1917 until his death in 1942, who advocated labour reform and had founded the Jamaica Representative Government Association in 1921.

The custos concluded that 'this disturbance is due to the economic conditions of this neighbourhood being exploited by the radical political element', conditions that he admitted were 'deplorable'. He commented that the area had not shared in the 'Banana Prosperity', that this 'portion of the parish is gradually going back to bush', and those people who had not already left 'have become poorer.... Their suffering and poverty is not a sudden thing of today, they have endured it for a generation with patience which entitles them to a degree of appreciation'.[23]

The claim that the Falmouth strike was prepared is supported by evidence of other 'agitation for increased pay on the part of loaders and stevedores' in Port Antonio and Kingston, which led to some shots and injuriesin the latter. Governor Denham met with representatives of the leading shipping firms on 29 May and was 'satisfied that the agitation is largely fomented by a rowdy and disorderly element'.[24] On 18 July he reported there had been 'no recurrence of the disturbance at Falmouth or elsewhere' and that most of the 32 people convicted, out of 38 defendants, at Falmouth were imprisoned for between 3 - 12 months.[25] The Colonial Office commented ominously that the police were justified in shooting at Falmouth, but that 'armed forces should never fire over the heads of a crowd. If it becomes necessary to fire, the officer in command should, when it is possible, point out one or two ringleaders and have them shot. Aim should be taken at the lower part of the body'.[26]

No specific organisation resulted from these disturbances in 1935, but the next year the most important trade union to date, the Jamaica Workers and Tradesmen Union (JWTU), was founded and peasant unrest developed in the countryside. The JWTU, formed in 1936 and registered in 1937, was led by two men, A.G.S. Coombs and H.C. Buchanan, who played a pioneering role in organising labour in Jamaica over the next few years. Allan George St Claver Coombs, born of poor peasant parents in St Ann parish in 1901, served in the Jamaican police force from 1919 until 1922 and then in the West India Regiment until 1926. Working as a contractor for the Public Works Department, he started the union among his own labourers in May 1936.[27] A couple of weeks later, on 4 June, hunger marches by the unemployed took place in Kingston, followed by several in Spanish Town, on 9 September, 9 October and 14 November, led by L.W. Rose, a shoemaker and UNIA organiser, and L.E. Barnett, who had returned from Costa Rica where he had been vice-president of the Limon Federation Union. One of the marchers, when offered lunch by the chairman of the St Catherine Parochial Board, responded,

> We are Naked...our children are naked, we are turned out of shelter, our families are turned out of shelter because we cannot pay the landlords their rent. What we do need is not the little lunch suggested but that the Parochial Board does find work, begin its work of magnitude and employ us now.[28]

On 23 November Coombs met members of the Ex-British West Indies Regiment Association and the Masons Cooperative Union[29] at Liberty Hall, the UNIA meeting place in Kingston. They created a council of action to organise more hunger marches to put pressure on the government. Coombs led a march of the unemployed in Kingston on 30 December, but the deputy mayor, Dr

Oswald Anderson, advised them to turn back. When they hesitated, the police charged them and injured two men before they dispersed. Coombs later described the event to the Moyne Commission:

> The people all unarmed were only carrying flags and banners bearing the words 'Starvation, Nakedness, Shelterless'. The Union Jack was torn in pieces. The batons and clubs of the police were brought in play mercilessly on the people, while extra armed men kept the people covered with rifles, bayonets and pistols, while the poor and unfortunate people recieved [sic] their floggings which necessitated many going to hospital for treatment.[30]

Coombs responded by placing an advertisement in *Plain Talk* on 2 January 1937, calling for people from all over the island to come forward and join the JWTU because the key was in organised labour: 'the workers should organize solidly, because it is only through organization that any group of people can achieve success'.[31] Six months later, Coombs described the dock workers whom he was organising:

> Women and children are among the banana carriers, pregnant women included. I stood up for about half an hour watching, the carriers running and trotting all along. The loaders receive the bananas with 'lightning' speed and accuracy, their clothing soaked with perspiration. The big bosses and managers paced lordly up and down the piers with their hands in their pockets, laughing and chattering with each other, while tourists take photographs of the workers, clad in tattered garments.[32]

By this time Coombs had been joined in his efforts by Hugh Clifford Buchanan, 'Jamaica's first active Marxist'.[33] Buchanan was born on 29 January 1907 and left his home at May Pen at the age of 12 to live with an aunt in Hanover. At age 16 he migrated with her to Cuba and there he learned the trade of brick mason and came to understand the Cuban sense of self-respect that was a source of powerful nationalism there. In December 1937, just a few months before the labour rebellion, he wrote to the new progressive paper, *Public Opinion*, comparing Cuban nationalism with the lack of such feeling in Jamaica:

> The illiterate Cuban *guajiro* beats his breast with pride and declares: 'I am a Cuban....' This pride of even the most illiterate Cuban is due to the fact that at a certain time in the past they rose and did something monumental. The deeds of a Maceo, a Marti and a thousand patriots who distinguished themselves in the struggle are written in prose, and poetry, and in the text books of their schools. It is the source of a never-ending folklore, the vital chord to which every Cuban responds. 'La Independencia' even though reduced to a solemn farce by the strangle-hold of Wall Street, is nevertheless the motive force, the ideal of a nation of progressive people less than one hundred miles from us.[34]

Buchanan may have had contact with Cuban Communists but it is more likely that he was active there in the UNIA. According to Richard Hart, Buchanan was introduced to Communism in Jamaica by Cleveland Antonio King, another Jamaican who had lived in Cuba and had been a member of the Communist

Party there before returning home. Buchanan borrowed Marxist literature, including Lenin's *The State and Revolution*, from Audley Thomas, a senior civil servant in the Department of Education.[35] In 1937, Buchanan met Richard Hart, then a young law student, and before the end of that year they were meeting in Jamaica's first Marxist group with Wellesley A. McBean, Frank Hill, Albreath A. Morris, T.G. Christian, Cecil Nelson, and Lionel Lynch. Morris and Christian were tally clerks on the wharves and Lynch was a longshoreman and stevedore who had been introduced to Communism while resident in the USA. They were soon joined by others, including Arthur Henry, who had been a railway fitter and an engine-room oiler on Canadian boats.[36]

Hart writes that the group was 'loosely centred around Buchanan', but it was Hart himself who became the most important Jamaican Marxist. Born in 1917, Richard's father was Ansell Hart, a solicitor. Richard was privileged enough to attend Munroe College and then spend three years at a minor English public school before entering the University of London in 1935. He returned to Jamaica in 1936, and became articled as a clerk in his father's firm. He had taken little interest in politics when in England but by 1937 was convinced he was a Marxist[37] and, as part of the growing agitation of local intellectuals, started writing letters and articles for newspapers. Frank Hill was a journalist who was one of the founders of *Public Opinion*, a progressive weekly started in February 1937, along with O.T. Fairclough, a Jamaican who had worked in Haiti, and H.P. Jacobs, a teacher from England who was Audley Thomas's brother-in-law. Another focus of middle-class reform was the National Reform Association (NRA), which held its inaugural meeting in March 1937. Noel N. Nethersole, a solicitor, became its president and the secretary was Ken Hill, Frank's older brother. In 1937 Ken Hill had started the Jamaica Chauffeurs' Union for taxi and lorry drivers and the Motor Omnibus Drivers' Association, while F.A. Glasspole, an accountant, organised shop assistants and clerks in Kingston and became secretary of the Jamaica United Clerks Association.[38] Thus by 1937 these people had formed a radical, socially active network.

These middle-class Jamaicans were trying to find a role in and provide leadership for the growing discontent in the colony, but they were not always trusted. At an early meeting of the NRA, on 28 April 1937, a popular Garveyite street orator, St William Grant, appeared and pointed an accusing finger at the dignitaries on the platform, demanding 'Are you leaders of this movement prepared, if need be, to die for the masses?'[39] Buchanan, who had joined the NRA immediately and was elected to its executive council, was certainly more radical than most of its members. A columnist wrote in *Plain Talk* in August 1937, 'Must it be understood that this lofty association intends to reform the already poverty stricken inhabitants of this island through the opinion and sentiments of a few aristocrats thrown on them?' [40]

An attempt to launch a Jamaicans' Labour Party was made in April 1937, but when Norman Washington Manley, the colony's leading barrister and founder of Jamaica Welfare, was asked to stand as its candidate at the forthcoming Kingston and St Andrew Corporation election, he refused. Earlier he had turned down Fairclough's invitation to become president of the NRA, saying, 'The problems of Jamaica, my dear Fairclough, are social and economic, not political'.[41] Manley had won the trust of the colonial officials and was careful to keep it. Governor Denham described Manley in July 1937 as 'the ablest Jamaican of today...very helpful, sane and conservative...not a controversialist nor a politician, though a man of strong – but I believe loyal – views'.[42] So, although some people were trying to create a more openly political movement in 1937, others, including Manley, continued to drag their feet. Between December 1937 and April 1938 there was a lively debate about the need to form a political party, and what kind of party it should be, in *Public Opinion*. Participants included Fairclough, Buchanan and Hart, and three leading members of the New York based Jamaica Progressive League (JPL) that was formed in 1936: W. Adolphe Roberts, Wilfred A. Domingo and Jaime O'Meally, the latter two former Garveyites. These people expressed strong nationalist and sometimes Marxist, sentiments in debating issues of socialism and self-government for Jamaica. By the middle of 1938, however, this debate was overtaken by events. The situation changed dramatically – and so did Manley's attitude to political activity.

The two most serious attempts to organise working people before 1938 were by the JWTU and the Poor Man's Improvement Land Settlement and Labour Association (PMILSLA). The peasants' economic distress was evidenced in their inability to pay an annual land tax of 1s. for every £10 in value. By the end of March 1937 the total arrears was £125,043 and the number of peasants imprisoned for non-payment increased from 57 in 1934-35, to 116 in 1935-36 and 153 in 1936-37.[43] In 1935 a group of peasants in Golden Grove, St Thomas, a centre of Howell's Rastafarians, formed the Tax and Rate Payers Association. They called on the government for help, demanding a land settlement scheme, better roads and water supplies and books for schoolchildren, but by 1936 they had faded from sight.[44] More serious was the PMILSLA, founded early in 1938 in Clarendon and led by Robert E. Rumble. A poor peasant who had worked in Cuban canefields in the 1920s, Rumble returned to Jamaica in 1932 and by 1937 was writing about 'the oppression of these iron-handed landowners in these parts of Clarendon'. He declared, 'We want no more landlords'.[45] Some land-hungry peasants who occupied land at Trout Hall and Cocoa Walk were arrested and tried. The PMILSLA, claiming a membership of 800, petitioned the governor on 23 April 1938:

> We are the Sons of slaves who have been paying rent to Landlords for fully many decades we want better wages, we have been exploited for years and we are looking to you to help us. We want a Minimum Wage Law. We want freedom in this the Hundredth year of our Emancipation. We are still economic Slaves, burdened in paying rent to Landlords who are sucking out our vitalities.[46]

Though Rumble appealed to the colonial authority as if it were a benevolent power above the local landlords, his tone was radical, and the demand for a minimum wage reflected the imminent proletarianisation of the peasantry and the discourse of modern labour reform. Many peasants believed, moreover, that 99-year leases had been given to landlords at the time of emancipation and that the land was due to pass to its rightful owners, the descendants of the former slaves. This radical interpretation expressed the peasants' class grievances and a historical desire for compensation as well as further politicising them, but Rumble's organisation did not expand beyond the parish of Clarendon and it was swallowed up by the general rebellion in 1938.[47]

The JWTU, meanwhile, was trying to organise all kinds of workers on an islandwide basis. Coombs and Buchanan, financially pressed, accepted the assistance of a money-lender, William Alexander Bustamante, who became treasurer of the union in 1936. Born with his father's surname of Clarke on 24 February 1884, Bustamante subsequently created shadowy legends about his past. His father was the half-brother of Norman Manley's mother, so these two leaders of modern Jamaica, sharing a grandmother, were half-cousins.[48] Bustamante went to Cuba in 1905, moved to Panama two or three years later, returned to Cuba in 1919 or 1920, and tried a dairy business back in Jamaica in 1928. By 1932 he was in New York, calling himself Alejandro Bustamanti, but he finally returned to Jamaica, not notably prosperous, in 1934.[49] He became a prolific writer of letters to the press,[50] and by May 1936 was speaking at meetings of the middle-class citizens' associations, which had grouped themselves into a federation the previous month and were intended to promote civic improvements.

During 1937, while Coombs and Buchanan were trying to organise dock workers, railwaymen and banana workers in Kingston, Spanish Town, Port Maria and Oracabessa, Bustamante made several trips to the rural areas. When news came of the labour rebellion in Trinidad, Bustamante wrote to *Plain Talk*:

> We too in Jamaica must organize, unite, stick together, stay united to obtain a living wage and better treatment both from government, from the so-called Captain of Industries and other employers, and until then we will never [be] worth being called a people.... Labour of every class in this Island, white collars etc, I exhort you to organize. I will go [to] any part of this Island as I have been doing paying my own expenses to speak to you, to tell you the necessity and the beauty of Labour Organizations.[51]

In 1937 Bustamante began to establish his reputation, which may be characterised either as that of an inflammatory demagogue or as the workers' fearless champion. The workers grew increasingly militant, there was a one-day strike in the railway locomotive workshops on 12 July, several strikes among workers on banana estates in St James parish in September, and the banana loaders' strike in Oracabessa in October; and Bustamante got more publicity and rapidly became known as a labour leader.

Post has summarised succinctly the importance of the relations between the JWTU and Bustamante at this time, both for the individual and for the organisation of Jamaican labour:

> To the Union he brought his financial backing, his energy, and his capacities as a crowd-puller, with his commanding presence—tall, with a shock of hair— distinctive voice and rhetorical flair. For his part, he seems to have found in the Union two things, a chance to give the most effective expression to his pity for the poor and exploited and an organisation which he could dominate.... As for Jamaican labour, it found in Bustamante 'the Chief', 'Busta', 'Labour Leader No.1', the man who was to lead it to apparent triumph and ultimate tragedy.[52]

Bustamante's ego and ambition created a crisis in the JWTU and friction developed because Bustamante wanted to become president. Coombs acknowledged he was losing authority to his treasurer and on 12 October he resigned as president and handed the position to his rival. However, Coombs 'never fully relinquished his claim to the leadership',[53] and in November Bustamante, facing opposition from Coombs' supporters, quit the union altogether. Bustamante had his own supporters, however, and the JWTU was badly divided. Buchanan attacked Coombs and resigned as general secretary in November and L.W. Rose, the vice-president from Spanish Town, also resigned. This was a serious split in the labour movement because at this time the JWTU claimed 88 per cent of the 1,080 members of the registered trade unions in the colony.[54] In late January 1938 a compromise was reached when Percy A. Aikan, a railway electrician who had been a leader of the railwaymen's strike at the end of the First World War, was made acting president, but the rivalry between Coombs and Bustamante re-emerged a year later in the struggle to control organised labour after the rebellion.

In September 1937, Governor Denham noted 'increased activity on the part of the various labour unions'.[55] The JWTU won a victory in St James in October when the banana growers agreed to pay carriers 2d. a stem in place of the former 1d., but the banana loaders' strike in Oracabessa later in the month petered out when the union could not persuade workers in Port Antonio and Port Maria to refuse to handle the diverted fruit. A union meeting at Port Antonio on 22 October was broken up by hired thugs and the police failed to intervene. This happened again on 28 January 1938. When unorganised workers on Serge Island sugar estate in St Thomas went on strike at the end of 1937, the JWTU was not involved. The strikers demanded 2s. for harvesting a ton of cane instead of 10½d., which was what the estate was paying. On 5 January some 1,400 strikers armed with sticks and cutlasses virtually shut down the parish of St Thomas. Bustamante, no longer a trade union official, offered to be a mediator but when the workers were told the employer was willing to pay only 1s. per ton they rejected the offer and Bustamante and the owner had to retreat with a police escort. A reinforcement of 50 police was brought from Kingston to quell the ensuing unrest in which 34 strikers were injured and 60 arrested.[56] This pattern of escalating violence was repeated on a greater scale within three months at Frome in Westmoreland parish, at the other end of the island.

It is now clear that the strike that erupted at Frome at the end of April 1938 was a continuation of the labour unrest and trade union politics that had been emerging for some months, but at the time many people were surprised by the event and amazed at the scale of the violence. Governor Denham's long message to the Legislative Council in March made only a brief comment about unemployment and no mention of labour relations. On 17 April 1938 Denham sent a telegram in response to what he called 'incorrect and misleading' statements by 'one Bustamante a local publicity seeker' concerning thousands of hungry schoolchildren. He assured the Colonial Office that 'Government is fully alive to present situation which does not appear to give any cause for alarm'.[57] Denham was not ignorant of the situation, nor was he as complacent as this telegram sounds. He was an active and liberal governor, as far as colonial governors in the 1930s could be, and had been involved in many relief efforts since his arrival in Jamaica in 1934. Legislation had been passed on workmen's compensation and slum clearance, and he had raised a loan of £2 million for land settlement schemes and irrigation projects, as well as building houses, schools, roads and hospitals. An effort had been made to create more jobs through public works and in the first months of 1938 several projects were started, including road improvement, building the new Palisadoes Airport and clearing slums in west Kingston. Nevertheless, Denham's claim that his 'Public Works Extraordinary programme amounting in coming year to over £170,000 will afford considerable relief to unemployment situation'[58] suggests that he was trying to reassure the Colonial Office that because he was doing his job they would not get trouble in Jamaica similar to what had occurred in Trinidad and Barbados in 1937.

On 20 April Bustamante, speaking to an estimated 2,000 people on North Parade in Kingston, described the governor as a 'misfit as an administrator', but he was careful to aver that he was 'not advocating a revolt'.[59] The next week Bustamante, who had won the trust of many poor people, spoke to an even larger crowd. A few days later, however, when the working people of Jamaica started their great rebellion in Frome, they did so without his leadership.

Though the various parts of the Jamaican labour rebellion were actually closely interrelated, for purposes of clarity we may distinguish between three chief locations and phases: first, the riot and strike at Frome Estate in Westmoreland between 29 April and 2 May; second, the protests, strikes and uprising in Kingston between 2 and 28 May; and third, the many demonstrations, riots and 'rolling strikes' throughout the island between 23 May and 11 June. Some of these events were organised and involved people we have already identified as labour leaders, but most were spontaneous responses with only local and anonymous leadership. Before the second week in June this rebellion had wrung several concessions from the colonial government and had promoted Bustamante and Manley to the status of leaders of the labour and nationalist movement.

The 'Frome Affair', which started with a riot and developed into a strike, began because of anger about 'the dilatory payment of wages earned'.[60] On the afternoon of Friday 29 April the estate workers were paid more slowly than usual and, in the opinion of the commissioners who enquired into the disturbances,

> it was not unnatural that those who were waiting to be paid became impatient and discontented. The discontent resulted in the throwing of stones and in an attack by some of the labourers on the pay office. The discharge of several shots from a revolver to scare those who were committing these acts and to protect the clerks in charge of the cash did not improve the situation.[61]

Though order was temporarily restored, some workers were angry and many were still unpaid when the office was closed at 10.30 pm. The next morning the estate manager failed to satisfy the workers and tension increased. In part, the immediate cause of the problem was bad management, and specifically 'the ingrained habit of estate operators of disregarding the convenience or point of view of labourers under their supervision',[62] but there was more to it than that, and the incident at the pay office was simply the spark that ignited some very dry tinder.

The small riot at the Frome Estate pay office became a strike and then a large-scale violent confrontation because the hopes and expectations of hundreds of poor workers had been raised and then frustrated. The British sugar company, Tate & Lyle, having bought several properties in Jamaica, was scrapping some smaller factories and consolidating its facilities by establishing a large new central factory at Frome. The West Indies Sugar Company, a subsidiary of Tate & Lyle incorporated on 22 May 1937, controlled Frome, Bluecastle, Friendship, Shrewsbury, Masemure and Mint estates in Westmoreland, Prospect in Hanover and Monymusk in Clarendon, a total of 61,500 acres.[63] As part of its modernisation plans the company announced it would also be building housing for its employees and schools, churches and a hospital, all to be free to the workers and their dependants, as part of a £500,000 investment. An announcement in *The Daily Gleaner* to this effect on 26 March, and rumours of higher wages of up to 4s. or 5s. per day, encouraged the migration of hundreds of desperate workers, but the wages actually paid were less than half what was expected. Moreover, more workers came than would be hired, which was perhaps intended by the management, and even those who were hired did not have secure tenure.

Construction workers and general labourers were hired out of the great pool of available workers according to the company's needs of the moment, so the labour force was expanded one week and reduced the next, with a good deal of turnover and uncertainty among workers. Thus, at the end of March the labour force was 632, and this went up to 780 on 13 April and 911 on 20 April, but fell to 758 on 27 April, just before the riot began, and again to 380 on 11 May.[64] Accommodation for the permanent workers was poor and those people who were casually employed or still looking for work had to live in temporary shelters outside the estate. As Post writes, 'The Frome project reproduced in a microcosmic and intensified form, therefore, the situation of the Jamaican working class—poor living conditions, exploitation, those who were fortunate enough to have jobs feeling the hot breath of the reserve-army of labour always on their necks'.[65]

The mobility and the concentration of these workers facilitated their politicisation, even though it was hard to organise such a casually employed and mobile group of workers. The JWTU had not campaigned at Frome Estate but some of the workers there had surely 'been exposed to its message'.[66] The construction work had been over-advertised to ensure a large pool of labour but the belief that pay rates would be higher may have resulted from rumours spread by unionists as much as by management. When the workers went on strike they demanded $1 a day, just as the dock workers had in Falmouth three years earlier. When the company offered a revised scale of pay and hours of work, amounting to 2s. for a ten-hour day with an extra 4d. per hour for overtime for general labourers, the workers asserted that 'it did not substantially differ from the existing one, refused to accept it and the dissatisfaction was intensified'.[67] Not only were these rates less than the workers had expected, but they also objected to the arbitrary cutting of their pay, by sums ranging from 3d. to 6d. per day, so they did not always receive what they believed to have been agreed and earned. The confrontation intensified as cane fires were started[68] and police reinforcements rushed in. 'The representatives of Tate & Lyle were determined to stand firm against the strikers' demands and the colonial state was there to back them up to the full. But the strikers too were in a determined mood'.[69] What began as an industrial dispute quickly became a violent confrontation. Perhaps, in this highly volatile situation and in the absence of any institutions or processes of mediation, the violence that transpired was inevitable.

Armed black policemen, commanded by white expatriate officers, faced about a thousand strikers who were armed only with bits of wood, iron pipes and stones. A *Daily Gleaner* reporter witnessed the scene on 2 May. He heard glass at the old factory being broken and moved out of what he anticipated would be the line of fire.

> Behind me, I hear rifle firing, followed by shrieks and cries.... I can see men on the ground. Some are motionless, others are staggering to and fro or crawling away on their hands and knees. The strike has culminated in stark tragedy. A few minutes later I hear that three are dead, eleven wounded and that the police are making arrests.[70]

By the end of the day four people were dead, three of them shot and one bayoneted by the police. Two of these were women, one of them old and the other pregnant. Somewhere between 14 and 25 people were reported wounded (including five policemen) but, as it was believed that people seeking medical attention for injuries would be arrested, the wounded were probably more numerous. According to the newspaper, 96 people were arrested up to noon on 3 May.[71]

People in Kingston responded to the news from Frome promptly. A protest meeting at North Parade on the evening of 2 May attracted 3,000 people and St William Grant led a march to the office of the *Jamaica Standard* to draw its English editor's attention to the conditions of Jamaica's working poor.[72] Bustamante left Kingston that night and, arriving at Frome on the morning of 3 May, conferred with the manager and endeavoured to play a mediating role. The *Gleaner* reported that he was satisfied by the medical facilities and promises of housing offered by the company but told the manager that the 2s. per day offered to workers was not adequate, and that there would not be 'peace at the factory so long as that scale of pay existed'.[73] As Hart points out, Bustamante was at Frome in 'the role not of a trade union leader representing workers but of a mediator between capital and labour'. [74]

Grant, meanwhile, led another protest march in Kingston, and some people from the horrific area known as the Dungle (a dunghill of refuse in western Kingston) insisted on taking reporters from the *Gleaner* to see where they had to live. On 4 May Bustamante, who had returned from Frome where the workers had accepted the company's offer, spoke at a meeting in Kingston sponsored by the Social Reconstruction League, led by a former policeman called Barrington Williams. Though Governor Denham considered Bustamante's speeches at meetings attended by as many as 3,000 persons to be 'distinctly inflammatory' and probably seditious, he decided to continue to watch him closely but not to arrest him. Denham believed that such a 'premature action might only result in creating a still greater amount of unrest and suspicion amongst the ignorant classes' while enhancing Bustamante's reputation.[75] Denham appears to have been trying to learn from what had happened in Trinidad and Barbados the previous year.

Despite public meetings and sporadic strikes of dock workers in Kingston, there was a relative lull in the rebellion for almost three weeks. There were marches of the unemployed on 9 and 13 May and the crowds became less orderly as tensions rose.[76] Buchanan, who was trying to organise the Jamaica Artisans' Federated Association after he left the JWTU, was active in Trench Pen, a slum area of Kingston where there was dissatisfaction with the hiring practices of labour contractors.[77] A crowd of 2,000 made some labourers on a public project quit work, but Bustamante 'helped quiet things down'.[78] On 14 May Buchanan and Stennett Kerr Coombs, who was not related to A.G.S. Coombs, brought out the first issue of the *Jamaica Labour Weekly*, the masthead of which displays a map of the island and two clasped hands, one black and one white, and the slogan, 'Workers of Jamaica Unite!' Though they never printed more than a couple of thousand copies this paper was, according to Hart, 'widely distributed throughout the island' and became 'a very popular voice of the workers'.[79] While calling for unity, the paper did not call for action, but advised the 'Fellow Workers' only to 'wait and watch'. But on 21 May the Kingston dock workers struck again and the rebellion intensified.

Dock workers on Lascelles Wharf had protested the use of stevedores from Curacao on 10 May and others struck at Grace's Wharf, demanding increased lunch hour rates.[80] Workers on the United Fruit Company's wharf then demanded 1s. per hour instead of 9d. and, as the strike spread, ships were diverted to Port Antonio in Portland. Meanwhile, people in Kingston followed the news from Frome where, on 19 May, the first lot of workers charged with riotous assembly had been convicted and sentenced, with prison terms ranging from 30 days to a year.[81] On Sunday, 22 May, Bustamante and Grant encouraged the dock workers to hold out for higher wages. American seamen were offered 5s. per hour, five times what the Jamaican workers were demanding, to unload the *Veragua* but they refused when they received a telegram from the National Maritime Union urging them to support the strike. The vice-president of the NMU since 1937 was a Jamaican Communist, Ferdinand Smith.[82] Grant, speaking to a large crowd of strikers, with the police in attendance, was reported to have said, 'We want better living conditions... we want our police to be better paid, we want the store clerks to be better paid, we want the ordinary Jamaican to get the wages of Englishmen'.[83] It has been suggested that Grant may have influenced the police not to interfere in the early stages of this strike,[84] but it is equally likely that Denham still hoped to avoid a repetition of the violence in Trinidad and Barbados in the previous year. Be that as it may, the situation on the waterfront became more disorderly the next morning and the police then reacted with force.

By 8 a.m. on 23 May, according to the report of the official enquiry, Disorder...became general and the Police were insufficient in numbers to control the situation. Persons of all classes going to business were set upon, public property was destroyed, streets blocked and tramcars attacked. A hostile mob entered the Sewage Pumping Station and drove out the staff and another took possession of the Gold Street Power Station of the Jamaica Public Service Company. Several thousand persons collected in Harbour Street where Bustamante and Grant were endeavouring to hold a public meeting and refused to disperse at the request of the Police. They were eventually dislodged by a baton charge undertaken by 60 officers and men of the Police who were subjected to a rain of stones and brickbats.[85]

Bustamante, having been rebuffed as a mediator by the employers, was 'firmly committed to siding with the striking waterfront workers' by 23 May.[86] That morning, he threatened 'to tie up every port in the Island' and the strike quickly spread among other workers. The street cleaners, who demanded a pay increase to a minimum of 30s. per week, with overtime for work on Sundays and public holidays, had stopped work on the previous day, and by 11 am all the bus and tram services in the city ceased as the operators stopped work. Strikers moved through the city, closing down businesses, calling out other workers, stoning the police and erecting barricades.

Richard Hart walked through the streets of Kingston that day and recorded what he saw in his diary the next day:

> Bands of workers closed all shops throughout the city. Was standing at door of Scotland's when small body of about twelve young men came up from Harbour Street and ordered his assistants to close the shutters. One shutter was closed and then about nine or ten police charged. The band scattered, and one man got hit over the head with a truncheon....

> Outside Jamaica Fruit Bustamante and Grant were holding a meeting. There was a large crowd completely blocking the street. There was a detachment of police east of the meeting... Bustamante finished his address and he and Grant moved east along Harbour Street. Some of the crowd started to follow. Then the police executed an absolutely unprovacated [sic] charge with batons, laying into men, old men and women indiscriminately....

> [After 11.30 am] Proceeded up King Street to South Parade where Bustamante, Grant and others were holding a meeting from the statue. Bustamante told everyone to go home. On the statue there was a man who was offering to assist the strikers with food...Bustamante then tried to get the people to sing 'God Save the King', but very few obliged, and the meeting ended. The crowd however did not disperse....

> It was now about [noon].... There was a body of police, at a rough guess about 60 to 80 formed up at the junction of Temple Lane and the Parade.... They spread across the road and advanced in a solid line mercilessly wielding their batons. They went right across clearing the Parade. I saw a ragged, bare-footed woman beaten till she fell to the ground, and the policeman stood over her and struck her across the back of the neck and shoulders as she lay there.... Another man was beaten badly and I saw him being escorted to safety between

Bustamante and Grant (the Police did not touch them)...he was in a pretty bad way when Grant was helping him along.

In the wake of the police came four (or five) little army trucks manned by soldiers in tin helmets. The trucks lined up opposite and south of the statue, facing the Orange Street side of the parade.

The police then formed up and systematically cleared the park working from south to north. As I with the rest was driven towards the north of the park, I saw stationed there some of the little army trucks manned by soldiers. Most of the soldiers in the trucks had rifles....

Bustamante and Grant were...walking side by side...down the side of the park on East Parade...A crowd began to follow but a body of police drove them back with batons. My companion and I were...turned back by the police....

We...went west along North Street to the Hospital as far as we could go. There was a guard of soldiers and police. The Laboratory was in a sorry state. Every window was broken... [When the government epidemiologist drove his car through the demonstrators and knocked down three women], the strikers had cut up rough and he had drawn a gun and shot someone. He had escaped into the laboratory and the mob had besieged the place...The police and soldiers had arrived and driven the people off.[87]

A crowd of 500 marched up from west Kingston, playing drums and singing 'Onward Christian Soldiers'. Others marched into the west 'to stop the country buses before they pulled out at three o'clock'.[88] The police were reinforced by six platoons of British troops from the Sherwood Foresters who were stationed in Jamaica. These drove the strikers from the power house, the railway station, the telephone company and the sewage works. By the end of the day the 400 police and 235 troops had been joined by some 400 special constables.[89] More barricades were erected across the roads to stop the movement of police and soldiers, and even when there was no barricade the amount of rubbish in the roads slowed traffic. Hart noted 'a mass of debris of all sorts, stones, rocks, an old motor car chassis, the body, an old engine, garbage cans, and God knows what else'. [90]The striking sanitary workers had left rubbish bins in the streets and these were overturned. People frequently fought back, stoning the police and smashing street lamps to hamper the patrols at night. The city was convulsed in a virtual insurrection. The official report records:

There were minor clashes between the Police and the populace throughout the day.... In Kingston from 6 pm on the Monday to 6 am on the Tuesday morning the city was patrolled by units of Police, Local Forces and Special Constables. They were frequently attacked by mobs concealed in dark lanes and alleys, which occasionally fired shots but in the main relied on stones.... During the night three Chinese grocery shops were set on fire.... By 2.30 am the city was quiet.[91]

Meanwhile, unrest and strikes spread to other places, such as Spanish Town and Montego Bay, and Llandovery and Drax Hall estates in St Ann parish.[92] To contain the unrest, the government recruited many 'light complexioned members of the upper and middle classes' as special constables because these people, with 'guns in their hands', could be relied on to subdue 'the rebellious black masses with enthusiasm'.[93] These 'Specials', who were responsible for many of the casualties, were undoubtedly hated by ordinary Jamaicans. As the violence escalated the social lines hardened, and as those lines hardened the violence escalated. When the number of special constables enrolled reached almost 5,000, however, they included many 'black men with a more mercenary motivation'.[94]

On 24 May, which was ironically the old Empire Day, the unrest continued and so did the violence. 'Crowds began to gather in the capital early in the morning and police and military were engaged throughout the day in breaking them up.... Military trucks patrolled the streets at frequent intervals'.[95] At about 9.15 am a police patrol was stoned when it tried to disperse a crowd at the corner of Princess and Heywood Streets. The police fired into the crowd and also into the upstairs window of a nearby house, fatally wounding a woman who was looking on.[96] At about 10 am a woman and her nine-year-old son were shot dead, and her six-year- old child seriously wounded, when police and special constables opened fire in Matthews Lane. A *Gleaner* reporter called it 'a scene of indescribable confusion. The remaining members of the unfortunate family were screaming hysterically while police clubbed men and women who assembled in the lane'.[97]

Bustamante and Grant, who had been prevented from addressing a crowd on the Spanish Town Road west of Kingston, went to the Fire Brigade headquarters where the firemen were demanding higher pay and threatening to strike. The governor decided to have them arrested, though Bustamante was offering to represent the firemen who did not actually decide to strike 'until after their attempt to enlist Bustamante's support had been frustrated'.[98] Bustamante and Grant were charged with sedition, inciting people to assemble unlawfully, and refusing to move on when ordered to, and were taken to jail. With Bustamante and Grant in jail, Norman Manley took a more prominent role, but, like Bustamante at the beginning, as a mediator rather than as a labour leader.

Manley was at Frome on 23 May, representing the West Indies Sugar Company at the Commission of Inquiry. Recalled to Kingston by a telegram, Manley 'perambulated' in the city on 24 March and in 1969 he recalled seeing 'knots of silent sullen people waiting in ugly frame of mind. I did not at all like what I saw'.[99] He spoke with the governor, who refused to release Bustamante but convinced Manley to intervene in the waterfront dispute. A special court was assembled at the central police station at 10 pm and Bustamante's lawyer, J.A.G. Smith, applied for bail, but it was refused. By the time that Manley's interview with a *Gleaner* reporter was carried in the paper on 25 May, announcing that he had 'placed his services at the disposal of the working classes to present their cases to the employers and the authorities',[100] the jailing of Bustamante had itself become a grievance. Manley said he was 'convinced that Government is anxious that the people should have an opportunity of making representations...and that one of the greatest difficulties in the way of any desire on the part of Government to assist in these troubles is the difficulty of finding persons who are willing to assist the labouring classes and putting forward their grievances'.[101] Bustamante was willing, of course, but the government would not yet let him out of jail. Manley recorded in his diary that he thought this was a mistake because 'a martyr was being made'.[102] The unrest persisted, meanwhile, as strikes were reported on 24 May among bus operators and road workers. A patrol of police and special constables was stoned in Spanish Town and four more people were injured, one by a bayonet and three by gun shots, by military patrols in Kingston.[103]

On 25 May there were further signs of the strike spreading. Dock workers at Bowden and Port Morant in St Thomas refused to load bananas, and strikers demonstrated at Highgate in St Mary and Bog Walk in St Catherine. The sugar factory at Monymusk Estate, Clarendon, was closed by a strike and there was a hunger march in Montego Bay.[104] Special constables, commanded by the estate manager at Caymanas, shot and wounded six workers, three of them seriously. The manager said that 'a gang of hooligans' had taken 'control of the whole estate', so he 'read the Riot Act and then ordered my Special Constables to clear them out'.[105] The class nature of this confrontation is quite transparent.

In Kingston shop assistants and the subordinate staff at two hospitals came out on strike and the tram and bus operators of the Jamaica Public Service Company decided to continue their strike.[106] Bustamante and Grant were again refused bail after a crowd was dispersed by armed force from the central police station. The governor declared a state of emergency, and Manley met representatives of several groups of workers as well as employers. It was clear that the Kingston waterfront strike was the key to the whole situation and Manley arranged to meet the dock workers at No.1 Railway Pier on the following morning. Before the meeting, Hart and Buchanan tried to persuade Manley that he should not advise the dock workers to give up their strike until Bustamante and Grant were released, but Manley recorded in his diary that he spoke 'bluntly' with them. He had negotiated an offer of an increase from the employers and he and E.E.A. Campbell, a lawyer of the citizens' associations, intended to convey this to the strikers' meeting. Buchanan quickly printed up a leaflet and distributed hundreds of copies on the waterfront :[107]

MANLEY AND CAMPBELL CANNOT BE TRUSTED

TOOLS OF THE CAPITALISTS

AWAY WITH THEM

SUPPORT BUSTAMANTE AND GRANT

At the mass meeting on 26 May the strikers, led by W.A. Williams, who had emerged during the strike as the longshoremen's leader, refused to resume work so long as Bustamante and Grant remained in jail. Manley's advice that they should accept a wage increase of 2d. an hour and return to work was firmly rejected. According to the *Gleaner*, the workers chanted, 'No work, no work', and 'We don't want 1s. an hour. We want Bustamante'.[108] While Bustamante was becoming a martyr and the hero of the workers' cause, as Manley had feared, Manley had put himself in the role that, ironically, Bustamante had first sought, namely as a mediator between capital and labour.

When Ken Hill, the secretary of the National Reform Association, suggested to Williams and other waterfront strikers that they should form a trade union, Bustamante indicated through his solicitor, Ross Livingston, that he was willing to be their president. 'In this way', Livingston announced, 'there will be a legal and organized body ready to hand to negotiate with wharf owners and shipping companies and Government'.[109] At the height of the rebellion, therefore, Manley's offer to be a mediator was accepted by the government and employers but rejected by the waterfront workers, who propelled Bustamante into the role of labour leader. This laid the foundation for the Bustamante Industrial Trade Union.

HMS *Ajax* arrived from Bermuda on 26 May, and street cleaners and bus drivers, under police guard, returned to work in Kingston. There were large demonstrations in Spanish Town and on nearby estates in St Catherine, requiring the despatch of soldiers and special constables. Several people were wounded in confrontations as 'every inch of ground' was contested by the demonstrators and some of the armed forces were injured by 'heavy missiles'.[110] There were new strikes at Richmond in St Mary, May Pen in Clarendon, and Bog Walk in St Catherine, as well as Montego Bay and Kingston. Some working-class women who had started cooking free meals for the waterfront strikers in Kingston were assisted by middle-class people, including Edna Manley, Norman's wife. Truck loads of bananas and coconuts were donated and sent from rural areas and by 27 May some 1,500 midday meals were provided for strikers in Kingston.[111] The rebellion was not only spreading and remaining militant, it was also becoming more organised.

Governor Denham, like Governor Fletcher in Trinidad the previous year, seemed to think that a combination of conciliation and intimidation would end the rebellion. So, as the presence of the warship added to the show of force and the government again opposed bail for Bustamante and Grant, Denham announced the appointment of a board of conciliation whose task would include bringing about settlements of labour disputes 'so as to secure continuation of work' and making recommendations 'to relieve unemployment'.[112] As no institution for the settlement of labour disputes existed before 1938, O.W. Phelps is correct in concluding that the appointment of this board was 'the first indication of official acceptance of negotiation between employers and employees as a basis for industrial peace, instead of reliance solely upon force'.[113]

While the Royal Navy was preparing to protect the wharves and 'to relieve police and troops for duty outside Kingston if the situation became worse in the country',[114] the conservative *Gleaner* portrayed Manley as 'every working man's friend', in preference to Bustamante. Manley announced the creation of a labour committee 'to represent the different groups of workers before the Conciliation Board and to negotiate on their behalf', to help organise trade unions, to draw up recommendations for labour reforms and 'to try and lay a foundation for a genuine Labour Party in Jamaica'.[115] Richard Hart, who was a member of that committee, concludes that at this point 'Manley saw his role to be merely that of an adviser, albeit a most influential adviser, and an advocate serving the workers, and the functions of his Labour Committee as temporary',[116] but it seems clear that Manley had by then become committed to a more overtly political strategy. Hart and Buchanan's Marxist group decided to cooperate with the labour committee which met in Manley's chambers on 27 May; this marked the beginning of an important coalition. At the meeting of waterfront workers that morning Manley defended himself against the accusation that he was a tool of the capitalists, saying 'I do not represent more companies than I represent poor people in our law courts'.[117] However, the workers remained determined to make no deals until Bustamante and Grant were released. That night, Manley visited Bustamante in prison and got 'satisfactory assurances' that he would not make trouble if released. He then went to King's House and reassured the governor, noting, 'We agree Bustamante to come out next day'.[118]

On Saturday, 28 May, bail was granted at a specially arranged court session, described by Manley as a 'farce' and by Hart as a 'ridiculous charade'.[119] It must have become clear to the governor that there was more chance of the unrest continuing if Bustamante and Grant remained in jail than if they were released. All charges against them were subsequently dropped.[120] Shortly after 4 pm Bustamante arrived with his lawyers, Manley and the mayor at No.1 Railway Pier, to be greeted by a crowd of 15,000. Bustamante claimed credit for getting an increase in their overtime rates above what Manley had negotiated, though he had been in jail when this concession was made the previous day at a meeting of the conciliation board. Having impressed the workers that he was able to get them more than Manley, he urged them back to work. The strike was promptly called off. Manley recorded in his diary, 'Smith and Bustamante rush off in enthusiastic crowd. I go home sadly. The first round is over'.[121] Manley and Bustamante then worked with the conciliation board to settle more claims for wage increases and negotiate an end to other strikes, including that of the daily labourers of the Public Works Department. Meanwhile, A.G.S. Coombs led a JWTU team in Montego Bay, where they won a round of pay increases for banana carriers, wharf workers, stevedores and waterworks labourers.[122]

Though Kingston became quieter after 28 May, other parts of the island remained in turmoil for two more weeks. Important as the events in the capital were, and they clearly shaped the future of Jamaican politics, Post is right in emphasising that what happened in the rest of the island, particularly among banana workers and small peasants, was equally important for understanding the nature of the labour rebellion. This was recognised at the time by the English journalist, William Makin, who wrote on 31 May:

> The disturbances which have been going on for some days in the country have astonished those who imagined that once the strikes in Kingston were settled, the whole island would be quiet and peaceful. But it must be remembered that the real unrest and discontent began in the country, and it is likely that it will be some days before it ends in the country.[123]

The country around Mandeville in Manchester was full of demonstrators on 30 May, and roads were blocked and fires started as they moved towards the centre of town. Roads were blocked and telephone wires cut in the area of Santa Cruz and Black River in St Elizabeth, and banana workers and carriers went on strike in several places in St Mary, St Catherine and Portland. By the first week of June, there was evidence of rebellion in every parish.

Just as in St Kitts in 1935, workers marched from estate to estate, singing songs and waving sticks, calling out their fellows in a series of rolling strikes through the countryside. Sometimes they stopped cars and demanded money, and sometimes they looted groceries and fired canefields, but there is little evidence that they committed serious violence to persons. A strike at Prospect Estate in Hanover on 2 June seems to typify the spontaneity of this unrest. About 1,000 workers gathered at the factory where the manager addressed the strikers and offered a 25 per cent increase in wages and better working conditions. The offer was refused and when the crowd raided the kitchens for food, five constables were unable to prevent them. Only when reinforcements arrived in the afternoon was the crowd dispersed.[124] Some clashes were more violent , however, especially when Sherwood Foresters and special constables supported local police in clearing road blocks and dispersing marchers. At Balaclava in St Elizabeth, a man was wounded when police opened fire at a roadblock, and two strikers were badly wounded at Richmond in St Mary. That parish was described as being 'like an armed camp' and a serious incident occurred in Islington on 3 June. A crowd of about 100 strikers from nearby estates had cut telephone wires and gathered in the town. When police arrived and tried to disarm them, one man, Edgar Daley, refused to give up his stick, saying, 'No, not a rass. You have you gun. I have my stick'. He wrestled the policeman to the ground, was bayoneted and had his back broken by rifle butts.[125] The crowd surrounded the police and stoned them. The police fired, killing four people, Caleb Barrett, Archibald Franklin, Felix McLaglen, and Thadeus Smith, and wounding others.[126] Near St Ann's Bay a crowd of about 40 people armed with sticks and cutlasses invaded the Greenwich Park property and demanded land. An armed party was sent to drive them out.

More roads were blocked, wires cut and clashes occurred in the next few days. William Makin wrote on 4 June that 'the country districts of Jamaica are blazing with discontent and outbreaks are occurring with disconcerting frequency'. Though Bustamante and Manley travelled round the island trying to get the strikers to accept the offers made by planters and the conciliation board, many refused to accept such settlements. According to Makin, 'The men argue that it is not a question of the day's wages being insufficient, but that the amount of work available is insufficient'.[127]

Since Governor Denham had died after an operation on 2 June, the colonial government was in the hands of C.C. Woolley as acting governor. He continued the combination of intimidation and conciliation, but with important new initiatives. On 5 June, while the *Ajax* moved to Montego Bay, having left two platoons of marines in Kingston, Woolley made a dramatic announcement that £500,000 was to be spent on a land settlement scheme in a 'New Deal' for Jamaica. Though, as Ken Post writes, 'this announcement was the decisive factor in bringing the rural rebellion to an end',[128] the unrest and suppression continued for several days, and the official report described 6 June as 'the worst day in the parishes when the disorders reached their climax'. The Sherwood Foresters deployed patrols through the parishes of Clarendon, Manchester, St Ann, St Mary and Portland on 6 June and two platoons arrived in Savanna-la-Mar at dawn on 7 June to deal with widespread unrest in Westmoreland. Determined strikers at Worthy Park Estate in Lluidas Vale were fired on and several wounded, another striker manning a road block at Jericho was wounded, and a woman was killed and at least one person wounded at Tryall in St James where strikers had occupied the estate yard. An armed party going to rescue an estate owner and his staff in Trelawny was ambushed by a crowd rolling boulders down a hill on to a road. When the crowd was fired on, one person was killed and others wounded.[129] Similar incidents occurred, with more shootings, in Hanover and St James over the next few days, but by 11 June the labour rebellion had petered out. In response to the acting governor's request, however, another company of British troops arrived in Jamaica on 20 June.

According to the commissioners' report, eight civilians had been killed (in addition to the four killed at Frome), 32 wounded by gunshots and 139 'otherwise injured', while 109 of the government's forces were injured and none killed.[130] In Jamaica, as in the other labour rebellions, it is clear that most violence against people was committed by the forces of law and order. Of some 745 persons who were prosecuted, 480 were convicted and given punishments ranging from 'admonished and discharged' to 9 months imprisonment with hard labour.[131] The price of the labour rebellion was high in another way, too, namely the implicit rivalry that emerged between the two cousins, Bustamante and Manley. Their temporary coalition barely hid deeper divisions that were to emerge in the following year and that subsequently split the labour and nationalist movement in Jamaica. This was already apparent at the meeting on 28 May, when Bustamante had just been released from jail and claimed credit for obtaining a better deal for the waterfront workers than Manley had been able to. He told the crowd that he was glad Manley 'came down to enter the breach' during his enforced absence, but also made it clear that he himself was their only real leader: 'I was glad that he tried to do something to help you, but I was more glad that you all refused to work. When you did this, you gave definite proof that you respect your leader and that you accept but one leadership'.[132] This autocratic style defined Bustamante's leadership of the labour movement from the beginning.

The martyred hero became the dictatorial leader soon after the labour rebellion. Even those, like Hart and Buchanan, who were concerned about Bustamante's authoritarianism, decided to support him. Hart writes that they were concerned that the workers, inexperienced as they were, did not as yet 'have a clear understanding of their strength as a class, and still saw their struggle in terms of response to a messiah. Bustamante was the personification of their will to resist oppression and fight for their rights'.[133] Hart wrote to O'Meally in New York on 1 June 1938:

> The comet-like rise of Alexander Bustamante, Usurer, discredited officer of the Jamaica Workers and Tradesmen's Union, to the rank of deity among the masses, is nothing short of a miracle.... But...it would be definitely foolish to oppose him now. He has taught the people the strength of unity, and that unity exists in loyalty to him alone. He has the power to organise the people into unions now, and must be assisted to that end. Therefore, most of us, from the extreme left to the centre, are prepared to back him.[134]

Moreover, the left acknowledged that, such was Bustamante's popularity at the time, they would cut themselves off from the masses if they opposed him. Consequently, Buchanan accepted the post of general secretary, Ken Hill became a vice-president, merging his small unions with the BITU, and Lionel Lynch became an organiser in Portland, in Bustamante's growing union.

An advertisement, drawn up by Bustamante's solicitor, Livingston, appeared on 9 July: 'Look Out for the Name "Bustamante" on All His Unions'.[135] When Bustamante announced he would organise five trade unions, beginning with the Bustamante Maritime Union, they were conceived as his unions in a proprietorial sense and he expected to receive loyalty and obedience from the members. Hart writes that 'Bustamante did not regard a trade union as belonging to its members.... He conceived of a union as something more in the nature of a business and saw himself as its proprietor'.[136] This was true from the start of his unions and it remained true. When his union was registered on 23 January 1939, under the Trade Union (Amendment) Law 1938, it was as the Bustamante Industrial Trade Union. The rules constituted him as its president for life, and gave him power to control its funds and to appoint the committee of management.[137]

The distinctive forms of the labour rebellion in the country parts and the urban areas of Jamaica, particularly Kingston and Montego Bay, reflect the variations in the relations between capital and labour and the consequent differences in consciousness and organisation of the working people. These differences, in turn, correspond with the various ways in which the rebellion ended in these areas. Whereas the urban areas, in which waterfront workers were the militant vanguard, reached a temporary resolution of their demands around 28 May with concessions made to organised labour and the consequent strengthening of trade union organisation, the rural areas remained in turmoil, led by the strikes and demonstrations of banana workers and small peasants, until news spread about the acting governor's land settlement scheme after 6 June. The aspiration of most of Jamaica's rural population to an independent way of life based on small farming was apparent before legal emancipation in 1838 with the persistence of maroon communities and of a 'proto-peasantry'[138] that grew provisions for their own consumption and for marketing even while they were still enslaved. The promise of emancipation and the high expectations created by the former slaves' pioneering of banana production were increasingly frustrated by the development of large-scale capitalist marketing and plantation agriculture, backed by the colonial state. This frustration lay behind Rumble's protests and the intense rebellion in rural areas of Jamaica in 1938, particularly around the banana estates in St Ann, St Mary, Portland and St Thomas.

Acting Governor Woolley, shaken by the intensity of this rural rebellion, had grasped at the idea of land settlement, an idea that had been around in official circles since the Norman Commission recommended in 1897 'the settlement of the labouring population on the land as small peasant proprietors'.[139] Land settlement schemes had been discussed extensively and even tried on a small scale during Governor Denham's tenure. A few weeks before the rebellion a memorandum about unemployment in Jamaica assured that 'the additional land settlement schemes undertaken are proving of assistance to the agricultural population'.[140] Nevertheless, Post's description of Woolley's promised 'New Deal' as 'a desperate expedient'[141] is appropriate in the sense that this was a hasty response, made without consulting his superiors in London, rather than a well-planned policy. Captain C.H.L. Woodhouse of HMS *Ajax* reported:

> By Saturday, 4th June, 1938, it was clear that Monday, 6th June, 1938, was likely to be a critical day in the country districts. There was apprehension that murderous attacks might be attempted on the white population in isolated positions and extensive blocking of roads, cutting of telephone wires and blowing up of bridges was anticipated.[142]

While there is no evidence of the attacks on people or 'racial animosity' that the colonial officials feared,[143] many roads were blocked, telephone wires cut and bridges damaged as the rebels tried to stop the movements of police and troops.

The intolerable pressure on the peasants and their experience of proletarianisation under conditions of casual and impoverished employment intensified their desire for land and made them listen to the acting governor's offer. As Post writes, 'When the banana workers struck and demonstrated they did so for land, even if their immediate demands were for higher wages'.[144] Woolley offered land, and also promised tools, seed, livestock, advice and a new government department to provide them. Special editions of the Sunday papers and meetings organised by local authorities publicised the scheme. A *Gleaner* headline on 6 June proclaimed the scheme would 'make people independent landowners'.[145] Bustamante and Manley supported it, saying, 'This new hope for Jamaica must not be dashed by acts of violence',[146] and Woolley was able to report on 7 June that his announcement had been 'well received' and the disturbances were diminishing. [147]

The banana workers, unlike the waterfront workers, still hoped to avoid proletarianisation, so the promise of a land settlement scheme appealed to them, and the administration calculated that access to a bit of land would not only keep the rural poor from starvation but would also deter further unrest. So, while the urban workers and sugar workers, who were more remote from the possibility of tilling their own land, moved towards unionisation in the struggle for better wages and working conditions, the banana workers, in contrast, aspired to revert to their peasant status. We may conclude, therefore, that the outcome of the rebellion produced not only divisions within the movement toward organised labour but also reinforced the divisions between those workers who were more and those who were less proletarianised.

Though the crisis had passed by 10 June, when the newspapers reported that a Royal Commission would investigate conditions throughout the West Indies, the colonial government and capitalists were shaken by the great rebellion and were afraid of new disturbances. Specifically, they were concerned about the coming hundredth anniversary of emancipation, on 1 August, and anticipated land invasions by people who believed rights in land should now revert to them. The *Jamaica Standard* reported on 25 May that tenants in upper Clarendon, encouraged by Rumble's PMILSLA, were refusing to pay rent to their landlords and that, in anticipation of acquiring formal ownership on 1 August, they were putting up fences and were even offering to pay taxes on their land in advance.[148] In June and July the acting governor and the Colonial Office were taking this matter seriously:

> In the Clarendon district there had been a no-rent campaign since the beginning of the year, and labourers have already staked out their plots and endeavoured to induce Government tax-collectors to accept land-tax on these plots in order to establish a claim to them at zero hour. It is said that owners who will not hand over are to be massacred.... If this is true it would explain the anxiety of the Officer administering the Government to have a warship available on 1st August.[149]

There is no evidence that any widespread plot existed, however, and Woolley reported,

> August 1st passed off very quietly, much to my relief. I think the people understand now that we are not going to tolerate any further disturbances. We took every precaution of course and the Police, Military and some 2,000 Special Constables took up 'battle' positions. There were no attempts at seizure of land as had been anticipated.... I think the worst is over, although there is a tremendous amount of mopping up to be done.[150]

Part of the mopping up involved Rumble. The government, fearing that Rumble's message might spread, arrested him on charges of committing an act of public mischief by inciting people to abstain from paying rents that were legally due. He was tried in December 1938 and sentenced to six months of hard labour.[151]

While Bustamante was busy creating a trade union in his name and style, Manley founded the People's National Party (PNP), initially an organisation related and complementary to his cousin's union. Manley acknowledged that Bustamante had become 'Jamaica's Labour Leader by the only test which matters and that is the support and confidence of labour'.[152] In the tradition of British Fabian socialism, Manley created a reform-oriented party that would appeal to elements in the middle class as well as cultivating a working-class base through Bustamante's union. When the PNP was launched in Kingston on 18 September 1938, the principal speakers were Manley and Sir Stafford Cripps, the prominent British Labour MP who happened to be on holiday in Jamaica. Bustamante, who was on the platform, was not invited to speak and 'he never played an active part in the affairs of the PNP'.[153]

Whereas Bustamante's initial political orientation was entirely 'labouristic' and limited to trade union activity, Manley's was more 'nationalistic' in the sense that he 'saw the trade union organisation as a bridge between the middle class movement for self-government and the working class movement which implied social and economic reconstruction. He saw these as two sides of the same coin'.[154] Manley's social background, education and professional experience all made him more cautious than Bustamante and he was careful to maintain his acceptability to the employers and government. Even after having launched the PNP, 'his nationalistic ideas were still undergoing a process of hesitant formation and development'.[155] In his oral presentation to the West

Indies Royal Commission, given on 14 November 1938, Manley stated he was against immediate self-government and that he was prepared to see suffrage limited by a literacy test. He eventually agreed that adult suffrage without such a test would be preferable only after being prodded to do so by the commissioners.[156] While it was common for educated middle-class Jamaicans like Manley to have such reservations about the qualifications of the masses to choose their government, his response was hardly what one would expect of a socialist and nationalist leader. When universal suffrage was proposed by J.A.G. Smith in the Legislative Council, it was approved by 12 votes to 1 on 13 December 1938, and even the nominated conservatives supported the motion. At the PNP's first annual conference, held in Kingston between 12 and 14 April 1939, Manley supported the goal of achieving 'a parliamentary democracy on the lines which obtain in other self-governing units of the British Commonwealth', but when Britain declared war on Germany in September he persuaded the PNP's Executive Committee to suspend agitation for self-government.[157]

Despite Manley's evident caution, the Marxist group had already decided to cooperate with his nationalist party while preserving their own separate identity as leaders of a socialist movement within the broad anti-imperialist front. As early as 1 June 1938, Hart wrote to O'Meally informing him of this decision: 'Mr Manley and Mr Fairclough are engaged in the formation of a Labour Party.... It will be the duty of all earnest members of the movement to keep it really alive from within, and that is the line we of the left have decided to take'.[158] This decision to work for unity, taken during the labour rebellion, was crucial in the subsequent shaping of the labour and nationalist movement in Jamaica. [159]

Meanwhile, repression continued. The Marxist group's newspaper, the *Jamaica Labour Weekly*, attracted the government's wrath over an article in the issue of 18 June, headlined 'Police Terror in St James. Innocent People Beaten and Shot. Jails Crowded'. The article made accusations about brutal activity by the special constables. 'Government is determined to kill every working man or woman...who raise their voices in defence of labour'.[160] Buchanan and Stennet Coombs, the editor and printer, respectively, were prosecuted for seditious libel. They were convicted in October and sentenced to imprisonment for six months. The paper was temporarily silenced, but Hart, with the help of Frank Hill and others, revived it on 17 December. Buchanan and Coombs were released on 3 April 1939 but they had quarrelled and the paper soon died.[161]

The chief problem of disunity at this time occurred within the trade union movement itself, in the continuing rivalry between Bustamante and A.G.S. Coombs, who was again president of the JWTU. On 30 November 1938 Sir Walter Citrine met with Bustamante, Glasspole, Campbell and others and urged them to form a trade union advisory council to coordinate their activities, but Bustamante declined.[162] Bustamante's union expanded rapidly in the second half of 1938. In November he claimed he had 50,000 supporters, half of them active members, but government figures suggested there were about 8,000 regular members, including 2,000 dockers and 4,000 agricultural, mostly sugar, workers.[163] Many local JWTU leaders had transferred their allegiance to Bustamante. L.W. Rose, who led the St Catherine branch of the JWTU, for example, was persuaded to switch unions and bring the membership with him, and he was rewarded by being appointed a vice-president in Bustamante's union.[164] The BITU was rapidly becoming the only major union, as Bustamante coopted or eliminated his rivals.

Coombs remained entrenched among the banana and dock workers in St James, however, so Bustamante sent Grant to Montego Bay in February 1939 to start organising a challenge. Grant was told by a member of the JWTU, an employee of the United Fruit Company, that the Bustamante union was not wanted there. An altercation developed and Grant sent for Bustamante who promptly demanded that the company dismiss the man. Coombs insisted that he be allowed to continue working and the company agreed, so Bustamante called a strike on the Montego Bay wharves. The Standard Fruit Company and Jamaica Banana Producers' Association wharves were closed, and the companies diverted their fruit to Kingston, but the United Fruit Company wharf remained open under police protection. Bustamante impulsively and autocratically called for an islandwide general strike, 'without any proper preparation or consultation with the workers'.[165]

Dock workers in Kingston and Port Antonio and sugar workers in St Thomas responded to Bustamante's call, and so did Governor Sir Arthur Richards who, just as impulsively, declared a state of emergency on 14 February and mobilised the local forces and special constables. Protection was given to strike-breakers on the wharves, where members of the Ex-Servicemen's Trade and Labour Union provided scab labour. Thus, a local dispute between unions, which had started as an altercation between two individuals, exploded within two days into a political struggle between the infant labour movement and the colonial government as a result of Bustamante's precipitate action.

The strike was a complete failure and some workers who had responded to Bustamante's call suffered victimisation. The weakness of the labour organisation and the inexperience of its leader were revealed, as Bustamante's 'ill-considered move...jeopardized the whole future of the new trade union movement'.[166] On 16 February Governor Richards assured the Colonial Office that 'while the strike is maintained in places it is generally losing ground and public opinion is against it'.[167] Manley tried to salvage the movement by proposing what Citrine had suggested earlier, namely the formation of a trade union advisory council. Bustamante and Coombs agreed and Richards accepted the idea. On 20 February the strike notices were withdrawn, Richards ended the state of emergency at midnight, and the next day the advisory council's formation was publicly announced, with N.N. Nethersole as its Chairman. At a public meeting at the Kingston Race Course on 25 February 1939, the chief speakers were Bustamante, Coombs and Manley. According to the *Jamaica Standard*,

> A historic scene was witnessed...when before thousands of labourers, shouting themselves hoarse, the union of Jamaica's two rival labour chiefs, Alexander Bustamante and A.G.S. Coombs was at long last accomplished as they shook hands, embraced warmly, and pledged themselves to fight together and as never before in the cause of labour.[168]

Richard Hart, who was the provisional secretary of the Advisory Council, describes this public reconciliation as one-sided because Bustamante was less generous to Coombs[169] than the latter was in his praise for Bustamante. 'The truce between Bustamante and Coombs had not solved all the problems of a divided labour movement, but it was a step in the right direction', according to Hart. However, Bustamante regarded the truce 'as a temporary expedient' to save him from the trouble caused by the failure of the strike he had so impulsively called.[170] Glasspole became the secretary of the Advisory Council in March and it was renamed the Jamaica Trades Union Council in April. The affiliated unions were the BITU, the JWTU, the Montego Bay Clerks Association, the Northern Longshoremen Union, the Northern Fruit Clerks Association, the Builders and Allied Trades Union and the Jamaica United Clerks Association.[171]

In March a group of union members, including Lionel Lynch, challenged Bustamante to democratise his union, as he had agreed during the negotiations in February, calling for the election of officers and for proper records of union decisions and activities. Bustamante's response at a meeting in Edelweiss Park was to call them 'tools of the capitalists'. The truce soon fell apart, as Bustamante broke with the Advisory Council and 'reverted to his own way of achieving unification under his personal control—the destruction of all other organisations'.[172] When Buchanan was released from prison on 3 April he was not reinstated as general secretary of the BITU, and the post went instead to J.A.G. Edwards, a former Garveyite who had been appointed to act in his absence.[173] The public passenger transport workers split with Bustamante and formed their own union, the Tramway Transport and General Workers Union, on 23 May. Their president was Ken Hill, who had originally led the bus drivers and had brought them into the BITU but had resigned as vice-president of the BITU on 17 April. The BITU was supreme, however, and on 24 May, in order to demonstrate its continuing support, a mass demonstration was staged, honouring Bustamante and Grant as the heroes of the previous year's labour rebellion.

At about this time the Marxists, who were then quite isolated, started the Jamaica Unemployed League (JUL), with Buchanan as secretary. During its brief existence, several leaflets were issued, demanding that relief workers should be paid at the rate of 3s. 9d. per day, as recommended the previous year by the Conciliation Board, and charging that the government was undermining the general level of wages by paying them only 1s. 6d. for an eight hour day, up to four days a week for a maximum of 6s. From 10 May demonstrations prevented the implementation of this scheme as so few workers signed on that the project could not be started. By 9 June the new labour adviser, F.A. Norman, had persuaded the government to announce a reduction of the daily hours to six and a free meal to supplement the 1s. 6d. daily rate, but the weekly maximum remained at 6s. Bustamante then encouraged his unemployed followers to accept these terms and begin to register.[174]

This issue became linked with the attempt by the principal shipping companies to employ members of the Jamaican Ex-Servicemen's Union (JESU) as strike-breakers. On 16 June a crowd attacked the JESU headquarters and threw stones at the police who opened fire on the crowd. The next day, the government mobilised 400 special constables and a battle ensued in Kingston between people protesting against the government's terms of relief work and the armed forces. On 18 June police escorting members of the JESU to work at No. 2 Pier at 7.30 am were attacked by a crowd of 600. When the police opened fire, one man, who the London *Times* said 'was not one of the rioters',[175] was mortally wounded. The governor proclaimed a state of emergency on 19 June, rushed through legislation to control public meetings and demonstrations, and ordered intensive patrols of the streets. The disturbances ended.

This violence, the worst since the 1938 rebellion, occurred at the confluence of two of the chief sources of conflict, the unemployed and the dock workers. Several hundred dock workers who had been victimised since the strikes of February were looking for work on the Kingston wharves. They refused to accept the terms the government offered for relief work and objected to their places being taken by members of the JESU, whom they saw as scab workers. Their bitterness and the subsequent violence reflected not only the divisions that characterised the working class but also the determination of the shipping companies and the government to keep wages low.

However, this also exposed one of the fundamental contradictions in the functions of the colonial state and contributed to the further politicisation of the working class. On the one hand, the colonial government was forced into expanding relief work for the unemployed. In January 1939 some 12,000-14,000 people were registered as unemployed in Kingston alone, out of perhaps 50,000 in the island as a whole.[176] After the experience of the labour rebellion in 1938, the colonial government took the advice of the Colonial Office to expand relief work as an 'insurance against disorder'.[177] However, the government, on the other hand, retained its role of helping to maintain a suitable supply of cheap labour for the employers, so it was essential that the rate offered for relief work should not compete with and drive up wages in the private sector. As the wages paid for casual employment in this sector were reduced to a minimum by competition, the relief worker had to be paid at less than minimal rates. Major Orde Browne had concluded that a rate of 12s. per week was just above the minimum subsistence level for a man without dependants, so the rate allowed for relief workers was to be no more than half that, namely a maximum of 6s. per week.

The unemployed not only resented these pitifully inadequate wages, but also resented the fact that the government gave armed protection to the strike-breakers who undermined their efforts to raise wages in the private sector. The contradictions of the economy were therefore forcing the colonial government into becoming a cut-rate employer at the same time that it maintained its role as the policeman of labour for private capitalists. It was therefore not just the economic conditions of a casual labour market, characterised by poverty and insecurity, but also the expanding and highly visible role of the colonial government that politicised the working class. The fact that the government could not meet the people's demands led to this synergy between the labour and nationalist movements, as it was widely believed that economic needs and reconstruction could not be achieved without self-government. However, by the middle of 1939, these two aspects, which should have come together, remained badly divided in practice. The TUC, which was led by PNP people, could not seriously rival the BITU on the labour front, while the nationalist movement, as represented by the PNP, had lost its roots in labour. These divisions remained a serious and persistent problem in Jamaica.

Notes

1. Hart 1988: 52.
2. Post 1978: 4
3. Holt (1992) provides a useful analysis of many of the key issues in the century before the labour rebellion.
4. Gov. A.F. Richards to MacDonald, 21 Oct. 1938, CO 318/434/8.
5. Maj. Orde Browne's provisional report, 25 Jan. 1939, CO 137/837/68989.
6. From Gov. to SS, 18 May 1938, CO 137/825/68729, quoted in Post 1978: 122.
7. Post 1978: 123.
8. In CO 950/110, quoted in Post 1978: 125.
9. Post 1978: 124.
10. *Ibid.*, 131.
11. Roberts 1957: 153.
12. Clarke 1975: 30.
13. Hart 1988: 63.
14. Eaton 1975: 23.
15. *Ibid.*, 24.
16. Post 1970: 195.
17. Hart 1989: 21.
18. Post 1970: 202.
19. Nettleford 1970; Campbell 1988.
20. Post 1978: 240.
21. The quotes in this account are from Inspector George O'Toole to Inspector General Owen F. Wright, 22 May 1935, enclosed in Gov. Denham to Cunliffe-Lister, 30 May 1935, and *The Daily Gleaner*, 30 May 1935, CO 137/806/68557.
22. Guy S. Ewen to Denham, 25 May 1935, enclosed in Denham to Cunliffe-Lister, 30 May 1935, CO 137/806/68557.
23. *Ibid.*
24. Denham to Cunliffe-Lister, 30 May 1935, CO 137/806/68557.
25. Denham to MacDonald, 18 July 1935, CO 137/806/ 68557.
26. Minute by F.J. Howard to Sir Cosmo Parkinson, 10 July 1935, CO 137/806/68557.
27. Post 1978: 242. Coombs died in 1969, without public acknowledgement of his pioneering role.
28. *Plain Talk*, 17 Oct. 1936, quoted in Post 1978: 243.
29. The latter may have been started by Buchanan who was a master mason.
30. Quoted in Post 1978: 244.

31. Quoted in Post 1978: 244.
32. Letter in *Plain Talk*, 19 June 1937, quoted in Post 1978: 137.
33. Hart 1989: 18.
34. Letter in *Public Opinion*, 18 Dec. 1937, quoted in Post 1978: 5-6.
35. Hart 1989: 18.
36. *Idib.* 19-20.
37. Post 1978: 225.
38. Report of the Trades Union Congress of Jamaica, 30 June 1946, for report to Conference on 21 Sept. 1946, in Hart's papers, Institute of Commonwealth Studies Library, University of London, M861 (hereafter Hart papers). However, Post cites the *Jamaica Standard*, 13 May 1938, that Hill started these unions in early May 1938 (Post 1978: 350).
39. *Plain Talk*, 8 May 1937, quoted in Post 1978: 219.
40. *Plain Talk*, 28 Aug. 1937, quoted in Post 1978: 219.
41. Quoted in Post 1978: 220.
42. Denham to Parkinson, 30 July 1937, CO 318/427/13.
43. Post 1978: 119.
44. *Ibid.*, 246-48.
45. Letter in *Plain Talk*, 20 Feb. 1937, quoted in Post 1978: 248.
46. Petition published in *Plain Talk*, 30 April 1938, quoted in Post 1978: 249.
47. Post 1978: 249.
48. Eaton 1975: 1.
49. *Ibid.*, 14-15.
50. Hill 1976.
51. *Plain Talk* 3 July 1937, quoted in Post 1978: 256.
52. Post 1978: 255.
53. Hart 1989: 30.
54. Bakan 1990: 101.
55. Denham to SS, 20 Sept. 1937, CO 137/820/68868.
56. Phelps 1960: 422.
57. Copy of 17 April telegram in Denham to MacDonald, 21 May 1938, CO 318/430/5.
58. *Ibid.*
59. *Jamaica Standard*, 21 April 1938, quoted in Post 1978: 276.
60. Phelps 1960: 424.
61. *Report of the Commission appointed to enquire into the Disturbances which occurred on Frome Estate in Westmoreland on 2nd May, 1938* (Kingston, 1938), p.1; hereafter, Frome Report.
62. Phelps 1960: 423.
63. Notes on Tate & Lyle's interests in the West Indies, 8 Feb. 1938, enclosed in Charles Watney to Ormsby-Gore, 15 Feb. 1938, CO 318/432/5.
64. Frome Report, p.8.
65. Post 1978: 277.
66. *Ibid.*
67. Frome Report.
68. As burnt cane can be salvaged if harvested quickly, the firing of canefields should not necessarily be understood as sabotage but may be a way for workers to try to hasten a settlement.
69. Hart 1989: 38.
70. *Daily Gleaner* 3 May 1938, quoted in Hart 1989: 39.
71. *Daily Gleaner* 4 May 1938.
72.

The editor, William Makin, wrote a book, *Caribbean Nights* (1939), about his Jamaican experience.

73. *Daily Gleaner* 4 May 1938, quoted in Hart 1989: 41.
74. Hart 1989: 41.
75. Denham to MacDonald, 21 May 1938, CO 318/430/5.
76. Phelps 1960: 425.
77. Post 1978: 277.
78. Phelps 1960: 425.
79. Hart 1989: 123.
80. St Pierre 1978: 185.
81. Hart 1989: 43.
82. Smith, born in 1893, worked for five years in the Canal Zone and 33 years in the USA, where he became vice-president of the NMU in 1937 and national executive secretary in 1939. Deported to England in 1951, he returned to Jamaica in 1952 and continued to be involved in trade union organising.
83. *Daily Gleaner*, 23 May 1938.
84. St Pierre 1978: 186.
85. *Report of the Commission appointed to enquire into the Disturbances which occurred in Jamaica between the 23rd May, and the 8th June, 1938* (Kingston, 1938), hereafter Jamaica Disturbances Report, pp.4-5.
86. Hart 1989: 48.
87. Hart's diary, typed copy in Institute of Commonwealth Studies library, University of London.
88. *Ibid.*
89. Phelps 1960: 426.
90. Hart's diary.
91. Jamaica Disturbances Report, p.5.
92. *Ibid.*, p.6.
93. Hart 1989: 52.
94. *Ibid.*
95. Jamaica Disturbances Report, p.6.
96. Hart 1989: 53.
97. *Daily Gleaner*, 25 May 1938.
98. Hart 1989: 54.
99. Manley (1973), quoted in Hart 1989: 55.
100. Quoted in Hart 1989: 57.
101. *Ibid.*
102. Nettleford 1971: 26.
103. Hart 1989: 60.
104. Phelps 1960: 427.
105. *Daily Gleaner*, 26 May 1938, quoted in Hart 1989: 60.
106. Hart 1989: 61.
107. *Ibid.*, 66.
108. *Daily Gleaner*, 27 May 1938, quoted in Hart 1989: 67.
109. *Daily Gleaner*, 27 May 1938, quoted in Hart 1989: 70.
110. *Daily Gleaner*, 27 May 1938, quoted in Hart 1989: 68-69.
111. Hart 1989: 69.
112. *Daily Gleaner*, 27 May 1938, quoted in Hart 1989: 73.
113. Phelps 1960: 428.
114. Jamaica Disturbances Report, p.7.

115.*Daily Gleaner,* 27 May 1938, quoted in Hart 1989: 74-75.

116. Hart 1989: 76.

117.*Ibid.,* 78.

118. Nettleford 1971: 27.

119. Hart 1989: 79.

120. Makin had earlier realised that Bustamante had actually 'discouraged rioting' and attempted negotiations. 'Bustamante may not be the leader that all men want,' he wrote, 'but he is the only leader available to them.' *Jamaica Standard,* 25 May 1938, quoted in Post 1978: 288.

121. Nettleford 1971: 27.

122. Hart 1989: 82-83.

123. Quoted in Post 1978: 282.

124. Jamaica Disturbances Report, p.10.

125. He was never able to work again and died a pauper; Hart 1989: 91.

126. Jamaica Disturbances Report, pp.10-14.

127.*Jamaica Standard,* 4 June 1938, quoted in Post 1978: 283.

128. Post 1978: 284.

129. Hart 1989: 94.

130. Jamaica Disturbances Report, p.1.

131.*Ibid.*

132.*Jamaica Standard* and *Daily Gleaner,* 30 May 1938, quoted in Post 1978: 291.

133. Hart 1989: 105.

134. Richard Hart to Jaime O'Meally, 1 June 1938, Hart papers.

135.*Jamaica Labour Weekly,* 9 July 1938, quoted in Hart 1989: 100.

136. Hart 1989: 102.

137.*Ibid.,* 104.

138. Mintz 1974: 151.

139. Lobdell 1988: 200.

140. Undated memo. prepared for answer to Parliamentary question by Mr Day on 30 March 1938, CO 318/427/3.

141. Post 1978: 293.

142. Quoted in Post 1978: 293.

143. Woolley to SS, 5 June 1938, CO 137/826/68868.

144. Post 1978: 296.

145. Quoted in Hart 1989: 97.

146.*Jamaica Standard,* 6 June 1938, quoted in Post 1978: 294.

147. Woolley to SS, 7 June 1938, CO 137/826/68868.

148.*Jamaica Standard,* 25 May 1938, cited in Post 1978: 249.

149. Minute by J.H. Emmens, 23 June 1938, CO 137/827/68868.

150. Woolley to Sir Henry Moore, 3 Aug. 1938, CO 137/826/68868.

151. Hart 1989: 96.

152.*Daily Gleaner,* 27 Aug. 1938.

153. Hart 1989: 118.

154. Nettleford 1971: 28.

155. Hart 1989: 114.

156.*Ibid.,* 115-16.

157.'This decision, though largely ignored in practice, was not formally reversed until the party's Second Annual Conference on August 28, 1940.' Hart 1989: 143.

158. Hart to O'Meally, 1 June 1938, Hart papers.

159. Domingo and O'Meally's JPL in New York joined Manley's new PNP in September.

160.Eaton 1975: 60.

161.An attempt to create a similar paper, called *The Worker*, edited first by Arthur Henry and then Frank Hill, lasted only a few weeks, between November 1939 and early 1940; see Hart 1989: 123-25.

162.Post 1978: 395.

163.Eaton 1975: 69.

164.*Ibid.*, 61.

165.Hart 1989: 127.

166.*Ibid.*, 128.

167.Gov. Sir Arthur Richards to SS, 16 Feb. 1939, CO 137/836/68868.

168.Quoted in Hart 1989: 131.

169.Bustamante is reported to have said, 'The reason why Mr. Coombs is here is not because I personally need him, but because it was necessary for all branches of labour to unite for the good of Jamaica.' Quoted in Eaton 1975: 76.

170.Hart 1989: 133.

171.Report of the TUC, 30 June 1946, Hart papers.

172.Hart 1989: 133.

173.*Ibid.*, 134.

174.Post 1978: 423.

175.*The Times*, 20 June 1939, quoted in Hart 1989: 135.

176.Post 1978: 420.

177.Quoted in Post 1978: 438.

Chapter TWELVE

Antigua

Labour unrest, though not a labour rebellion as such, occurred in Antigua, which was 'one of the more quiet areas of the region' between 1934 and 1938.[1] As elsewhere, earlier unrest had petered out without resulting in any lasting organisations. Workers used friendly societies and lodges for political and economic purposes in the early twentieth century. At one of these, the Antigua Progressive Union, there was in 1917 a discussion of wages and the Contract Act, the means by which the planters recruited and secured their labour. At the end of the First World War, a central factory was able to pay its workers slightly higher wages than the planters who owned small estates, so many workers felt the estate owners were not paying them enough. One estate worker recalled bitterly, 'After the nega reap the cane, the estate owner use to collect the money for it from the factory and pay the croppers what the owner decide was enough. Crop after crop them robbed us'.[2] In 1918 some sugar workers went on strike and battled against the police. As old Samuel Smith recalled, the reinforcement of the police by the militia and the defence force made it, in Antigua as elsewhere, more of a racial confrontation:

> The massas call out the militia and when they come the riot really spread. No longer was it riot between the Point people and the police, now it was between nega and white. The militia and the defence force—except for a few high-coloured police—was all white.[3]

After reading the Riot Act, the armed forces fired on the demonstrators and several people were wounded. According to Smith, people were intimidated by this violence:

> I think it was after the riot that the people of Antigua got to be afraid of guns. Everything went still. Small farmers decided to make out, no more public grumbling from them. Them just grunt and bear it. No more refusal to work from anybody—at least that I know of—for quite a while.[4]

One of the workers' leaders in 1918 was George Weston, who subsequently became a vice-president of Garvey's UNIA in New York. On return visits to

Antigua he spoke of Garvey and pan-Africanism at the local UNIA branch, trying to keep alive a degree of community politicisation.

An effort to create an organisation oriented toward the working class was made by Harold Wilson when he formed the Antigua Workingmen's Association (AWA) in 1933, but it 'had only a small impact'.[5] While the labour rebellions elsewhere between 1934 and 1938 largely passed Antigua by, people were certainly aware of them. The governor of the Leeward Islands reported that, before the rebellions in Trinidad and Barbados in 1937, a strike among Antiguan dock workers at the end of April 'collapsed after small increases of pay were given and alternative supplies of labour found', but that there was 'an indefinite restlessness' among Antiguan workers.[6] At the end of July, he reported anxiously that 'no immediate indications of trouble are evident but that possibility cannot be excluded'.[7] From the opposite end of the social spectrum, Samuel Smith recalled,

> news were reaching Antigua of disturbances in the other islands, something that the Antigua planters take very seriously. A whole lot of them gather at the great house at Collin's to talk about the riots in the other islands. At that meeting the bakkra pledge to do everything to keep that kind of thing from reaching Antigua.[8]

The Contract Act was repealed in 1937 and the colonial government announced the Antigua Recovery Programme that included a small land settlement scheme for peasants and an expansion in public works activities, such as road construction.[9]

The visit of the Royal Commission to Antigua stimulated labour activities and the formation of the first trade union. In the early months of 1939, labour unrest was reported to be common, 'with sporadic strikes in numerous sections of the labouring community'.[10] On 27 March a dispute at the Antigua Sugar Factory started a wider disturbance. The strikers wanted to form a union to represent them in their demand for higher wages but, according to Governor Lethem, 'it does not appear that this embryo trade union had in any way engineered the strike'.[11] On the evening of 28 March a pay rise of 20-25 per cent was conceded and work resumed but the next day workers at a smaller factory, known as Bendals, went on strike to claim a similar raise. Workers from the factory joined field workers from various estates and waterfront workers, and some travelled in bands armed with sticks and cutlasses from one estate to another to promote a general strike. Some cane fires were set and work stopped for two days. The police and defence force were mobilised, reinforced by an officer and ten men from St Kitts, and despatched to the estates. Eleven arrests were made, but there were no violent confrontations. Two weeks elapsed before these factory workers received a small raise and returned to work, but other workers got no increase. Lethem admitted that the wages of agricultural workers were 'definitely low' but thought the estates could not afford to pay more. Bendals, which was already in difficulties, soon sold out to the Antigua Sugar Factory. On 9 April the dock workers and porters went on strike, demanding a substantial raise. After a committee of inquiry was appointed they returned to work on 12 April. An increase was granted, though not so much as was demanded. On 3 May the Antigua Sugar Factory workers struck again, but the government insisted this was 'utterly irresponsible' and they returned to work immediately. [12]

The labour officer, who had been appointed in November 1938, failed to win the confidence of either the employers or those who were emerging as labour leaders, and in May the members of the Legislative Council who had been elected in 1936 voted against him. One of these men was Reginald Stevens, a middle-class politician, described by Smith as a 'brown-skinned man' and 'a big man in the Odd Fellows Lodge'.[13] Soon after the commission's visit, during which Sir Walter Citrine spoke of the value of trade unionism, Norris Allen, who had experience of unions in the United States, brought together several men to create the Antigua Trades and Labour Union (ATLU). These men included Stevens, who became the first president, Berkeley Richards, the general secretary, Harold Wilson of the AWA and Vere Bird, who later replaced Stevens and soon became the chief figure in Antigua's politics. The Trade Union Act, No. 16 of 1939, was modelled on British legislation and contained 'provisions for the immunity of trade union funds in relation to actions for tort and for permitting peaceful picketing'.[14] The ATLU held its first annual conference in February 1940 and was officially registered on 3 March 1940. The creation of the ATLU, which 'marked a very important turning point in the political organization of Antigua workers',[15] thus came about relatively peacefully, but these developments in Antigua were largely the result of the impact of the labour movement in the British Caribbean as a whole.

Notes

1. Henry 1985: 84.
2. Smith and Smith 1989: 129.
3. *Ibid.*, 131-32.
4. *Ibid.*, 133.
5. Henry 1985: 83.
6. Gov. of Leewards to SS, 29 July 1937, CO 318/427/11.
7. Gov. of Leewards to SS, 30 July 1937, CO 318/427/11.
8. Smith and Smith 1989: 142.
9. Henry 1985: 85.
10. Gov. Lethem to SS, 19 March 1940, CO 318/439/12.
11. Lethem to SS, 8 Nov. 1939, CO 152/485/61760.
12. *Ibid.*
13. Smith and Smith 1989: 144.
14. Lethem to SS, 19 March 1940, CO 318/439/12.
15. Henry 1985: 86.

Chapter THIRTEEN

Guyana

Although Guyana[1] did not experience a massive labour rebellion such as occurred in Trinidad, Barbados or Jamaica, it certainly shared the characteristics and consequences of similar rebelliousness in the 1930s. Indeed, the history of persistent labour militancy and labour organisations is longer in Guyana than elsewhere in the British Caribbean.

Walter Rodney writes critically of the tendency among those who trace the origins of trade unionism in Guyana 'to skim over the last decades of the nineteenth century'[2] and to commence with the years after the First World War or, sometimes, to start with the riots of 1905. Certainly, 'it was in the late nineteenth century that the modern political economy of Guyana took shape', and this constitutes the context within which the Guyanese working people began to shape itself into a class, as Rodney eloquently describes, through extensive political struggles. However, as he himself writes, in the 1905 riots 'spontaneity was much more evident than organization',[3] so the history of organised labour may be said to have commenced in 1919 with the formation of the British Guiana Labour Union (BGLU).

The strikes, demonstrations and riots of 1905 did indeed 'set the stage for advance toward trade union organization',[4] but such organisation emerged on a lasting basis only in 1919. Subsequently, a series of sporadic but persistent strikes and demonstrations by the Guyanese working people gave rise to the formation of 12 more trade unions in the 1930s. While Guyana has the longest history of continuous organised labour and a record of great labour militancy, by 1939 the labour movement was not as strong there as it was in Jamaica or Trinidad. Among the reasons for this are that Guyanese labour organisations came to reflect the racial or ethnic segmentation of the population and they were not linked to any broader nationalist movement in the colony at that time. There were, however, growing links between some labour organisations in Guyana and those in other West Indian colonies, and these links were largely inspired and promoted by Guyana's labour leaders. It was in Guyana, in this period, that the foundations were laid for the Caribbean Labour Congress.

Guyana is an unusual part of the British Caribbean, less because of its continental location than its population distribution. Apart from the indigenous people of the interior, most of the colony's population became concentrated in the coastal belt that was drained and cultivated to produce sugar. While the overall population density remained low, therefore, the pattern of colonisation concentrated about 90 per cent of the people into the 4 per cent of the total land area that constitutes this coastal belt. The planters maintained political hegemony after the termination of apprenticeship in 1838 and used a combination of legal sanctions and massive immigration to keep their control over labour. Protracted strikes on the sugar estates by former slaves in the 1840s were defeated and planters reduced wages and turned to indentured immigration from Madeira, Africa, China and India. Portuguese immigration peaked in 1846 and African and Chinese immigration virtually ceased in the 1860s, but Indian immigration continued until 1917. The several thousand indentured immigrants who were brought to Guyana in the 1840s were so successful for the planters that annual shipments occurred without interruption between 1851 and 1917. The introduction of a further 228,743 Indians in this period dramatically changed the racial and cultural composition of the colony's population. By the 1890s the newer immigrants amounted to 43.6 per cent of the total population and the fact that they were brought to Guyana in order to supplant the former slaves and to reduce their wages 'created an atmosphere of suspicion and animosity between these ethnic sections'. [5]

Though all these working people were being exploited, they were pitted against each other in ways that tended to increase competition and communalism. However, actual conflict was minimal. As Brian Moore argues, the absence of serious communal conflict between Guyanese of Indian and African origin in these early decades 'did not mean an absence of serious conflict...at a localized and individual level'. Moreover, 'the incidence of communal conflict was kept to a minimum by the high degree of physical separatism which characterized the coexistence of these two large differentiated ethnic groups, but which at the same time accentuated and perpetuated their social and cultural differences'.[6] Tragically, one of the ideas that these people came to share, which was derived from the dominant colonial culture, was that racial differences and identities were primordial and paramount. To the extent to which this idea was shared, then, it promoted ethnic divisions in the colonial society, including divisions in labour organisations. Despite the fact that the working people of Guyana were in the same leaky colonial boat, or perhaps because they were put in the situation of competing with each other for their places in that boat, their labour organisations came to reflect the ethnic segmentation of the wider society, and the more divided the labour movement, the weaker it was.

The discovery of bauxite about 70 miles up the Demerara River from Georgetown led to the establishment of the Demerara Bauxite Company, a subsidiary of Alcan/Alcoa, and the company town of Mackenzie, now Linden, during the First World War. In the 1920s and 1930s, however, the Guyanese economy remained largely agricultural, producing chiefly sugar and rice. In 1931, only 2,867 labourers, or less than 3 per cent of all wage-earners, worked in mines and quarries, compared with 46 per cent in agriculture.[7] The vast majority of sugar and rice workers were Indian, some of them immigrants who still spoke only Indian languages. Though unindentured Indian adults resident on the estates already outnumbered indentured immigrants by 1880, the last indentures were cancelled on 15 April 1920.[8] The interests of the Indian indentured workers were supposed to be looked after by an official Protector of Immigrants until the post was abolished in 1932. The presence of such indentured labour had a depressing effect on wage rates not only because they were the lowest paid workers but also because of the fact that these bound labourers reduced the ability of other workers to bargain for wage increases.

The combination of low wages and a sharp rise in the cost of living during the First World War led to many labour disturbances and the creation of the BGLU in 1919, but no other union was registered in the 1920s. The dramatic effect of falling sugar prices in the depression after 1929 provoked demonstrations in Georgetown in February 1930, and on 28 January 1931 a second trade union, the British Guiana Workers' League (BGWL), was registered. Led by A.A. Thorne, a Barbadian, this union lasted until 1951, but its membership was less than 500 until the 1940s. Most members were sugar factory workers, or municipal, hospital and other government employees in Georgetown, and were predominantly of African descent.

As the depression worsened, hundreds of Guyanese migrated to Georgetown to look for work, thereby increasing job competition in the capital. The government started some road work to relieve unemployment in 1930 but paid only 50 cents for a nine hour day. In 1931 the BGLU pressed for a dole for the unemployed, and when the colonial government rejected this demand the union continued to agitate. A march was held on 11 May 1933, and a rally was planned in Georgetown for 1 August, the anniversary of emancipation, 'to celebrate National and International Day of Solidarity'. The BGLU's publicity called for workers to prepare themselves for the coming struggle: 'Emancipate yourself from Imperialist and Capitalist economic slavery'.[9] Governor Denham dictated that 'no demonstrations would be allowed' and 'everything passed off quite quietly'. Nevertheless, Denham was concerned about the situation and felt that without 'the assistance given from home for works to relieve the situation... there would undoubtedly have been disturbances to be quelled by force'.[10] On Monday, 14 August, the BGLU organised a token 'Down Tools Day' as part of their struggle for an eight hour day and a 44-hour week, without a reduction in pay. Though the 'Down Tools Day' did not have the intended impact on the Legislative Council, which met on the next day, a strike among sugar workers at Diamond Estate, demanding the removal of the manager and large wage increases, continued until early in October.[11] Members of the East Indian Association, a largely middle-class group, provided food for the strikers and asked the government to support arbitration. The strike ended without violence, but 17 employees were convicted of intimidating non-strikers in the fields. According to the governor, 'The influence of Mr Critchlow and his supporters has undoubtedly been considerably weakened by the failure of the demonstration and strike', but he continued to be concerned that the thousands of unemployed in Georgetown 'form ready material on which agitators can work'.[12] A Workmen's Compensation Ordinance was passed in 1934, but its value was limited as about 75 per cent of the workers, including all agricultural and domestic workers, were excluded.

The depression persisted through the mid-1930s. In 1935 the yield of sugar per acre reached 3.02 tons, a record, and the total output was another record, namely 178,041 tons, compared with the previous record of 148,634 tons in 1932. However, while the total yield and the yield per acre increased substantially in the 1920s and 1930s, the falling price of sugar meant that the gross receipts for sugar, and even of sugar per acre, were falling. Thus, the average annual gross receipts for sugar per acre between 1921 and 1928 were $166.70, whereas between 1929 and 1935 they were $117.70, though the average yield per acre in those periods had increased from 1.96 tons to 2.55 tons of sugar.[13] The sugar workers were producing more sugar, and producing it more efficiently, but they continued to receive the same low wages. The result, in terms of housing, diet and nutrition was appalling. Many sugar workers continued to live in run-down and overcrowded barracks left over from the indenture period, surrounded by stagnant water and without adequate sanitation or water supplies. A visitor to Guyana in 1936 reported that 'The diet is mainly starch foods.... Milk foods are lamentably lacking...generally speaking, a child once weaned never tastes milk again'. And, as someone in the Colonial Office noted on this report, 'milk is beyond the reach of the labouring classes, even where available'.[14] As the economic crisis continued, serious disturbances broke out on several sugar estates in 1934 and 1935.

In the 1930s Indians, who formed 42.3 per cent of the Guyanese population, constituted 44 per cent of all wage earners. However, they were overrepresented in sugar and rice production and underrepresented in most other occupations: 75 per cent of all agricultural wage earners were Indian, whereas they were only 19 per cent of wage earners in the public services, clerks and shop assistants and transport workers, 14 per cent of mechanics, artisans, and engine drivers, 8 per cent of domestic servants, and 2 per cent of wage-earners in mining, quarrying and forest work. [15]

Not only was there a great deal of ethnic segmentation of wage-earners between economic sectors but there were also substantial differences in the occupations and wages paid within these sectors. Resident estate labourers were almost entirely Indian but many non-residents who lived in villages worked in the factories or cutting the cane, and a higher proportion of these were of African descent. Whereas the average annual wage for all workers in the sugar industry in 1935 was said to be $112, that for Indians was less than $98, so the minority of sugar workers who were of African descent were better paid. Moreover, while the average earnings of all workers increased slightly between 1931 and 1935, those of Indians declined. The average weekly earnings of Indian resident labourers between 1925 and 1928 was $2.03, corresponding to annual average earnings of $105.69. This fell to $1.92 and $99.84, respectively, in 1929, and fell further to an average of $1.74 weekly and $90.27 annually between 1930 and 1934. The agitation and strikes in 1934 and 1935 raised these rates slightly in 1935, to $1.88 and $99.76, respectively, but this was still less than the workers had received ten years before. There were also significant wage differentials between occupations on the sugar estates. For example, the best paid African male cane cutters in 1935 could earn $1.39 per day, while Indian male cane cutters received no more than $1.05 per day. All other African male field workers (including punt loaders, cane transporters, fork and shovel workers, trench cleaners and weeders) received 61-82 cents per day and Indian male field workers were paid 52-77 cents per day for the same jobs. Women field workers' pay ranged from a maximum of 90 cents for Indian cane cutters to a minimum of 24 cents for those who worked at grass banking. In the factory, average daily earnings (not distinguished by the workers' ethnicity) varied from $1.05 for fitters to 50 cents for unskilled labourers, with engine drivers, blacksmiths and carpenters receiving 73, 89 and 90 cents, respectively.[16]

The distinctions and competitions between workers made it extremely hard to organise labour across ethnic lines, even in the general economic crisis of the 1930s when the vast majority of the working people, whether employed or unemployed, and whatever their skill, ethnicity or gender, suffered so badly. The fact that Guyanese sugar factory workers and cane cutters of African descent did join Indian sugar workers on several occasions and that there were no reported cases of conflict between these communities, is eloquent testimony to the growth of class consciousness in Guyana in these years.

Surprisingly little has been written about the labour rebellion in Guyana in the mid-1930s. Some Colonial Office files were destroyed[17] but much material remains on industrial unrest and labour disturbances in these years. According to a report by J. Nicole, a county inspector and district commissioner, 'there was a noticeable undercurrent of unrest' on several sugar estates in September 1934.[18] The trouble began at Plantation Leonora on the West Coast of Demerara, one of several estates owned by the Demerara Company and managed by the local agents, Sandbach, Parker and Company, whose relations with Leonora dated from the nineteenth century. On 7 September about 600 shovelmen quit work and complained to Mr Lywood, the manager, about the price being paid, which would not enable them to earn more than 20-24 cents per day. They also complained that the work was not priced when it was allocated, that the overseers and deputy manager cursed workers unnecessarily, and that the head driver, Hassanalli, 'was overbearing and did as he pleased'. Nicole added that he thought the removal on the same day of the three senior staff members, to whom the workers felt 'they could carry their troubles', and the refusal of the new manager to participate in a system by which labourers contributed from their wages to a local Hindu temple, contributed to the trouble. This is a fairly typical mixture of grievances, including as it did concerns over pay rates and relations with management. It is clear that the workers felt abused in several ways. On 10 September, a 'noisy and excited crowd of over 1,500' demanded Hassanalli's immediate dismissal and, saying that they did not want the manager or his deputy on the estate either, roughed them up and drove them off. Nicole sent for 12 police to keep order but the strikers refused to return to work until 12 September, after Hassanalli had been dismissed and the deputy manager had quit the firm. But that same day 200 people left work when a driver assaulted a labourer. They returned only after Nicole told them the driver had been charged with assault and locked up. These workers, in the absence of any formal procedures for expressing their grievances, were finding an effective way of dealing with abuses by management.

On 21 September, between 250–300 workers, shovelmen, punt-loaders and weeders, from Plantation Uitvlugt, owned by Booker Bros, which owned and managed most of Guyana's plantations, came to Nicole. They, too, 'complained about the low prices paid for work and the fact that work was not being priced when allocated'. The next day the whole estate was on strike and when the manager tried to re-start grinding over 2,000 strikers 'made an ugly rush towards the factory'. Nicole called for 'every available man to come armed with ammunition' and the factory was started under 'a strong armed guard'. The workers, like those at Leonora, 'complained against several drivers and the punt-loaders asked for adjustments to their pay, hours of work and the amount of load per punt'. Some of these demands reflect the distinctive nature of the organisation and tasks of sugar production in Guyana, but the general problem was essentially the same as elsewhere, namely too little pay for too much work and resentment about the abusive behaviour of supervisors.

No sooner had the workers at Uitvlugt returned to work on 24 September than, the next day, those at two other estates, De Kinderen and Tuschen, also belonging to Booker Bros, went on strike. The manager at Uitvlugt claimed his workers had 'gone absolutely mad' and had tried to beat him. By 26 September all three estates were on strike and pickets turned back the few who turned up to work. At De Kinderen, Nicole found a large and threatening crowd and when he urged them to return to work 'about a dozen men, blacks and East Indians, shouted that they must not believe me and that no one must work'. The next day some strikers assaulted a driver and two workers whom they 'suspected of carrying news to the Manager'. Three people were arrested that night and, after 'several displays of force' and three more arrests, the people 'were subdued and frightened'. What Nicole's report shows is that, though the workers could still be forced into submission, there was in 1934 a mood of anger and a willingness to engage in militant action on the estates.

The acting governor commented early in 1935 that, while these disturbances had never got 'out of hand', they, as well as other disputes on other estates in the colony, showed there was 'a growing spirit of unrest amongst the labourers'. He attributed this in part to the new generation of Indian workers, Guyanese Indians who could read and write English and who 'are beginning to realise the benefits which can be obtained by collective bargaining'.[19] Resentment about the arrogant style of supervision, along with the demand that workers be informed about the rate of pay at the time tasks were assigned, were major sources of dissatisfaction, and a contributing factor was that the workers knew many managers had been paid considerable bonuses in the previous two or three years and felt 'it should be also possible to increase slightly the wages paid to them'.[20] Finally, the acting governor thought that managers on the sugar estates should deal with most 'ordinary labour troubles' without invoking the aid of government and should seek police protection only as a last resort if life and property were threatened.

It is well known that serious trouble, which might otherwise have been avoided, may be created by the premature interference by Police Forces.... The premature invoking of outside assistance must have the effect of reducing the authority of the management over its employees.... It is quite evident that the troubles which recently occurred on the West Coast, Demerara, were the result of tactless handling by those in authority. [21]

These remarks proved prophetic of the tragedy at Leonora in 1939. However, while such tactless handling surely contributed, the fact that the troubles were more deeply rooted became evident as they spread in 1935.

Heavy floods on the East Coast of Demerara in January 1934 had destroyed some of the small farms and livestock of workers in that area, making them even more dependent on wage labour. Several hundred villagers, mostly of African descent, obtained government work repairing sea defences until March 1935, but had to then join all the others who sought employment in that year's sugar harvest. The workers anticipated it would be a bumper year because they could see 'the unprecedented heavy stands of cane'[22] resulting from the enrichment of the land by the floods, and they expected a share in this apparent prosperity. Agents of the BGLU had been active in the area and Critchlow was said to have encouraged the sugar workers to hold out for better wages at harvest time. While the demand for higher wages was a major factor in these disturbances, understandably, as most people's wages had been declining since 1929, at least as important was the workers' resentment about the way they were treated by the drivers and managers. Many of the disputes were triggered by anger about the way they were paid, or because wages they thought were due were withheld, added to which was the abuse they suffered. What lay behind this growing unrest was generally a combination of demands for better pay and working conditions along with demands for rights as workers and dignity as human beings.

In no case did the BGLU call a strike, nor were these workers organised; on the contrary, their actions seem to have been almost entirely spontaneous and local, though there was a certain amount of imitation by the workers of adjacent estates and villages. We can also see that various categories of workers were joining together and increasingly forging a common purpose and united strategy; between field and factory workers, estate residents and villagers, women and men, and Guyanese of African and Indian origin. Though some workers did intimidate others to join them in strike action from time to time, the only recorded violence was that directed against their supervisory personnel, often Europeans, who were sometimes beaten and humiliated. However much the plantation system had divided these workers in the past, their actions in this period indicate a growing class consciousness as they united against managers, employers and police. The lines that were hardening in the course of these confrontations in the 1930s were class not ethnic lines.

The labour unrest in September and October 1935 was described as 'continuous though sporadic'.[23] There were strikes on the West Coast of Demerara and in Berbice but the most militant were on the East Coast of Demerara. On 30 August workers at Plantation Leonora, where there had been trouble the previous year, complained that their head overseer, Mr Rigden, was 'too pressing' and demanded his removal. They said he habitually cursed and abused them and was 'cruel' to them. They also complained that they were not told the price to be paid for task work until it was almost completed and objected to the long hours in the factory, and that mule boys who got home at 1 am and had to be out again by 3 am were getting only two hours sleep in 24. 'Most stress however was laid upon abuse by Mr. Rigden whom they wanted dismissed'.[24] On 2 September, the workers, armed with sticks, said that 'if Mr.

Rigden was not off the estate by 11 a.m. they would make a row',[25] and everyone went on strike. The next day a deputation of 300–400 strikers met the estate's attorney at the district commissioner's office. There they raised more complaints, including some about the treatment of women, saying in particular that old women should not have to walk long distances to get to their assigned work places and that pregnant women should be allocated lighter work. The main complaint was still about Rigden's abusive behaviour, but the attorney refused to dismiss him. Later that day some canefields were fired and over 1,000 tons of cane burnt. Work did not resume in full at Leonora until 10 September.

The commissioners concluded that another contributory cause of the strike at Leonora was the system called 'Jeribandan', by which workers were defrauded of part of their earnings by drivers who assigned their cronies to complete other workers' tasks at the end of the week and then took a portion of the pay. This was a widespread abuse on sugar estates where the workers were assigned tasks that would take several days to complete instead of daily tasks. All the workers involved in this strike were Indian, and it is clear that men spoke up for women and village people spoke up for estate residents. The latter is particularly significant as estate residents, who were the tenants as well as the employees of the estate, felt so vulnerable to victimisation that not a single one came forward to give evidence to the commission about any of the disturbances. The commissioners bluntly stated that the obvious reason was their fear, 'the fear of retaliatory action and possible eviction from house and subsistence plot with but three days notice…and the knowledge that no alternative means of earning a livelihood is readily available'.[26] (In this connection it is worth noting that three lawyers of the British Guiana Sugar Producers' Association were present at all the commission's meetings, which would have intimidated many workers, particularly the estate residents.) A few villagers did come forward, however, presumably because they felt a little more independent. One of these was a man named Basdeo who, with his brother Arjun, had taken prominent parts in the strike at Leonora in 1934. After being refused employment at Leonora he had sought work on an estate in Berbice, some 60 miles away, under an assumed name, and had succeeded in this for seven weeks. When a suspicious manager had his photograph taken to verify his identity, Basdeo returned to his village near Leonora, but found it hard to earn a livelihood. He and three other villagers, Assick, Sookdeo and Manna Singh, 'expressed the hope after giving their evidence they would not suffer through having come forward'.[27] The commissioners heard complaints of Rigden's 'harsh, exacting, autocratic and unsympathetic treatment'. A woman, for example, complained that he had caught her fishing and destroyed her seine, then fined her husband 2s. and told him that if he did not like it he could leave the estate. The commissioners concluded that such acts would 'account for the animosity directed against the perpetrator culminating with a unanimous wish for his removal'.[28]

These examples are included at some length because it is through such details that we learn more of what the workers had to contend with and why they responded as they did. There is often a sense of accumulated frustration, of a whole series of overlapping complaints that spill over from work situations to community and social life, any one of which may not seem major but that together eventually tip the balance and provoke the workers to risk strike action. It is also clear, in Guyana as elsewhere in the 1930s, that the workers had no other recourse so long as there were no established procedures or institutions to enable them to express their grievances without fear of victimisation. This left strike action as virtually the only way they could get something done about their problems.

Several other strikes occurred in the next few weeks on Plantations Vryheids Lust and La Bonne Intention between 11 September and 20 October, at Plantation Enmore between 18 and 24 September, at Lusignan between 7 and 17 October, at Plantation Ogle between 8 and 15 October, at Plantation Farm between 15 and 22 October, and also at seven plantations in Berbice between 11 and 14 October.

At Vryheids Lust the shovel gang, comprised entirely of Indians, stopped work when told the price offered, and a few days after threatened to beat Ramsingh, a driver who was cheating them. Others demanded increases in the rates for loading a punt, for half-banking and planting. The manager made some small concessions and suspended Ramsingh on half pay pending investigations into his conduct. On 30 September, a gang of cane cutters refused the rate offered and demanded to know the price before they commenced work. One of the problems, the commissioners thought, was that 'the growth of cane is often very unevenly distributed in fields and that a flat rate might operate very unfairly to workers'.[29] These cane cutters, who were all villagers and mostly African, made sure estate workers would not be brought to cut the canes, saying that 'they had planted the canes and were not going to permit others to reap them'.[30] On 2 October, 22 policemen were brought in to escort 80 estate workers to cut cane but some of the villagers chased them off. The next day the manager agreed to a higher rate as the canes were deteriorating and there was then 'a scramble for the work'. News then came that some gangs intended to stop the factory, so more policemen were brought to the estate. A crowd of about 400 strikers, armed with sticks and cutlasses, waving flags and beating drums, got into the factory and stopped the mills, but when the manager pleaded with them that the estate could not afford to pay any more the factory was re-started and the demonstrators quietened down. When ten mounted and forty armed police arrived, however, the strikers got angry and accused the manager of being responsible for this, which he denied. At La Bonne Intention, as at Vryheid Lust, workers complained about a driver and wanted him dismissed, but the manager informed them that he kept fines in his own hands and the driver was not in any way responsible.

At Plantation Enmore grinding started at the end of August. On 18 September some punt loaders demanded an increase from 9 cents to 10 cents for loading each ton of canes. The 15 punt loaders on the estate earned an average of 94.6 cents per day, so each person was loading over 10 tons of cane per day. They also complained about the long hours they had to work to earn these wages. The manager declined to make any increase, so that afternoon the punt loaders went to the cane hoist at the factory and stopped all the work. Two of them attacked a driver and broke his arm. At the district commissioner's request, 24 policemen arrived on the estate and the trouble escalated. The punt loaders were joined during the night 'by Blacks and other East Indians from adjacent villages'.[31] They picketed the entrance to the estate, cut the telephone wires and set fire to several acres of cane. When the manager tried to re-start the factory the next morning the strikers objected, shouted down the manager and the district commissioner, and 'all work on the estate was paralysed'. At 9.30 pm the electric wires were cut, plunging the factory and managerial staff residences into darkness, and more canefields were set on fire. The strikers were using their own methods of counter-intimidation. At the strikers' request, the member of the Legislative Council for the East Coast Demerara District and an Indian doctor, Dr Jung Bahadur Singh, who was the member for Western Demerara, visited the estate to investigate the complaints. In addition to demanding a general increase in wages, the strikers now asked for the dismissal of the deputy manager who was said to use 'bad language to their wives'. The next day they were told their complaints were not justified. An attempt by the strikers to involve the workers at the neighbouring estate, Non Pareil, failed because they had just got a wage increase. On 23 September, 'a large force of police' arrived early in the morning to ensure the re-start of grinding, 'the crowd melted away', and people returned to work.

At Lusignan a group of cane cutters, described as half–blacks and half–East Indians, demanded an increase in pay and the manager promptly raised their rate from 36 cents to 40 cents per opening. These men agreed to this, but soon the manager encountered about 120 other workers, beating drums and waving red flags, who demanded $1.08 an opening and a flat rate of 24 cents for cutting all canes. When the manager said that he could not agree to such a rate, they said they would not go to work and nor would anyone else. Soon after, the place was deserted and at 9 am about 100 strikers 'forced their way into the factory, drums beating, flags flying and waving cutlasses'.[32] They kept up the demonstration for about 15 minutes, with no violence and then 'danced themselves out of the factory'. By the time they returned, five police had arrived and they were kept out. They then went behind the factory, stopped a string of loaded punts and released the mules. It was not until 17 October, ten days later, that the factory could work again. On 16 October a crowd of strikers beat an overseer and forced him to march in front of them, naked to the waist and carrying a red flag. These strikers, who were Africans from nearby villages, armed with sticks and cutlasses, were shouting: 'Bad Abyssinia, all you white bitches got no business here our country you go back where you come from'.[33] One man, named Murray, ordered the overseer to dance to a drum and when he said he did not know how, they 'gave an African exhibition dance' round him, but let him go when armed police arrived. After several arrests were made, and under an armed guard of 12 police, work resumed the next day.

On Plantation Ogle on 8 October, the punt loaders obtained an increase from the manager, simplifying the payment system by eliminating extras and bonuses, and receiving instead a flat rate of 48 cents per punt, as they demanded. The next morning some shovelmen took an overseer's saddle off his horse and threw it into a trench. A 'gang of East Indians and Blacks' beat the deputy manager and forced him to carry a red flag at the head of their procession. Between 200 and 300 strikers, 'waving cutlasses and sticks and carrying red flags', said they wanted more money and the deputy manager and a driver named Manoo dismissed, as these people ill-treated them. They complained also about not being told the price before they started work, that the wages for field labour were insufficient, that they had to pay rental for their rice lands while these were free on other estates, that there was favouritism in allocating work, that reductions were made from men's wages when their wives did not work regularly, and that women were required to do unsuitable work in the water. The manager found that Manoo had indeed been 'showing favouritism' so he was transferred, but he declined to dismiss his deputy. The strikers were not satisfied so, carrying a banner saying 'War Declared', they barricaded the bridge to the estate to try to prevent mounted police from entering and prepared to 'rush the factory'. They quieted down when the police arrived, however, and a few days later, after they were told that the deputy manager was going away on leave and that some wages were to be increased, work was resumed.[34]

On Plantation Farm on 15 October, a crowd of workers, led by a former policeman named Joseph Barlow, shouted at the manager, 'We want more money'. When he said their demands were unreasonable, they shouted 'Slavery done long time' and became 'threatening in their demeanour'.[35] The next day two overseers were assaulted and by 18 October police were stationed on the estate and the overseers were sworn in as special constables. By 22 October work was returning to normal. One of the workers, a shovelman named Soobrian Singh, later gave evidence that workers felt that they could not ask for more money because if they did the overseer and driver 'would tell such a man "no work for you" ', so they could only make demands when they were emboldened as a group: 'when the strike come on they get a little pluck otherwise the game would have continued so always'.[36] Barlow himself testified that they had actually planned to strike, having decided on 12 October that if they were not told the price of work for new tasks on 15 October they would strike. He also objected that the manager had implied that if they did not like the price they should take their wives to the bars in Georgetown where they could earn money as prostitutes. 'I turned to him and said "Oh, you take us then to make slaves", and he said yes if we does not know that we are still slaves. I said if we are slaves then nobody goes to work and I will see that no man work'.[37] Barlow, who was described by the commissioners as 'a capable and industrious worker', said he went about persuading people to stop working because of these insults.

These examples show that much of the labour unrest on these Guyanese estates was about how the workers felt they were treated. Workers demanded wage increases and better working terms and conditions, of course, but they were often provoked into strike action by the attitudes and abuse of the drivers, overseers and managers who carried on in a manner reminiscent of the days of slavery and indentured labour. The workers were sensitive to this and in 1935 a good deal of their militancy and some of the symbolic acts of resistance they displayed were focused on the issue of authority and their struggle for rights at the workplace, including the right to be treated with respect as human beings.

Governor Northcote reported that Guyanese people of African origin were 'most powerfully affected by [the] Italian Abyssinian conflict which presents itself to them as [a] colour question',[38] and attributed the assaults on European estate officials to this. While there is some evidence that anger about this colonial war was a contributing factor, it would be an error to deny that the behaviour of these managers was itself a reason, as Northcote implied. Opinion about the Abyssinian invasion reinforced the workers' anger about the racism that was deeply rooted within the culture of the British colony itself and that was manifested so frequently in labour relations on the plantations. The BGLU's publicity that 'employers are making too big profits and labourers are getting too little pay'[39] and that the start of the harvest was the best time to strike, was certainly another reason for the timing of these strikes. Having started on the West Coast of Demerara the action spread to the East Coast and then to Berbice in October, 'actuated no doubt by rumours that substantial increases in remuneration had been wrested from employers in this way'.[40] The governor acknowledged that the practice of not fixing the price of a task before the worker had 'gone aback' to start 'prejudiced the labourer', but his response to the prolonged unrest was to issue a proclamation on 17 October, make many arrests, enlist 100 extra police and put the militia on standby, after which, he said, 'the situation rapidly improved'.[41]

The strikers' tactics suggest a growing militancy, beginning with a verbal expression of demands backed up by strike action, and then often continuing by invading factories and firing canefields. Telephone lines were cut on five estates and roads were blocked with felled trees and barbed wire, and some bridges were destroyed. The inspector general of police commented on the similarity of the strikers' tactics to those used during the 1924 strikes, in which 'East Indians and persons of African descent banded together for a common purpose...waving red flags, beating drums', and creating a common tradition of resistance and rebellion. He added that with armed and truculent crowds of between 200-700 people, 'a mere demonstration of force was not sufficient to set down the steadily rising tide of unrest'.[42] Given the scale of the unrest and the intensity of feelings involved, there seems to have been very little actual violence, by either strikers or police, in 1935 but the Governor and his police chief were clearly prepared to use more force to suppress the growing disturbances if they felt it necessary.

The persistence of low wages, long hours of work, irregular employment and ill-treatment by supervisors caused continuing discontent and strikes on the sugar estates, but the BGLU and BGWL remained small and their activities were chiefly in Georgetown.[43] On 7 October 1936 Critchlow sent a letter to several firms, asking for higher wages for dock workers and stevedores. He argued that a reasonable living is 'made difficult owing to the limited number of days per month during which these labourers are employed'.[44] The speeding up of their work and the smallness of the gangs resulted in 'excessive physical strain on the workers...[and] fewer days' work being available to them', as three days' work was compressed into two. Critchlow asked for an increase in the size of the gangs from three to four men, an increase of stevedores' wages from $1.60 to $1.80 per day, with double time for night and holiday work, and of dock workers' wages from $1.12 to $1.28 per day for men and from 84 cents to 96 cents for boys. The employers, while admitting that wage rates had remained stationary since 1922, said it was 'impossible to contemplate any increase in the wages paid on the wharves'.[45] The strike called among the wharf workers of

Georgetown lasted from 26 October to 10 November but was unsuccessful because 'many unemployed took advantage of the strike situation to obtain work' and the police ensured that the situation remained orderly.[46] The number of unemployed workers in Georgetown continued to rise in 1936 and 1937: on 31 December 1937 there were 5,047 people registered at the government labour bureau and 3,403 of these were described simply as labourers.[47] The absence of a strong union and the police protection provided for strike-breakers meant that the competition provided by the unemployed people in the town, many of them migrants from depressed rural areas, undermined the efforts to raise wages and improve working conditions on the wharves.

In September 1936 a Colonial Office minute on the commission's report into the 1935 disturbances commented that 'present conditions in the sugar industry preclude a cash rise in wages, but...some shortening of hours *without* reduction of wages seems to me unavoidable'.[48] The official noted that the hours worked by field labourers, mule boys and factory workers were far too long, particularly in relation to their income, and that such conditions 'cannot be allowed to continue.... In the absence of a powerful trade union movement which could bring pressure to bear on the employers...authority must be set up to watch over the interests of the labourers'. The official was concerned not only about the workers' low wages and long hours but also by their obvious fears of retribution from management if they complained about their conditions. He commented that all the managers of the estates who gave evidence and said that the disturbances had surprised them, were either 'liars, or...extraordinarily ignorant of the feeling among their employees'. These comments, which were made before there was a strong union movement anywhere in the British Caribbean and even before the major labour rebellions in Trinidad, Barbados and Jamaica, indicate that some people in the Colonial Office were thinking that something had to be done about the exploitation and oppression of Caribbean workers. Another minute, written four months later, when it was anticipated that the price of sugar would rise, argued that the Colonial Office should press for 'action to improve the working conditions throughout the sugar producing Colonies', as the industry was dependent on government policy by way of preferences:

> Every endeavour should be made to ensure that a full share of the benefits of those improved conditions [in sugar prices] is passed on to the labourers, partly in increased wages, and, perhaps more important, in better conditions, shorter hours, etc, throughout the Colonial sugar industry. Present conditions vary no doubt, and perhaps they are not everywhere as bad as in British Guiana, but I am sure that they are everywhere capable of improvement.[49]

While this sense of paternalistic responsibility was being expressed in the Colonial Office, a new union emerged in Guyana, the most important to be formed in the 1930s. This was the Manpower Citizens' Association (MPCA), formed in 1936 and registered on 5 November 1937. The MPCA focused on organising the sugar workers, especially the field workers, and it grew rapidly. Founded and led by Ayube M. Edun, the president, with the assistance of Harri Barron, general secretary, and C.R. Jacob, treasurer, the MPCA claimed about

10,000 members in 1939 and 20,000 by 1943.[50] Edun and Jacob were already well known as advocates of the political rights of Indians. Jacob, a merchant and elected member of the Legislative Council, was president of the East Indian Association and wrote articles for the *Guiana Review* calling for Indian communal representation. Arthur Lewis wrote in 1939 that the Indian workers were easier to organise than the African because they have 'a greater sense of national solidarity, being bound together by their own languages, religions and social customs'.[51] Though these languages, religions and customs actually divided the Indians in many ways, a communal feeling of being not-creole may have contributed to the MPCA's success in organising them. Though there were some people of African descent in the MPCA, this union was seen from its inception as a largely Indian organisation.

Meanwhile, some other trade union leaders were active in voluntary associations that were largely composed of and oriented towards people of African descent. Critchlow of the BGLU, for example, was involved in the Negro Progress Convention, founded in 1922. Six other trade unions, registered in 1938, organised primarily African Guyanese workers in Georgetown: the British Guiana Seamen's Union, the Transport Workers' Union, the Post Office Workers' Union, the Subordinate Medical Employees Union, the British Guiana Congress of General Workers and the Subordinate Government Employees Association, registered respectively on 16 February, 23 March, 30 June, 28 September, and 3 and 6 October.[52] The most important of the four small unions registered in 1939 was the British Guiana Clerks Association.[53] What was emerging in the late 1930s, then, was a trade union movement that was largely divided along ethnic lines, and some of the leaders of the trade unions were also leaders or active members of ethnic associations.

In a confidential section of his report on labour conditions, Orde Browne noted that in his first general meeting with all the unions the MPCA, which he described as 'overwhelmingly Indian', was 'conspicuous by its absence'. He commented, 'While the various trade unions all stoutly maintain their disregard of racialism, there is a very perceptible mistrust between brown and black', and a rivalry that could all too easily be aggravated if employers took advantage of it 'for purposes of strike-breaking, a quite possible development which would...produce most mischievous results'.[54] The ever-present danger was that racial divisiveness would permeate down the society from the top and that the resulting disunity of labour would negate efforts to achieve progress for all Guyanese working people.

The number of labour disputes, which had declined in 1936 to two and in 1937 to four, rose sharply in 1938. Between January and September 1938 there were 30 disputes involving over 12,000 workers. None of these strikes was called by the MPCA, but the union became involved in negotiations. When strikes happened in June, the MPCA advised the workers to return to work while it secured wage increases for them by negotiation.[55] Most of the strikes involved demands for wage increases, but seven of them included calls for the dismissal of unpopular heads of gangs. The Sugar Producers Association (SPA) complained that the activity of the MPCA was affecting the white staff on the estates and that some were quitting as the workers became 'more and more truculent'.[56] The racist attitudes of the planter class and their managers was made shockingly explicit in an exchange with Citrine during the Royal Commission's visit to Guyana between 27 January and 20 February 1939. The SPA memorandum to the commission referred to the workers' requirements as 'food, shelter, bright and attractive clothing, a little spare money for rum and gambling, and the opportunity for easy love making'.[57] A mass meeting was held in Georgetown on 12 February to protest against these remarks and Citrine attacked the president of the SPA, Frederick Seaford, for the planters' profiteering and exploitation of labour. Seaford tried to defend himself by saying that his remarks were directed only at Guyanese of African descent, not at Indians, and accused Citrine of threatening the 'well being of the colony' by setting up 'labour against capital'. The terms of this debate, which had 'all the ingredients for a powerful class reaction against entrenched, external capital',[58] could have clarified the real bases of exploitation in Guyana. However, the commission hearings were overtaken by a major strike and rebellion at Plantation Leonora, which had been the scene of strikes in 1934 and 1935.

A strike by a shovel gang on 14 February was preceded by a complaint by the 15 firemen at the Leonora factory on 13 February that they worked an hour longer than other factory workers. They worked for 11½ hours per day, in two shifts. While their request for an hour's extra pay was being considered they returned to work. The next day, the 80 or 90 workers on shovel gang No. 2 complained to Lywood (the same manager as in 1934) that their rate of pay was so low that they could not earn an adequate sum in the course of a week. They spoke to the district commissioner who advised them to accept the rate offered. Dissatisfied, the men said that they wanted to speak to Edun, president of the MPCA, and that they would go to Georgetown to see the Royal Commission.

On 15 February no field workers turned out to work and entrances to the estate were picketed. At 7.40 am, while a small deputation went to see Edun and the Commissioner of Labour in Georgetown, the police prevented a large crowd from boarding the train, so they left on foot, shouting that they would go to Georgetown. Before 11 am they had reached Vreed-en-Hoop where a party of police stopped them. At noon Jacob, the MPCA's treasurer, arrived and heard the workers' complaints about rates of pay, hours of work and the method of marking punts. Jacob said he would make representations on their behalf and advised them to go home and await results. When he returned to Georgetown, 'the crowd became more disorderly' and tried to board the ferry to cross the river but the police prevented them.[59] The crowd was reinforced by a party of women who arrived at Vreed-en-Hoop at about 1.30 pm. Later in the afternoon the crowd 'tried to push through the police cordon' to cross to Georgetown, 'but at no time used any form of violence'.[60] Arrangements were eventually made to take them back to Leonora by train, which left at 5.33 pm. Over 30 police were present and, apart from one isolated incident, it was said that no violence was used on either side. Meanwhile, Edun and Jacob told the SPA that they wanted to be able to carry on negotiations on the estates whenever disputes arose, because Lywood had said they could meet the workers only on the public road. The problem was that the SPA had not yet recognised the MPCA as a legitimate union, so the MPCA's officers, rather than pressing the specific demands of Leonora's workers, were using the dispute to struggle for recognition and their right to organise on the estates.

On 16 February about 200 factory workers turned up and were working at about 8 am when a crowd of 70-100 strikers entered the factory and, without violence, got them to leave. This action was so orderly that some of the strikers even assisted a panboiler to remove sugar before he left the building. At 8.20 am, after the strikers, now joined by the factory workers, had left the building, 19 police arrived, armed with rifles and greenheart batons. Their bus was pelted with missiles and a large crowd gathered on the road by a bridge at the entrance to the factory. When District Superintendent Weber arrested five men the crowd attacked the police and demanded their release. People complained that PC Bijadder had injured a man and some strikers threatened him. At about 10.30 am another 12 police, also armed with rifles, arrived. The prisoners were released on bail at about 11 am and the crowd moved away from the factory.

Some strikers then approached the manager's house and the police who were sent to guard it were stoned and their bus's windshield was broken. Some workers said they had come because the manager had agreed to inspect the site where they were working, others demanded more pay, and some asked to be allowed to see Edun and Jacob. The MPCA officials had communicated that 'they were unable to attend on the estate without full recognition by the management'.[61] When the manager spoke to the strikers they threw things at him and the police escorted him back to his house. The district commissioner arrived at about 2 pm. His explanation that Edun and Jacob could not come because 'the estate authorities would not permit them to enter on the estate'[62] was unpopular and the police drove the crowd back with fixed bayonets. A police car drove up at 2.30 pm, was attacked and damaged, and the occupants injured. When the police threatened to fire on the crowd, some people shouted, 'You are not allowed to shoot', and 'don't be frightened, they cannot shoot', 'the riot act has not been read and they cannot shoot'.[63] But when the police raised their loaded rifles to the 'present', a large part of the crowd moved away, towards the factory.

The situation at the factory was quiet until after 3 pm. Among the eight police then guarding the factory was the same PC Bijadder. As the crowd approached the factory, he separated from the other police and fled across the road to a shed. Some strikers followed him while others pelted the remaining police on the bridge. The police fired some shots in the air but with no apparent effect. Fearing for the safety of Bijadder, Weber gave orders to his men to fire on the ringleaders. Several shots were fired, both by the police on the bridge and those who had followed Bijadder. Four people were killed, one of them a woman named Sumintra, four more were admitted to hospital with bullet wounds, and at least six others were injured. Of the 32 police who were on duty, 23 were said to have been injured to some degree. No more shots were fired and the crowd almost immediately dispersed. Edun arrived at about 5.30 pm, met a large number of people whom he said were then very quiet, and spoke to them at the Hindu temple before they went to their homes.[64] Work resumed at Leonora the following day.

The commission appointed by Governor Sir Wilfred Jackson to enquire into the Leonora disturbances met for 12 days of hearings. The commissioners concluded that the firemen had acted 'reasonably' on 13 February, and that their action 'appears to have been symptomatic of a more general discontent with conditions rather than a contributory cause of the strike'.[65] They thought that the members of the shovel gang who were dissatisfied with their rate of pay and went on strike on 14 February 'felt that they had legitimate cause for complaint' and that they were 'not altogether unreasonable' in assuming the manager had prejudged the matter and was trying to trick them back to work without any better rate when he agreed to inspect the field. They found no evidence of 'any deliberately concerted or organised determination' either among the workers or by people from off the estate to develop a more general strike. The march towards Georgetown and the more general strike resulted rather from 'an infection of immediate discontent which spread through the estate' after the shovel gang failed to get satisfaction. The commissioners concluded that the strike was caused by 'a general feeling of discontent with wage rates, earnings, hours of labour and conditions of living' throughout the colony, by an awakening and intensification of that discontent through the formation of trade unions, the unrest in neighbouring colonies, and the proceedings of the Royal Commission, by the immediate grievance, 'genuinely felt', by a section of the estate workers, by the failure of the manager 'to meet this grievance in a sufficiently conciliatory manner', and, finally, by:

> The absence of any effective means whereby the trade union would have been enabled to make representations directly to the management on behalf of these labourers at the time when the grievance first arose and to secure at that time adequate investigation of the matter in dispute.[66]

Though the commissioners believed that the police had used 'proper and necessary' force against the strikers, it is clear from their report that the intervention of the police so early in the dispute contributed to the rebellion by provoking the strikers. The commission report states clearly that there was no violence, nor was any intended, even when the field workers persuaded factory workers to cease work and join them, until after the police arrived.

> The determination of the crowd which had now gathered to effect a complete stoppage of work but not at that time, it would appear, to commit acts of violence led them to resent the arrival of the police upon whom assault was immediately made by the throwing of missiles at the bus which conveyed them.[67]

The efforts of the police to clear the factory and make arrests 'further incensed the crowd who then resumed their attack on the police with greater violence'. Though the police were within the law in repelling these attacks, their methods of dealing with the strikers created still more resentment and anger against particular policemen, like Bijadder, who took part in the arrests and used their large greenheart batons too vigorously. When the escalating violence resulted in threats to Bijadder, and perhaps also to burn the factory, the police prepared to fire on the crowd. Though the commissioners supported the order to fire at the so-called ringleaders in these circumstances, they concluded: 'There is no sufficient evidence from which we can conclude that any of the persons who were killed or injured by rifle fire were actually engaged at that moment in acts of violence'.[68]

One must conclude, as the commissioners did not, that the presence of armed police at an early stage of a labour dispute in which there has been no violence to persons or damage to property was perceived by the strikers as inappropriate and an attempt to intimidate them. The fact that the manager could bring the police on to the estate so promptly, while at the same time denying access to their chosen representatives in the MPCA, who could have helped to negotiate a peaceful resolution of the dispute, incensed the strikers, quite understandably. The readiness of the police to intervene in a labour dispute on behalf of management further identified the interests of capital and the colonial state in the strikers' consciousness.

In this way, the evolution of a labour rebellion out of a small labour dispute, and of a national incident out of a local problem, such as occurred at Plantation Leonora, itself became a factor in the emerging identity of the labour movement and the anticolonial movement, though the latter did not really begin in Guyana until the 1940s. The death of several strikers, who were not themselves involved in acts of violence, at the hands of the police further confirms this identity in the consciousness of the working people, as the martyrs of the Leonora rebellion become part of Guyana's nationalist history.

Soon after the Leonora rebellion, on 2 March 1939, the SPA agreed to recognise the MPCA 'for purposes of collective bargaining, giving it the right to negotiate in any case of dispute, and to hold meetings on the plantations'.[69] The commissioners expressed the hope that 'more orderly negotiation and settlement' of disputes would result and that the MPCA would use its influence to control and limit work stoppages, of which there had been 37 in 1938, involving a loss of 147,461 aggregate working days.[70] The SPA was also concerned about the security of its factories. The recognition of the MPCA as representing the largely Indian field workers, while the BGWL represented the more African factory workers, encouraged a division among estate workers as a whole, a division that actions such as the Leonora rebellion seem to have transcended, if only temporarily. The joining together of field and factory workers in a more general strike at Leonora indicates the development of a class consciousness that, by bridging ethnic divisions, created unity among labour *vis-à-vis* management. This was exactly what the president of the SPA told the Royal Commission would be 'most disturbing to the well being of the colony', meaning the well–being of the SPA and their shareholders.

One positive consequence of the strike and the subsequent recognition of the MPCA, which was surely not intended by the SPA, was the facility and encouragement it gave the union to organise and unite field workers throughout the colony. 'Union recognition throughout the industry made possible communication between sugar workers throughout the country. A unity of purpose, and at times of action, thus developed among the plantation labour force that had never been possible in Guyana before'.[71] However, the rapid growth of the MPCA after 1939 came at the expense of a broader, more inclusive labour unity precisely to the extent to which it was seen as a union of Indian workers under Indian leadership. Labour organisation in Guyana, because it 'started from the assumption of ethnic separation...became a vehicle for ethnic interest'.[72] The early trade unions of Guyana, instead of overcoming the ethnic divisions of the colonial society, reflected and ultimately reinforced them, to the long-term detriment of the society.

Notes

1. Now formally called the Cooperative Republic of Guyana and known as British Guiana between 1831, when berbice was united with Essequibo and Demerara, and independence in 1966
2. Rodney 1981: 219.
3. *Ibid.*, 221.
4. *Ibid.*, 219.
5. Moore 1987: 178.
6. *Ibid.*, 184.
7. Figures from the 1931 census.
8. Rodney 1981: 34.
9. BGLU fliers, 14 July and 1 Aug. 1933, CO 111/712/15140.
10. Denham to Parkinson, 25 Sept. 1933, CO 111/712/15140.
11. Denham to Cunliffe-Lister, 17 Oct. 1933, CO 111/712/15140.
12. *Ibid.*
13. Calculated from figures in 'Report on Sugar Industry in British Guiana' by J. Sydney Dash, 24 Feb. 1936, enclosed in Gov. Northcote to J.H. Thomas, 5 March 1936, CO 318/421/3.
14. Notes on a recent visit to British Guiana and the West Indies by Sir Edward Davson, 29 May 1936, CO 318/423/4.
15. Data from 1931 census and 1936 Economic Survey, enclosed in Orde Browne's provisional report to SS, 18 Oct. 1938, CO 111/756/60338.
16. Figures from Report of the Commission of enquiry into the 1935 Disturbances, 24 Aug. 1936, (hereafter Report of 1935 disturbances), CO 111/732/60036, pp. 7, 30.
17. For example, CO 345/28 refers to 1934 'Industrial unrest' file 35156 as destroyed, and CO 345/29 refers to two files for 1936, 'Lucius O'Brien, activities of. Suspected of Communistic activities & requests that enquiries be made into his past activities', file 60148, and 'Political situation', file 60206, which were also destroyed.
18. Report by J. Nicole, 3 Oct. 1934, enclosed in Act.-Gov. Sir Crawford Douglas-Jones to Cunliffe-Lister, 24 Jan. 1935, CO 111/726/60036.
19. Douglas-Jones to Cunliffe-Lister, 24 Jan. 1935, CO 111/726/60036.
20. *Ibid.*
21. *Ibid.*
22. Report of 1935 disturbances, p.4.
23. Gov. Sir Geoffrey Northcote to SS, 17 Oct. 1935, CO 111/726/60036.
24. Report of 1935 disturbances, p.18.
25. *Ibid.*, p.19.
26. *Ibid.*, p.16.
27. *Ibid.*, p.21. The commissioners, by publishing their names, would scarcely have helped them.
28. *Ibid.*, p.21.
29. *Ibid.*, p.21.
30. *Ibid.*, p.22.
31. *Ibid.*, p.23.
32. *Ibid.*, p.24.
33. *Ibid.*, p.25.
34. *Ibid.*, p.26.
35. *Ibid.*, p.27.
36. *Ibid.*, p.27.

37. *Ibid.*, p.28.
38. Northcote to SS, 17 Oct. 1935, CO 111/726/60036.
39. Northcote to H. Beckett, 18 Oct. 1935, CO 111/726/60036.
40. Report of 1935 disturbances, p.29.
41. Northcote to Thomas, 7 Dec. 1935, CO 111/726/60036.
42. Report of W.E.H. Bradburn, 15 Nov. 1935, enclosed in Northcote to Thomas, 7 Dec. 1935, CO 111/726/60036.
43. Northcote to SS, 17 Feb. 1936, CO 111/732/60036.
44. Letter from Hubert Critchlow, 7 Oct. 1936, enclosed in Northcote to Ormsby-Gore, 4 Dec. 1936, CO 111/732/60036.
45. Report of meeting, 19 Oct. 1936, enclosed in Northcote to Ormsby-Gore, 4 Dec. 1936, CO 111/732/60036.
46. Northcote to Ormsby-Gore, 4 Dec. 1936, CO 111/732/60036.
47. Report of the Government Labour Bureau, enclosed in Gov. to SS, 12 Feb. 1938, CO 318/427/3.
48. Minute by J. St J. Rootham, 29 Sept. 1936, CO 111/732/60036.
49. Minute by S. Caine, 22 Jan. 1937, CO 111/732/60036.
50. Chase n.d.: 85.
51. Lewis 1977: 25.
52. Orde Browne's provisional report, 16 Oct. 1938, enclosed in Orde Browne to SS, 18 Oct. 1938, CO 111/756/60338, and Chase n.d.: 90.
53. Chase n.d.: 92.
54. Orde Browne's provisional report, 16 Oct. 1938, enclosed in Orde Browne to SS, 18 Oct. 1938, CO 111/756/60338.
55. Lewis 1977: 26.
56. Memorandum enclosed in Edward J. King, secretary of W.I. Committee, to private secretary of SS, 7 June 1939, CO 111/758/60036/1.
57. Quoted in Chase n.d.: 94.
58. Cross 1988: 300.
59. Report of Leonora Enquiry Commission, 23 March 1939 (Georgetown, 1939), CO 111/762/60270, hereafter Report of the Leonora Commission, p.5.
60. *Ibid.*, p.6.
61. *Ibid.*, p.8.
62. *Ibid.*, p.8.
63. *Ibid.*, p.9.
64. *Ibid.*, p.13.
65. *Ibid.*, p.15.
66. *Ibid.*, p.16.
67. *Ibid.*, p.18.
68. *Ibid.*, p.22.
69. Lewis 1977: 26.
70. Report of Leonora Commission, p.23.
71. Walker-Kilkenny 1992: 8.
72. Cross 1988: 304-05.

Comparisons and Conclusions

Despite considerable diversity in the British Caribbean, there is a degree of unity that enables us to conceive of these various colonies as parts of a regional whole. Important as the individual rebellions are in the social and political history of each country in which they took place, the impact of the rebellions as a whole was greater than merely the sum of the parts. In this final section, in which we examine some of the common causes, characteristics and consequences of these rebellions, we will see that they constitute a kind of watershed in the region in much the same way that legal emancipation did one century earlier. I mean a watershed not in the extreme sense of everything changing, because there were important continuities after 1939 just as there were after 1838, but in the more limited sense that after these events, and largely because of them, the political culture and institutions of the British Caribbean were irrevocably changed in several crucial ways.

Caribbean intellectuals as different as C.L.R. James and W. Arthur Lewis recognised the epoch-making nature of these events at the time they occurred, but it is now possible, over a half century later, to understand the period in a different fashion. James and Lewis hoped that the birth of this workers' movement would not only give rise to labour and political reforms but would also form the basis of a new nation. They differed in their political responses to this project, but they shared the goal of a free West Indies. Though we must now admit that this project was aborted, it was nevertheless a real project at the time.

In *The Black Jacobins*, published in 1938, James wrote his analysis of the Ste Domingue revolution that produced the first independent Caribbean nation in 1804 because he believed there was a parallel, and a lesson to be learned, in the way the Haitian people had transformed themselves while breaking out of the old colonial system. James believed that this had to be a revolutionary struggle. Lewis, whose *Labour in the West Indies* was published by the Fabian Society in 1939, was a reformer who believed that the liberalization of the political system, along with economic growth and social welfare, would promote the development of the West Indian people. Like James, Lewis understood the transformative political influence of the labour movement in the 1930s and hoped it would provide the basis for the aspiration to West Indian nationhood. He concluded his pamphlet: 'The Labour Movement is on the march. It has already behind it a history of great achievement in a short space of time. It will make of the West Indies of the future a country where the common man may lead a cultured life in freedom and prosperity'.[1] More than half a century later, when each of the former colonies has gone its separate way to nationhood, it is hard to comprehend the strength of this West Indian aspiration. But if we fail to comprehend it we will also fail to comprehend the regional dimension that was part of the movement at the time it took place. The embryonic aspiration to West Indian nationhood that was encouraged by the labour movement in the 1930s and 1940s subsequently became fragmented and frustrated in the 1950s and 1960s. A comparative and regional analysis of the labour rebellions between 1934 and 1939 is therefore essential for the further understanding of this whole historical process.

First, the common causes of the labour rebellions include the impact of the economic crisis in the capitalist world, known as the great depression, and the related reduction of opportunities for labour migration and the return of many migrants to their countries of origin. Further, changes were occurring within colonial policies, particularly with regard to labour reforms and the return of the elective principle on a limited suffrage, that encouraged people in the British Caribbean to demand further reforms. While British legal and political institutions were slow to change in the colonies, and generally lagged behind the liberalisation of the metropole, some British companies were modernising more rapidly in terms of technology than in their labour relations. Finally, the deeply rooted colonial political culture, based upon racism and rigid social hierarchies, was being challenged in the 1930s by the influence of various ideologies, including Garveyism and Ethiopianism, on the one hand, and Fabian socialism and Marxism, on the other. Though these factors had varying degrees of impact in different places, they were present more or less throughout the British Caribbean in the 1930s.

The great depression, which was an international catastrophe, shattered the dependent monocrop economies of the Caribbean. About half of the 2½ million people in the British Caribbean were then engaged in agriculture, many of them dependent still, as they had been for a century, upon seasonal wage labour on the sugar plantations. Endemic unemployment and underemployment, resulting in widespread and persistent poverty, became suddenly worse in the 1930s. Sugar workers and their families throughout the Caribbean suffered, as did those who depended on forest products in Belize or bananas in Jamaica. Everywhere employment was intermittent and insecure, wages were low and hours long, and working and living conditions were severe. Poor housing, malnutrition and ill-health conspired to produce declining living standards and social conditions, particularly for the children of the poor. The Royal Commissioners' account of the terrible conditions they saw in 1938 and 1939 was suppressed by the war cabinet for fear that it could provide useful material for 'enemy propaganda'. Lord Moyne agreed to moderate the tone of the report and to cut particularly dangerous sections, such as those on housing and the position of women, from the published document.[2]

The closing of work opportunities in Central America, Cuba, the Dominican Republic and the United States, and the return of many West Indians who had migrated to those places in the more prosperous 1920s, swelled the ranks of the unemployed in the 1930s. Many of these returning migrants, who may have had some experience of unionism and politics, often associated with the Garvey movement, became active in the labour rebellions in the British Caribbean, for example in Belize, St Kitts, Jamaica and Trinidad. The impact of the depression was not only direct, therefore, in terms of the deteriorating conditions affecting the working class, but also indirect in so far as it caused many people, who had been influenced by ideas that were then new and radical in the British Caribbean, to return home. Buchanan in Jamaica was one of the most prominent of these, but hundreds of others who have remained anonymous contributed to the labour rebellions through this period.

Changing colonial policies between the wars, particularly in the areas of labour reform and the legislative systems, had an impact throughout the British Caribbean, often provoking further demands rather than satisfying them. Differences existed in the legislative systems in these colonies, from Barbados which had never been a Crown Colony to Trinidad which had always been one. Most colonies had a semi-representative system in which part of the legislature was elected, and the other part was either official or unofficial but was nominated by the governor. Generally, the officials could prevail by means of the governor's veto and the Colonial Office was unwilling to give up this power. After Major Wood's report of 1922, however, some concessions were made to increase the popularly elected element, though still with tiny, restrictively-based electorates. Even in Jamaica, 'politically the most advanced of all the units, only one-twelfth of the population qualified for the taxpayers' franchise, while in all the colonies high property and income qualifications restricted candidacies for election to the legislative councils to the small groups of the well-to-do classes'.[3] Not surprisingly, 'all self-respecting West Indians despised'[4] this half-baked system and agitation for further reforms persisted throughout the 1930s.

The British labour movement's involvement in influencing its Caribbean counterpart began in 1925 when Critchlow of the BGLU participated in the British Commonwealth Labour Conference in London and in 1926 when Roberts attended the British Guiana and West Indies Labour Conference hosted by the BGLU. Lord Passfield, formerly Sydney Webb, the Fabian socialist who became secretary of state in the Colonial Office in the second Labour government in 1929, and his talented subordinate Dr T. Drummond Shiels, showed a commitment to reforming the archaic labour laws in the West Indies. Prompted by the conventions proposed by the International Labour Organisation, Passfield indicated to all the colonial governments that henceforth they would have to pay attention to the organisation and conditions of 'native labour'.[5] A Colonial Office Conference, held in June and July 1930, discussed a variety of topics, the most important of which was colonial labour reform. Passfield urged the colonial governments 'to deal...with Trade Unionism, and to provide for its organization'[6] and Shiels pressed them to repeal the obsolete master and servant ordinances that still defined a breach of contract by a labourer as a criminal offence.[7] West Indians who participated in this conference included Cipriani, Critchlow and Marryshow. There is no doubt that they felt encouraged by what they heard and returned home with renewed enthusiasm for their workingmen's associations and infant unions, but perhaps they had too much faith in what they thought the British Labour Party would achieve on behalf of the Caribbean working people.

The workingmen's associations of Trinidad and Grenada and the BGLU began to look to the British labour movement for guidance and assistance at this time. Even after the fall of the Labour government, the appointment of the young Malcolm MacDonald as secretary of state for the Colonies in June 1935 ensured that the concern with labour issues would not die. When, in response to the disturbances, Major Orde Browne was appointed labour adviser to the secretary of state in March 1938, the Labour Party, which had originally proposed such an appointment in 1936, welcomed the move. MacDonald advised Orde Browne to cooperate with Citrine and the TUC on colonial labour problems.[8] In December 1937 the general council of the TUC had established a new colonial advisory committee, the 13 members of which included Professor Macmillan, author of *Warning from the West Indies*, Dr Drummond Shiels, former under-secretary at the Colonial Office, C.R. Buxton, vice-chairman of the Anti-Slavery and Aborigines Protection Society, and Arthur Creech Jones, an influential Labour Party and trade union leader. This group not only began to shape the Labour Party's colonial policies but also sought to influence the new labour movement in the British Caribbean. On 31 March 1938, for example, a booklet for the guidance of colonial organisations, called *Model Trade Union Rules, Agendas, and Standing Orders*, was sent to all the known colonial unions[9] and in February 1939 Creech Jones sent his account of the British trade union movement to several Trinidadian labour leaders: C.R. Alexander of the SLWU, Rienzi of the OWTU, Francois of the NWCSA, and Patrick of the FWTU.[10] The paternalistic attitude of the British labour movement to its Caribbean counterpart took on an urgency after the labour rebellions when the British Fabian socialists became anxious that the Caribbean trade unions should be led by responsible people. Consequently, their advice and assistance were intended to guide and support those leaders whom they identified as responsible, at the expense of others.

This issue was especially salient in the late 1930s because of the revolutionary potential and radical ideological currents sweeping the entire Caribbean. While, in the British Caribbean, Marxism appears to have had an influence only in Trinidad and Jamaica in this period, which influence was quite circumscribed, Garveyism was both more widespread and more deeply rooted in the political culture of the region. Many labour leaders of the 1930s were followers or former followers of Garvey, some with experience in UNIA branches in Cuba, Costa Rica or the United States. So it was not only the ideas of Garvey that were important but also the experience of public speaking and organising, and of recognising the need for unity, self-reliance and solidarity. After the Italian invasion of Ethiopia, in particular, the pan-African and anti–colonial aspects of Garvey's philosophy became a major force in the labour rebellions. Members of the British labour movement, as well as colonial officials, were antagonised by what they saw as an anti-white racial hostility in this reaction because they were unwilling to acknowledge how deeply rooted and interrelated with the class struggle the phenomenon of race and racism is in Caribbean societies. The British government's failure to satisfy the people's growing political aspirations, the increasing unemployment and poverty in the great depression, the spread of new radical ideas that challenged the colonial political culture, and a host of local grievances specific to each place, gave rise to the labour rebellions across the region between 1934 and 1939.

This summary of the major causes of the labour rebellions indicates the need to understand the relationships between local and global, and between economic, political and ideological factors, as well as the need to see the interconnections of these colonies in the region.

Because many of the causes were common, there were also many characteristics common to these rebellions, in terms of issues and concerns, situations, tactics and responses. As is to be expected in an area of such widespread economic deprivation, two of the key issues that recurred repeatedly across the region were the demands for jobs and higher wages. Several disturbances began with demonstrations of the unemployed who demanded work or relief, and others were from people who demanded more regular and secure work. The extent to which the unemployed and employed united in these actions is impressive because it shows that working people understood the relation between their low wages and casual employment, as well as the threat to the efforts to raise wages that was posed by the reserve army of unemployed. Though some unemployed were recruited as strike-breakers, we see the working people struggling simultaneously for jobs, more security, shorter hours and higher wages.

These economic issues were not their only nor always their first concern. We see also, repeatedly, demands for the end to racial discrimination and abuse at the workplace and for the rights to organise and negotiate.These workers' rights became increasingly linked to demands for rights as citizens. These human rights issues were less often expressed as demands for specifically political rights, however, than for decent and respectful treatment as human beings. Over and over again, the working people of the British Caribbean, most of them the descendants of slaves and indentured workers, made it clear that they resented being treated as if they were still in bondage. Their view of themselves as free people, a century after the end of legal slavery, was inseparable from their sense of dignity and the respect that they, like all other people, deserved. For them, as for anyone else, self-respect depends largely upon the respect one receives from others, and the entire colonial system, economically, politically, socially, culturally and psychologically, conspired to deprive the majority of people of such respect. A century after formal emancipation, several factors conjoined, including the working people's economic deprivation, frustrated political aspirations, ideas about human rights and racial pride, and often their experiences overseas, to encourage so many people to struggle for these rights and this respect.

An important example of how the working people perceived and responded to this struggle has to do with their relations with the police and other armed forces. The police forces, and especially the various volunteer groups, were not only the front line of protection for colonial property arrangements and social institutions, they were also the visible embodiment of racial privileges and hierarchy, which were maintained through violence. The officers and volunteers were largely white or near white, from the privileged social sectors of the colony or from outside the society, while the rank-and-file were brown and black. To many working people the police constables, who were in other respects like themselves, may have appeared as traitors or mercenaries, paid and ordered to oppress their own people. But the greatest anger was directed against the volunteers, the militia and special constables, who were often the strikers' employers, managers and overseers, given license by the state to use violence against the workers. In these situations, time and again, the colonial power structure was dramatised and clarified. The employers and managers, who were often racially distinct from their workers, armed themselves and called for armed police as soon as a labour dispute began, and this was frequently enough to enrage workers who had until then been peaceful. The ready use of armed force to intimidate workers in a labour dispute itself became an issue as the workers struggled for the right to express and negotiate their grievances. If the strikers defended themselves or were provoked into attacking the police, this often led to bloodshed and escalating violence, and in many cases to the introduction of more armed force, including the British army and navy. Even before it reached such extremes, however, the escalation of the struggle made the role of the colonial state in relation to labour disputes quite transparent. As the conditions provoked the workers into disputes and rebellion, so the labour rebellions provoked the state to defend with violence the economic and social order.

We see a frequent pattern in these rebellions. A local and quite specific labour dispute, having to do with rates of pay or methods of payment, or an abusive overseer, or not enough work to go around, became a source of confrontation with management who promptly sought the backing of the police. The workers' tactics, which were generally peaceful, often included mass meetings, processions and demonstrations, sometimes with a petition to someone in authority, and strikes that frequently developed as 'rolling strikes' with occupations or sit-ins, as more militant workers encouraged others to join them in a more general strike to bring broader pressure to bear on the employers and the colonial administration. The workers, who began without legal or recognised representation or grievance procedures, often directed their frustration and anger at the police and special constables who were sent to intimidate them, and violence, once started, quickly escalated. The forces of law and order, therefore, often provoked violence and disorder and then suppressed it by arresting and shooting people. If the governor felt it necessary, he declared a state of emergency, enlisted volunteers and called in the navy and army to restore order. The courts subsequently convicted and sentenced many of the arrested people to make an example of them, while a commission of enquiry showed concern about the causes of the riots but expressed satisfaction that the police and volunteers had acted appropriately in difficult circumstances.

This brings us to the third aspect of the labour rebellions, namely their common consequences, which include the responses of the imperial system, and the institutionalisation of the labour movement and the development of its links with modern politics and nationalism. The responses of the various colonial governments were similar in part because some administrators, like Sir Edward Denham, went from one colony to another, and in part because all were following broadly defined Colonial Office policies for the region (and even for the entire imperial system). But they were also similar in large part because they followed the logic of a colonial system in which similar structurally and culturally defined conditions limited the options. One of the chief functions of the colonial state was to maintain the security of capitalist property, particularly important in the case of Trinidad's oilfields; and, in relation to that function, to ensure the supply of a cheap and manageable labour force. By the 1920s this could no longer be provided by enslaved or indentured labour, and the system of coercion codified by the Masters and Servants Acts that made workers' breach of labour contracts a criminal offence was under attack, even within the imperial government itself, by 1930. But it was the challenge to this system by the working people themselves, between 1934 and 1939, that provoked a crisis and exposed the contradictions within it.

The colonial governments throughout the British Caribbean responded to this challenge essentially in three ways: by police action, by making limited concessions, and then by trying to institutionalise and control the labour movement. First, police action, as we have seen, involved surveillance, intimidation, armed force and legal action through the courts. When existing laws were inadequate new ones were quickly passed in order to detain, punish and isolate the more radical elements and divide the movement. Such laws, which included new definitions of sedition and the prohibition of meetings and demonstrations, generally inhibited democratic discourse and procedures, as well as workers' rights.

Second, colonial governments made concessions to some demands, particularly for relief, by providing (or sometimes only promising) help in the form of relief work and land settlement to assuage a proportion of the working people and so to divert them away from the growing labour movement. This part of the strategy was begun early in Belize and became a widespread response as an insurance against disorder in Jamaica and elsewhere. As social welfare it became the central part of the colonial development and welfare programme throughout the British Caribbean after 1940. The launching of urgent relief schemes became a standard tactic for heading off disturbances and a key part of public welfare programmes for controlling the political responses of the poor. [11]

Third, the colonial governments appointed labour advisers and created labour departments, ostensibly 'to assist and guide the labouring classes in the formation of trade unions along the right lines'.[12] Where trade unions were still weak, however, the labour departments tended to dominate and control industrial relations and actually retard the development of autonomous trade unions by usurping their functions.[13] The paternalistic approach taken by the Colonial Office, in conjunction with the British TUC, sought to establish sound trade unions under responsible leadership. In July 1938 MacDonald circulated copies of the TUC's booklet, *Model Trade Union Rules,*"to all the colonies.[14] Several prominent British trade unionists and Labour Party leaders, including John Jagger, Sir Stafford Cripps, and, above all, Sir Walter Citrine, played a direct role in shaping labour organisations during their visits to the Caribbean. By mid-1939 the TUC, working in support of the Colonial Office, was engaged in a programme of activities that included the production of an *ABC of Trade Unionism for Colonial Unions* and the offer of scholarships to selected labour leaders to attend Ruskin College, Oxford. Working in conjunction with the new local labour departments, this programme was aimed at shaping the development of the Caribbean unions, to propagate what they defined as responsible trade unionism by emphasising 'the separation between industrial disputes and militant political action'.[15] The articulation of this goal and the creation of labour departments to implement it, was in response to the labour rebellions which had shown the possibility of a more radical labour movement, developing under leaders who linked it to a broad anti-imperialist project that could be both nationalist in orientation and regional in scope.

The logic of the colonial system meant that the Colonial Office and its local administrators had to retain their role of maintaining a suitable supply of cheap labour even when their more urgent task was to quash the rebellions and restore order. It was in this regard that the colonial governments became entangled in blatant contradictions. At the same time that they offered relief work, promised minimum wages and intervened in labour disputes in order to circumvent further rebellions, they could not do so in such a way that would antagonise the capitalist class. When Governor Fletcher and his colonial secretary chastised and offended the employers and shareholders of Trinidad in 1937 they were removed. Yet when the colonial governments intervened to keep wages low and workers disciplined, and paid miserable pittances for relief work so as not to compete with local employers, the workers quite reasonably resented them. Facing the crisis in the capitalist economy and an increasingly militant response from the working people, the colonial governments became more directly engaged in labour affairs, in some cases even becoming one of the largest employers in the colony[16] and not simply the means of ensuring a supply of labour to private capital.

The colonial state was pressurised, by the bankruptcy of the capitalist economy it was there to serve, to substitute a long-term relief work, public welfare economy while becoming more openly involved in disciplining the labour force that rebelled against its exploitation. As working people's demands rose, the role of the colonial government expanded and became more transparent, which only served to broaden the demands made of it. The structural conditions of the colonial economy, based as it was on the perpetuation of a cheap and casual labour market in which seasonal low paid work and frequent unemployment were the norm, denied the colonial government the possibility of meeting the people's economic demands, with the result that criticism was increasingly focused on the inadequacies of such government and the imperial system it represented. Thus, the increasingly obvious inability of the colonial governments to satisfy the people's demands fed the seeds of nationalism within the labour movement in the 1930s and the anticolonial and independence movements that followed. Despite the efforts of these colonial governments to divert or suppress such movements, through land settlement schemes or imprisoning the leaders, as we have seen, and despite the diversion of the war years when many colonised people rallied round the Union Jack, the momentum that was established in the labour rebellions between 1934 and 1939 developed into modern political parties, the evolution of self-government and constitutional decolonisation in the next 30 or 40 years throughout the British Caribbean.

As is well known, some of the leaders of these political parties and movements had already emerged by 1939, including Vere Bird in Antigua, Grantley Adams in Barbados, and Alexander Bustamante and Norman Manley in Jamaica. In many cases, such as Barbados, Belize and Jamaica, middle-class politicians used the trade unions as vehicles for their own advancement and the labour movement in these places lost autonomy. In some cases, such as Belize, Grenada and Guyana, the intimate connections between trade unions and nationalist parties did not emerge until the late 1940s and early 1950s. However, the analysis of these varied relations between trade unions and political parties in the British Caribbean in the 1940s and 1950s belongs elsewhere. Here it must suffice to say that there were already some crucial differences between the colonies by 1939. While trade unions were forming in most of the British Caribbean by that date, they remained weak in most places, such as Belize, St Kitts, Antigua and Barbados, and also in Guyana where they were sharply divided in terms of ethnicity. Unions were strongest in Jamaica and Trinidad, but whereas in the former one man had already come to dominate organised labour while his rival had formed a political party, in the latter there was a proliferation of trade unions without any political unity. These differences shaped the subsequent genesis of politics and the relations of political parties to trade unions, in those colonies.

Though these brief conclusions can only identify some of the chief consequences of the labour rebellions, along with their similarities and differences, something needs to be said about the regional nature of the movement at that time. While the institutionalisation of trade unions and their relations with political parties took an increasingly insular form, the aspiration toward some kind of regional movement was quite strong in 1939.[17] The first British Guiana and West Indies Labour Conference, organised and hosted by Critchlow and his BGLU in Georgetown in 1926, included representatives from Trinidad and Surinam. This embryonic regional labour organisation advocated broad social and political reforms within a federal concept of nationhood. Resolutions were passed recommending the introduction of compulsory education throughout the West Indies, along with workmen's compensation, an eight hour working day, minimum wages, non-contributory old age pensions, national health insurance and prison reform. The conference called for a federation of the West Indies and British Guiana, with some form of parliamentary self-government and dominion status. A committee was charged with drafting the rules for a Guianese and West Indian federation of trade unions and labour parties.

The second and third conferences were held in 1938, in Guyana in July and in Trinidad in November, with Critchlow of the BGLU, Thorne of the BGWL, Cipriani of the TLP, and Rienzi and Mentor from the OWTU. Messages were received from workers in Barbados, St Kitts and St Vincent, and delegates from Barbados attended the Trinidad conference.[18] The delegates reaffirmed their primary goal, namely 'To strengthen intercolonial solidarity of the workers in the various trade unions'.[19] The conferences aspired to embrace both trade union and broader political and cultural aspects of the workers' struggle. It was hoped to establish regular communication between this organisation and the British TUC, and the latter's general council agreed to send a representative to the West Indies. However, this regional labour congress remained at that time more of an aspiration than an institution.

Another aspiration towards regional unity manifested itself in 1938. Though it does not seem to have had a serious or organised basis, it shows that even some of the West Indians resident in Cuba shared in a federal ideal. In 1938, David S. Nathan, a Trinidadian resident in Guantanamo, Cuba, sent a resolution from the British West Indies Labour Party (BWILP), of which he was said to be the vice-president and Cipriani the president, to the Colonial Office. Nathan worked among West Indians in Oriente and Camaguey provinces. He claimed that the BWILP had received 'the endorsement and support of workers' in Belize, Guyana, the Bahamas, the British Virgin Islands and West Indies, as well as West Indians 'temporarily residing in foreign countries', to create a British West Indian government, with Cipriani as prime minister.[20] He wrote that the BWILP, 'situated in and around the Caribbean Sea', strongly protested 'the abuses of the capitalist class upon the workers' that were responsible for 'the revolution in the colonies during these several months'.[21] The British government took this seriously enough to make enquiries about Nathan in Cuba and Trinidad. Cipriani had apparently accepted Nathan's invitation to lead the BWILP but had not heard from him since.[22] When Nathan sent a Declaration of Independence on behalf of the BWILP to Washington in 1940, Cipriani repudiated the action.[23]

When the next regional Labour Conference was held, in 1944 in Guyana, representation included delegates from Barbados and Grenada. Resolutions were passed in favour of creating a West Indian federation with self-government and universal adult suffrage, the establishment of a minimum wage, a universal eight hour working day, and the right of public assembly and free and unimpeded movement of West Indians between the various territories. The conference resolved to pursue the closer cooperation between trade unions in the West Indies and Guyana.[24] The next year the aspiration was more fully realised when about 30 delegates, representing Antigua, Barbados, Bermuda, Grenada, Guyana, Jamaica, St Kitts, St Lucia, St Vincent, Surinam, and Trinidad and Tobago, met in Barbados and created the Caribbean Labour Congress (CLC).

Analysis of the history and significance of the CLC belongs in a larger study of which this is a part. Here it is only necessary to point out that the aspirations of the labour movement, that became organised in trade unions in the 1930s, towards closer regional cooperation and a federal ideal were institutionalised within a few years of the labour rebellions. Many of the participants in those events between 1934 and 1939, including Grantley Adams, Vere Bird, Hubert Critchlow, Richard Hart and Norman Manley, along with Robert Bradshaw, Albert Gomes, T.A. Marryshow and Hugh Springer, played leading roles in the development of trade unions and the CLC. Most of them, in the 1940s, saw the need for labour unity and West Indian unity as interconnected and interdependent. On the eve of the CLC conference in Jamaica in 1947, a few days before the Montego Bay Conference on closer union in the West Indies, Bird, then the president of the Antigua Trades and Labour Union, said that he wanted to see 'one big socialist labour union throughout the Caribbean.... We want a West Indian nation'.[25]

In these early years the labour leaders, who had not yet become insular nationalist politicians, still dreamed of a strong federal state, including Belize and Guyana, with full self-government and dominion status, that would be capable of planning regional economic development on behalf of the entire

West Indian working class.[26] Gordon Lewis wrote in 1968, 'The recognition of the seminal truth that only a unified Caribbean, politically and economically, can save the region from its fatal particularism is at least a century old'.[27] Though proposals about a federation started in the nineteenth century, it was not until organised labour emerged in the 1930s that the idea had a popular base. When the newly formed regional labour movement became divided in the late 1940s the federal ideal lost its labour voice, so the compromise federation that was worked out by middle-class politicians and British officials, without popular support, was doomed to failure. Nevertheless, the extent to which the movement that emerged from the labour rebellions of the 1930s included a regional impetus is an important part of the history of the Caribbean.

What were the chief achievements of the labour rebellions? They must include, of course, the formation of trade unions and the passage of a variety of labour reforms in the colonial legislatures. They must include also the new attention that the British government focused on its Caribbean colonies, marked by the Royal Commission of 1938-1939, and resulting in the Colonial Development and Welfare organisation and then, beginning in Jamaica in 1944, universal adult suffrage. Above all, however, the rebellions achieved a shift in the political culture, as the working people of the British Caribbean made it clear that they would no longer be defined as merely the cheap labour of sugar kings and oil lords. In Lamming's words, which were written with reference to Barbados but could apply throughout the region, there was after the labour rebellions a new 'confidence in very ordinary people that they could and should be heard by those who were called authority'. These people placed their demands for improved conditions at the centre of the Caribbean agenda, and their struggle for respect and a better life became the basis of modern Caribbean politics.

Notes

1. Lewis 1977: 52.
2. Correspondence and memoranda between Lord Moyne and the War Cabinet, 30 and 31 Jan. 1940, CO 318/443/6.
3. Lewis 1968: 102.
4. *Ibid.*, 100.
5. Circulars, Lord Passfield to all colonies, protectorates, etc., 19 Aug. 1929, CO 854/73, 12 March 1930, CO 854/173, and 29 Apr. 1930, CO 854/76.
6. Minutes of CO Conference, 23 June 1930, CO 854/173.
7. *Ibid.*, 10 July 1930, CO 854/173.
8. Basdeo 1983: 174-75.
9. CJP, RH, Mss Brit. Emp. S332, 14/1.

10. *Ibid.*, 14/4.
11. The general case about welfare as a means of social control is made in Piven and Cloward 1971.
12. Labour Department Annual Report, 1939, Belize.
13. Hamill 1978.
14. Circular, MacDonald to Governors, 12 July 1938, CO 854/110.
15. Susan Craig, "The Germs of an Idea" in Lewis 1977: 79.
16. In Belize, for example, by 1950 the Public Works Department alone employed 1,284 workers, exclusive of relief work, compared with 1,091 employed by the Belize Estate and Produce Company, the largest firm in the colony. Gov. R.H. Garvey's report on Economic Development and Employment, 30 Sept. 1950, CO 123/406/66985.
17. This topic was explored in a preliminary fashion in my paper, "The Caribbean Labour Congress and the Federal Ideal", presented at the 20th annual conference of the Association of Caribbean Historians in St Thomas, 27 March-2 April 1988.
18. Basdeo 1983: 257.
19. Chase n.d.: 75.
20. David S. Nathan to SS, 15 June 1938, CO 318/428/1.
21. Nathan to Ormsby-Gore, 12 May 1938, CO 318/428/1.
22. Act. Gov. John Higgins to MacDonald, 20 Dec. 1938, CO 318/436/1.
23. Gov. Sir Hubert Young to Lord Lloyd, 27 July 1940, CO 318/442/1.
24. Ashton Chase's notes on the conference, 28 Feb.-1 March 1944, FCBP, RH, Mss Brit. Emp. S365, 132. Chase was the conference secretary.
25. *Daily Gleaner*, 30 Aug. 1947.
26. The Federation of the West Indies that was created by an Act of the British Parliament in 1956, initiated in 1958, and disintegrated in 1962, lacked these features.
27. Lewis 1968: 343.

BIBLIOGRAPHY

Adamson, Alan H., *Sugar Without Slaves: The Political Economy of British Guiana, 1838–1904* (New Haven, Yale University Press, 1972).

Ashdown, Peter, 'Antonio Soberanis and the Disturbances in Belize 1934–1937', *Caribbean Quarterly* 24 (1978), 61–74.

'Race, Class and the Unofficial Majority in British Honduras 1890–1949', (unpublished PhD thesis, University of Sussex, 1979).

'Marcus Garvey, the U.N.I.A. and the Black Cause in British Honduras, 1914–1949', *Journal of Caribbean History* 15 (1981), 41–55

Bakan, Abigail B., *Ideology and Class Conflict in Jamaica: The Politics of Rebellion* (Montreal and Kingston, McGill–Queen's University Press, 1990).

Baker, Patrick L., *Centring the Periphery: Chaos, Order and the Ethnohistory of Dominica* (Kingston, The Press–University of the West Indies, 1994).

Basdeo, Sahadeo, 'The Role of the British Labour Movement in the Development of Labour Organisation in Trinidad 1919–1929', *Social and Economic Studies* 30:3 (1981), 21–41.

'The Role of the British Labour Movement in the Development of Labour Organisation in Trinidad 1929-1938', *Social and Economic Studies* 31:1 (1982), 40–73.

Labour Organization and Labour Reform in Trinidad, 1919–1939 (St Augustine, ISER, 1983).

Beckles, Hilary McD., *A History of Barbados: From Amerindian Settlement to Nation–State* (Cambridge, Cambridge University Press, 1990).

Corporate Power in Barbados: The Mutual Affair (Bridgetown, Lighthouse Communications, 1989).

Bolland, O. Nigel, 'The Social Structure and Social Relations of the Settlement in the Bay of Honduras (Belize) in the 18th Century', *Journal of Caribbean History* 6 (1973), 1–42.

The Formation of a Colonial Society: Belize, From Conquest to Crown Colony (Baltimore, The Johns Hopkins University Press, 1977).

'Systems of Domination after Slavery: The Control of Land and Labor in the British West Indies after 1838', *Comparative Studies in Society and History* 23:4 (1981), 591–619.

Belize: A New Nation in Central America (Boulder, Westview Press, 1986a).

'Labour Control and Resistance in Belize in the Century after 1838', *Slavery and Abolition* 7 (1986b), 175–87.

'The Labour Movement and the Genesis of Modern Politics in Belize', in Malcolm Cross and Gad Heuman (eds), *Labour in the Caribbean* (London, Macmillan, 1988a), 258–84.

Colonialism and Resistance in Belize: Essays in Historical Sociology (Benque Viejo del Carmen, Cubola Productions, 1988b).

'Society and Politics in Belize', in Colin Clarke (ed) *Society and Polilitics in the Caribbean* (London, Macmillan, 1991), 78–109.

'The Politics of Freedon in the British Caribbean', in Frank McGlynn and Seymour Dresher (eds), *The Meaning of Freedom: Economics, Politics and Culture after Slavery* (Pittsburg, University of Pittsburg Press, 1992), 113–46.

'The Social and Political Consequences of the 1931 Hurricane in Belize', unpublished paper, Association of Caribbean Historians, Mona, 1993.

Braithwaite, Lloyd, Introduction in Roy Thomas (ed) *The Trinidad Labour Riots of 1937* (St Augustine, UWI, 1987), 1–20.

Brecher, Jeremy, *Strike!* (Greenwich, Fawcett Publications, 1972).

Brereton, Bridget, A History of Modern Trinidad, 1783–1962 (Kingston, Heinemann, 1981).

Bryan, Patrick, *The Jamaican People, 1880–1902: Race, Class and Social Control* (London, Macmillan, 1991).

Buhle, Paul, *C.L.R. James: The Artist as Revolutionary* (London, Verso, 1988).

Campbell, Horace, *Rasta and Resistance: From Marcus Garvey to Walter Rodney* (London, Hansib, 1985).

Chase, Ashton, *A History of Trade Unionism in Guyana, 1900–1961* (Ruimveldt, New Guyana Company, n.d.).

Cheverton, R.L. and Smart, H.P., *Report of the Committee on Nutrition in the Colony of British Honduras* (Belize, Government Printer, 1937).

Clarke, Colin G., *Kingston, Jamaica: Urban Development and Social Change, 1692–1962* (Berkeley, University of California Press, 1975).

Craig, Susan, *Smiles and Blood: The Ruling Class Response to the Workers' Rebellion of 1937 in Trinidad and Tobago* (London, New Beacon Books, 1988).

Craton, Michael, *A History of the Bahamas* (Waterloo, San Salvador Press, 1986).

Cross, Malcolm, 'The Political Representation of Organised Labour in Trinidad and Guyana: A Comparative Puzzle', in Malcolm Cross and Gad Heuman (eds), *Labour in the Caribbean* (London, Macmillan, 1988), 285–308.

Cross, Malcolm and Heuman, Gad (eds), *Labour in the Caribbean: From Emancipation to Independence* (London, Macmillan, 1988).

Deerr, Noel, *The History of Sugar*, 2 vols (London, Chapman & Hall, 1949).

Dobson, Narda, *A History of Belize* (London, Longman Caribbean, 1973).

Drayton, Richard, and Andaiye, (eds), *Conversations: George Lamming: Essays, Addresses and Interviews 1953–1990* (London, Karia Press, 1992).

Eaton, George E. 'Trade Union Development in Jamaica', *Caribbean Quarterly* 8:1/2 (1962), 45–53, 69–75.

Alexander Bustamante and Modern Jamaica (Kingston, Kingston Publishers, 1975).

Elkins, W.F., 'A Source of Black Nationalism in the Caribbean: The Revolt of the British West Indies Regiment at Taranto, Italy', *Science and Society* 35:1 (1970), 99–103.

'Suppression of the *Negro World* in the British West Indies', *Science and Society* 35:3 (1971), 344–47.

Foster, Byron, *The Baymen's Legacy: A Portrait of Belize City* (Benque Viejo del Carmen, Cubola Productions, 1987).

Fraser, Peter D., 'The Immigration Issue in British Guiana, 1903–1913: The Economic and Constitutional Origins of Racist Politics in Guyana', *Journal of Caribbean History* 14 (1981), 18–45.

Frucht, Richard, 'A Caribbean Social Type: Neither "Peasant" nor "Proletarian"', *Social and Economic Studies* 16:3 (1967), 295–300.

Grant, C.H., *The Making of Modern Belize: Politics, Society and British Colonialism in Central America* (Cambridge, Cambridge University Press, 1976).

Hamill, Don, 'Colonialism and the Emergence of Trade Unions in Belize', *Journal of Belizean Affairs* 7 (1978), 3–20.

Harry, Carlyle, *Hubert Nathaniel Critchlow: His Main Tasks and Achievements* (Ruimveldt, Guyana National Service Publishing Centre, 1977).

Hart, Richard, 'Origin and Development of the Working Class in the English–speaking Caribbean Area: 1897–1937', in Malcolm Cross and Gad Heuman (eds) *Labour in the Caribbean* (London, Macmillan, 1988) 43–79.

Rise and Organise: The Birth of the Workers and National Movements in Jamaica, 1936–1939 (London, Karia Press, 1989).

Henry, Paget, *Peripheral Capitalism and Underdevelopment in Antigua* (New Brunswick, Transaction Books, 1985).

Herrmann, Eleanor Krohn, *Origins of Tomorrow: A History of Belizean Nursing Education* (Belize, Ministry of Health, 1985).

Hill, Frank, *Bustamante and his Letters* (Kingston, Kingston Publishers, 1976).

Hoyos, F.A., *Grantley Adams and the Social Revolution* (London, Macmillan, 1974).

Jacobs, W. Richard, 'Butler: A Life of Struggle', in *In the Spirit of Butler: Trade Unionism in Free Grenada* (St George's, Fedon Publishers, 1982), 32–44.

James, C.L.R., *Minty Alley* (London, Secker and Warburg, 1936).

The Black Jacobins: Toussaint L'Ouverture and the San Domingo Revolution (New York, Vintage Books, 1963; orig. 1938).

Johnson, Howard, 'Oil, Imperial Policy and the Trinidad Disturbances, 1937', *Journal of Imperial and Commonwealth History* 4:1 (1975), 29–54.

'"A Modified Form of Slavery": The Credit and Truck Systems in the Bahamas in the Nineteenth and Early Twentieth Centuries', *Comparative Studies in Society and History* 28:4 (1986), 729–753.

Joseph, Cedric L., 'The British West Indies Regiment, 1914–1918', *Journal of Caribbean History 2* (1971), 94–124.

Lamming, George, *In the Castle of My Skin* (London, Michael Joseph, 1953).

Lewis, W. Arthur, *Labour in the West Indies: The Birth of a Workers' Movement* (London, Victor Gollancz, 1939, rep. London, New Beacon Books, 1977).

Lewis, Gordon K., *The Growth of the Modern West Indies* (London, MacGibbon & Kee, 1968).

Lobdell, Richard, 'British Officials and the West Indian Peasantry: 1842–1938', in Malcolm Cross and Gad Heuman (eds), *Labour in the Caribbean* (London, Macmillan, 1988), 195–207.

Macmillan, W.M., *Warning From the West Indies* (London, Faber and Faber, 1936).

Makin, William J., *Caribbean Nights* (London, Robert Hale, 1939).

Mandle, Jay R., *The Plantation Economy: Population and Economic Change in Guyana, 1838–1960* (Philadelphia, Temple University Press, 1973).

Mintz, Sidney W., *Caribbean Transformations* (Chicago, Aldine Publishing Co., 1974).

Moore, Brian L., *Race, Power and Social Segmentation in Colonial Society: Guyana after Slavery, 1838–1891* (New York, Gordon and Breach Science Publishers, 1987).

Nettleford, Rex, *Mirror Mirror: Identity, Race and Protest in Jamaica* (Kingston, William Collins and Sangster, 1970).

Manley and the Politics of Jamaica: Towards an Analysis of Political Change in Jamaica, 1938–1968 (Mona, ISER, 1971).

Nicholson, Marjorie, *The TUC Overseas: The Roots of Policy* (London, Allen of Urwin, 1986).

Orde Browne, Major G. St J., *Labour Conditions in the British West Indies* (London, His Majesty's Stationery Office, 1939).

Piven, Frances Fox and Richard A. Cloward, *Regulating the Poor: The Functions of Public Welfare* (New York, Pantheon Books, 1971).

Phelps, O.W., 'Rise of the Labour Movement in Jamaica', *Social and Economic Studies* 9:4 (1960), 417–68.

Post, Ken, 'The Politics of Protest in Jamaica, 1938: Some Problems of Analysis and Conceptualization', *Social and Economic Studies* 18:4 (1969), 374–90.

'The Bible as Ideology: Ethiopianism in Jamaica, 1930–38', in C.H. Allen and R.W. Johnson (eds), *African Perspectives* (Cambridge, Cambridge University Press, 1970), 185–207.

Arise Ye Starvelings: The Jamaican Labour Rebellion and its Aftermath (The Hague, Martinus Nijhoff, 1978).

Ramdin, Ron, *From Chattel Slave to Wage Earner: A History of Trade Unionism in Trinidad and Tobago* (London, Martin Brian & O'Keefe, 1982).

Reddock, Rhoda, *Elma Francois: The NWCSA and the Workers' Struggle for Change in the Caribbean in the 1930s* (London, New Beacon Books, 1988).

'Transformation in the Needle Trades: Women in Garment and Textile Production in Early Twentieth–Century Trinidad', in Janet Momsen (ed.), *Women and Change in the Caribbean: A Pan–Caribbean Perspective* (Kingston, Ian Randle, and London, James Currey, 1993), 249–62.

Rennie, Bukka, *The History of the Working–class in the 20th Century (1919–1956) – The Trinidad and Tobago Experience* (Trinidad, New Beginning Movement, 1973).

Report of the First British Guiana and West Indies Labour Conference (Georgetown, British Guiana Labour Union, 1926).

Richards, Glenn, 'Collective Violence in Plantation Societies: The Case of the St Kitts Labour Protests of 1896 and 1935', Institute of Commonwealth Studies, University of London, unpublished seminar paper, 1987a.

"The Maddened Rabble": Labour Protests in St Kitts, 1896 and 1935', unpublished paper, Society for Caribbean Studies, Hoddesdon, 1987(b).

'Order and Disorder in Colonial St Kitts: The Role of the Armed Forces in Maintaining Labour Discipline, 1896–1935', unpublished paper, Association of Caribbean Historians, Mona, 1993.

Richardson, Bonham C., *Caribbean Migrants: Environment and Human Survival on St Kitts and Nevis* (Knoxville, University of Tennessee Press, 1983).

Panama Money in Barbados, 1900–1920 (Knoxville, University of Tennessee Press, 1985).

The Caribbean in the Wider World, 1492–1992: A Regional Geography (Cambridge, Cambridge University Press, 1992a).

'Depression Riots and the Calling of the 1897 West India Royal Commission', *New West Indian Guide/Nieuwe West–Indische Gids* 66:3, 4 (1992b), 169–91.

Roberts, G.W., *The Population of Jamaica* (Cambridge, Cambridge University Press, 1957).

Rodney, Walter, *A History of the Guyanese Working People, 1881–1905* (Baltimore, Johns Hopkins University Press, 1981).

Ryan, Cecil and Cecil A. Blager Williams, *From Charles to Mitchell*, Part 1 (St Vincent, Projects Promotion, n.d.).

Ryan, Selwyn D., *Race and Nationalism in Trinidad and Tobago: A Study of Decolonisation in a Multiracial Society* (Toronto, University of Toronto Press, 1972).

Samaroo, Brinsley, 'The Trinidad Workingmen's Association and the Origins of Popular Protest in a Crown Colony', *Social and Economic Studies* 21:2 (1972), 205–22.

Saunders, Gail, 'The 1942 Riot in Nassau. A Demand for Change?', *Journal of Caribbean History* 20:2 (1985–86), 117–46.

'The 1937 Riot in Inagua, the Bahamas', *New West Indian Guide* 62:3,4 (1988).

Bahamian Society after Emancipation: Essays in Nineteenth and Early Twentieth Century Bahamian History (Nassau, the author, 1990).

Singh, Kelvin, 'Adrian Cola Rienzi and the Labour Movement in Trinidad (1925–44)', *Journal of Caribbean History 16* (1982), 10–35.

'The June 1937 Disturbances in Trinidad', in Roy Thomas (ed.), *The Trinidad Labour Riots of 1937: Perspectives 50 Years Later* (St Augustine, Extra–Mural Studies Unit, University of the West Indies, 1987), 57–80.

Race and Class Struggles in a Colonial State: Trinidad 1917–1945 (Alberta, University of Calgary Press, and Kingston, The Press –University of the West Indies, 1994).

Smith, Keithlyn B. and Smith, Fernando C., *To Shoot Hard Labour: The Life and Times of Samuel Smith, an Antiguan Workingman,* 1877–1982 (London, Karia Press, 1989).

St Pierre, Maurice, 'The 1938 Jamaican Disturbances. A Portrait of Mass Reaction Against Colonialism', *Social and Economic Studies,* 27(1978), 171–96.

Sutton, James W., *A Testimony of Triumph: A Narrative of the Life of James Sutton and Family in Nevis and St Kitts, 1920–1940* (Scarborough, Edan's Publishers, 1987).

Thomas, Herbert, *Story of a West Indian Policeman* (Kingston, 1927).

Thomas, Roy (ed.), *The Trinidad Labour Riots of 1937: Perspectives 50 Years Later* (St Augustine, UWI, 1987).

Turner, Mary, 'Chattel Slaves into Wage Slaves: A Jamaican Case Study', in Malcolm Cross and Gad Heuman, (eds) *Labour in the Caribbean* (London, Macmillan, 1988), 14–31.

Waddell, D.A.G., *British Honduras: A Historical and Contemporary Survey* (London, Oxford University Press, 1961).

Walker–Kilkenny, Roberta, 'The Leonora Strike of 1939', *History Gazette* 46 (1992).

West India Royal Commission Report (London, His Majesty's Stationery Office, 1945).

Young, Virginia Heyer, *Becoming West Indian: Culture, Self, and Nation in St Vincent* (Washington, Smithsonian Institution Press, 1993).

INDEX